Community, Crime and Disorder

Community, Crime and Disorder

Safety and Regeneration in Urban Neighbourhoods

Lynn Hancock
Senior Lecturer in Criminology
Middlesex University
London

First published 2001 by
PALGRAVE
Houndmills, Basingstoke, Hampshire RG21 6XS and
175 Fifth Avenue, New York, N.Y. 10010
Companies and representatives throughout the world

PALGRAVE is the new global academic imprint of
St. Martin's Press LLC Scholarly and Reference Division and
Palgrave Publishers Ltd (formerly Macmillan Press Ltd).

ISBN 0–333–76149–9

This book is printed on paper suitable for recycling and made from fully managed and sustained forest sources.

A catalogue record for this book is available from the British Library.

Library of Congress Cataloging-in-Publication Data
Hancock, Lynn, 1964–
    Community, crime and disorder : safety and regeneration in urban neighbourhoods / Lynn Hancock.
        p. cm.
    Includes bibliographical references and index.
    ISBN 0–333–76149–9 (cloth)
    1. Crime—Environmental aspects—Great Britain. 2. Crime––Sociological aspects—Great Britain. 3. Inner cities—Great Britain. 4. Urban policy—Great Britain. I. Title.
    HV6177 .H36 2001
    364.4'0941—dc21
                                                    00–054530

10   9   8   7   6
10   09   08   07   06

Printed and bound in Great Britain by
Antony Rowe Ltd, Chippenham, Wiltshire

Contents

Figures and Tables

Acknowledgements

A great number of people deserve thanks for their help with the project upon which this book is based. Sadly, because ethical considerations require that certain individuals remain anonymous, I cannot mention them all personally. Indeed space would also prevent it. However, special thanks go to the Leverhulme Trust, Keele University and Middlesex University respectively for their financial support through the Leverhulme Special Research Fellowship Scheme. Thanks to Jean Cater at the Trust for her interest in the project. I am indebted to Kate Bowers and Alex Hirschfield of the Urban Research and Policy Evaluation Regional Research Laboratory (Department of Civic Design, Liverpool University) for their help with some of the data used in this book. Special thanks go to residents in and beyond the study areas in Merseyside, who must remain anonymous, but whose help and generosity made this research possible. Appreciation goes to all the individuals in the agencies who provided information and time. My closest friends (north and south) deserve more than their acknowledgement. I am grateful to many people who have generously given their encouragement and support, but special thanks to Sandra Walklate, Tim Hope, Tony Bottoms and Roger Matthews. Staff and students at Keele University and Middlesex, respectively, have in their various ways, and perhaps without knowing it, helped to clarify my ideas.

We are grateful to Charles C. Thomas Publishers, Springfield, Illinois, for permission to reproduce Figures 1 and 2 from A. Podolefsky and F. Dubow, *Strategies for Community Crime Prevention, 1981*, pp. 13 and 138.

1
Introduction: Urban Change and Crime

Many criminological researchers have turned their attention to the urban context of crime over recent years. In the United States a long tradition of research has focused upon neighbourhood change and its criminological consequences. For many the housing market was, and remains, pivotal to their undertakings (see Skogan 1990). In this context, of course, the private housing market is pre-eminent and the public sector highly residualized (Harloe 1995). British writers have drawn upon these traditions; identifying processes that are common to both sides of the Atlantic, and others that are not clearly reflected in the UK, in large part because of the relatively large social housing sector in this setting.

The local authority controlled housing sector has become increasingly residualized, and recommodified, over the last 20 or so years, but it remains problematic to apply American-based research to the British context in a straightforward fashion. Although residualization may be flowing from the logic of capitalist interests in Europe and the USA (Harloe 1995), there are 'nationally varying economic, political and housing market developments, patterns of urbanization, ideological factors, institutional arrangements and historical legacies' (Harloe 1995: 546), which have resulted in national variations in the provision of social housing. Indeed, there are many sub-national variations (Hancock 1996a). The overall context may be constraining, but these conditions are sufficient to create differences in the nature and pace of residualization (Harloe 1995). The factors leading to variance also have important consequences for the way we consider changes in housing provision and housing markets and, in turn, their relationships with neighbourhood decline, regeneration and crime.

In Britain, research has also demonstrated 'housing market' processes to be especially significant for determining crime patterns and offender rates, as their role in creating a particular concentration of 'at risk' groups of residents has been revealed (see Bottoms, Mawby and Xanthos 1989; Bottoms, Claytor and Wiles 1992; Foster and Hope 1993, for example). These studies have tended to focus on local authority controlled housing estates (Baldwin and Bottoms 1976; Bottoms and Xanthos 1981; Bottoms and Wiles 1986; Bottoms et al. 1989; Gill 1977; Barke and Turnbull 1992; Foster and Hope 1993, for example). In this context the notion of 'market' is problematic; we are often referring to 'means of access' to housing (see Rex and Moore, 1967) and, in particular, bureaucratic allocation processes.

Some writers, as I show below, have been concerned with changes in public housing provision and their impact on patterns of disadvantage and victimization. However, there have been few recent attempts to analyse other changes in housing policy for their criminological consequences. Some authors have recognized the importance of the changing balance of tenure for 'community crime careers', but they have mainly been concerned with two main tenure types found in the UK, owner-occupation and council renting (see Bottoms and Wiles 1986). Other forms of provision, such as that provided by the (non-profit) voluntary housing movement, have also been acknowledged (Bottoms and Wiles 1986). And, these contributions have been of enormous value. However, they have taken place in a different political and policy environment. One of the main aims of this study is to contribute to 'community crime career' (Reiss 1986) debates through an examination of these phenomena in the current context and over recent years. Thus, the growing role of housing association provision, and other changes in housing provision and consumption, are studied in an area where these processes are relatively well advanced. Many findings are applicable to other areas, at earlier stages in the trajectory of change.

This chapter begins by examining key changes in the urban environment in the UK; in urban governance and housing. It notes the links between new urban divisions and crime. It argues the importance of looking beyond social housing provided by the local authority when considering disadvantage and crime. It then considers the importance of community involvement in urban, including crime prevention, policies before discussing recent developments, including the Crime and Disorder Act (1998), and debates. The chapter outlines the approach adopted in this study, and concludes with brief information about its setting.

Urban change

While housing (markets, policies and housing management practices) has occupied a central role in explaining high rates of offending in certain areas of cities, these processes cannot be fully understood without some consideration of the changing structures of cities (Bottoms and Wiles 1995). The globalization of capital and culture; the decline of manufacturing, and the rise of service sector employment; the impact of new technologies (particularly on the ordering of daily life in time and space); and the 'hollowing out' of cities as populations leave decaying inner-urban cores to live, work and seek leisure on the urban fringe are of particular relevance to our understanding. These processes have led to new forms of social differentiation in the city; economic polarization between areas in cities is increasingly evident (Bottoms and Wiles 1995). The ways in which daily life is affected by these trends will vary across different societies, regions and cities. It is therefore important that these developments and their criminological effects are investigated empirically in a variety of cities (Bottoms and Wiles 1995). The complexity of such a research task is evidently great. In this light, Bottoms and Wiles (1995: 1.38) suggested we examine the 'consequences of late modernity for crime in our own city', exchange ideas, and formulate comparative research questions. A second aim of this research is to offer a contribution to such a research agenda.

Understanding changes at the local level

Changes at the global, national and city levels produce effects at the local level, and invoke the need to examine how they reveal themselves, are understood, and how they are responded to in high crime areas. Bottoms and Wiles (1992) assist us in the task of developing the empirical questions associated with such a study. They suggested that criminologists develop their understanding of community change and crime through an examination of the natural and built environment, the political, economic, social and cultural contexts of areas, and with the actions of individuals, organizations and corporate bodies within localities.

To disentangle the key processes involved in neighbourhood change and community crime careers, comparative neighbourhood studies are invaluable. For, as Massey noted, 'At any one time different areas may be changing in contrasting ways; different battles are being fought out, different problems faced' (1995: 113). Comparative approaches enable researchers to distinguish between core and divergent processes. Doreen Massey's discussion of the 'uniqueness of place' provides urban criminologists with useful insights when considering these matters; it can illuminate our understanding of community responses to crime, disorder, decline and regeneration. Similarly, variations in local organizations' responses to the agencies associated with the management of these phenomena are also informed by Massey's account. Put simply and briefly: Massey explains how localities are shaped by successive waves, or 'layers', of economic activity. Each new stratum brings with it possibilities for new forms of social organization, and positions of inferiority and strength compared with other areas. Spatial variations in class relations, created by productive arrangements in different localities, are significant for the evolution of social and political cultures. What is important is that these are shaped not only by the most recent wave of economic activity, but are fashioned by earlier modes of economic activity and social organization. Thus,

> Local changes and characteristics are not just some simple 'reflection' of broader processes; local areas are not just in passive receipt of changes handed down from some higher national or international level. The vast variety of conditions already existing at local level also affects how these processes themselves operate. (Massey 1995: 115–16)

Of course, wider cultural, ideological and political changes also shape social change in localities, but these too manifest themselves in a locality-specific manner (Massey 1995).

New rounds of investment affect the make-up of localities, but the existing character of a locality, which is shaped by earlier rounds of investment, influences their form. Moreover, Massey's analysis suggests that new layers of economic investment may reinforce or reverse an area's social and economic advantage or disadvantage (Massey 1995: 118). Massey's analysis therefore raises important considerations for analysts advocating some forms of urban policy as crime prevention. It also provides a framework for understanding how some urban regeneration or crime prevention policies produce unintended consequences in certain settings.

Changes in urban governance

Some writers, such as Donnison (1995), have advocated radical urban policies as a strategy to prevent crime through addressing social injustice, economic exclusion and political marginality, which lead to crime and victimization. British urban policies, from the 1980s, have often pursued much more limited aims, however. Indeed, they have sometimes produced effects in direct opposition to these estimable goals. Put another way, when urban authorities have pursued policies with the ostensible aim of ameliorating social and economic injustice, there is evidence (examined in this volume) to suggest that social divisions have sometimes increased, and low levels of community confidence, and other contradictory processes, have undermined their impact (see also Power and Tunstall 1997). Massey's framework facilitates our comprehension of these outcomes. Though the nature and form urban policy in Britain has taken, which has changed considerably over recent decades, is another useful starting point.

The shift in the locale of decision-making, away from locally elected councils, to Westminster, is central to our understanding of transformations in the way urban policy and urban service delivery is organized and funded in the UK. Though it precedes the election of the Thatcher government (Dunleavy 1980 in Blowers and Raine 1984) in 1979, this change in administration ushered in a fundamental shift in the manner and means of central government's control over local councils and their social and economic activities. In the period that followed, central government consolidated its power to determine the amount and direction of local spending, especially of Labour controlled authorities, most notably in the areas of housing, education and transport (Duncan and Goodwin 1988).

The arguments that accountability would be promoted at the local level, central government was promoting efficiency, and simplified structures needed to be developed, were used to justify the abolition of the six Metropolitan County Councils (MCCs) and the Greater London Council (GLC) in 1986; though most commentators argued that the unelected boards and the myriad arrangements which were put in place to carry out the functions of these bodies, resulted in a more complicated structure of functions, a diminution of accountability and further centralized power in Westminster (Clarke 1986). Redistribution of power, decentralization of decision-making, and the promotion of efficiency have also been the arguments put forward by central government during the drafting of legislation to privatize local government services in the 1980s (Parkinson 1988). Critics refuted the idea that decentralization of power was taking place. Instead, consumer power was described as being symbolic to the legislation (Parkinson 1988). One effect was the establishment of a number of new quangos, the promotion of some existing unelected bodies, and the elevation of private sector interests in policy-making bodies, who increasingly carried out functions previously in the domain of local authorities. Urban Development Corporations, housing associations, Task Forces, City Action Teams, Housing Action Trusts and City Challenge, for example, were favoured for providing housing and leading economic regeneration (Stoker, 1989). In an attempt to rationalize the myriad agencies and government departments involved in regeneration, the Single Regeneration Budget was established in 1994. This combined 20 of the earlier programmes, managed by 5 different government departments, under the auspices of the government's regional offices. The New Labour government indicated that there would be further changes to reshape the Single Regeneration Budget when it reported on its Comprehensive Spending Review in July 1998.[1] In sum, since 1979, the shape and mode of local governance changed markedly as boards of civil servants, private sector nominees and local government representatives formed into 'partnerships', and took on the responsibility of developing local urban policies. In education and social services, private, 'opted out', voluntary and, in the case of social services in particular, informal provision through the family, were promoted to supplant or compete with local government provision.

Changes in housing

These processes have been clearly reflected in the specific case of housing policy during the 1980s and most of the 1990s (Spencer, 1989). Successive pieces of legislation limited the autonomy of local authorities; their capacity to develop local housing policies (especially building programmes), in response to local assessments of need, collapsed. National priorities were enforced. Central government regarded local authorities as 'enablers' of services rather than 'providers' (Spencer, 1989; Bramley, 1993); planned public expenditure on housing declined, in real terms, by 60 per cent between 1979/80 and 1993/4 (Balchin 1995). Support for home owners through mortgage interest tax relief (MIRAS) increased from £1,639 million in 1979/80 to

£4,850 million in 1987/8 (Balchin 1995), and decreased during the 1990s to nearly £1.4 billion in 1997/8[2] as MIRAS was cut back. The financial cost of supporting tenants through Housing Benefit and rent rebates also increased dramatically – to £10 billion in total in 1997/8,[3] not least because of the promotion of 'market rents'.

Strict financial controls constrained the housing development activities of local authorities, and stock was removed through the 'right to buy' scheme, established by the 1980 Housing Act. Between 1979 and 1997 1.3 million tenants bought their homes,[4] which had a devastating effect upon the quantity of good quality stock to rent. Local authorities were prevented, for the most part, from spending their capital receipts from these sales on new house-building activities (Balchin 1995). The second Thatcher government, elected in 1987, promoted the removal of local authority stock by encouraging tenants to 'opt out' of local government controlled stock through Tenants' Choice, Housing Action Trusts and local authority voluntary transfers (under the provisions of the 1988 Housing Act). Between 1988 and 1998, 61 local authorities transferred their stock to a Registered Social Landlord.[5] Where stock remained under local authority control, the use of City Action Grants and Estate Action funding served to bring local authorities under central scrutiny (Spencer, 1989). These programmes have since been incorporated into the Single Regeneration Budget.

The touchstone of government policy was the promotion of home ownership. Housing associations and the private sector were encouraged to become the providers of rented housing for those unable to achieve homeowner status. An increasing proportion of total housing expenditure was channelled to housing associations, through the Housing Corporation, and for the first time in 1989–90 housing association construction of new homes exceeded those built by local authorities (Spencer, 1989). However, during the mid-1990s, there were cuts in government funding to the Housing Corporation to reduce the Public Sector Borrowing Requirement and, preceding this, subsidies to associations (Housing Association Grants) were systematically reduced from 1988 (Balchin 1995). Housing associations became increasingly reliant upon private finance to make up the shortfall left by the withdrawal of subsidies. Rehabilitation of older properties declined significantly, not least because of the greater financial risks associated with such properties; standards degenerated and rents increased (Balchin 1995). Housing associations became increasingly dependent upon private finance and many writers doubted their ability to replace local authorities as the main providers of social housing, especially as the economy grew and other investment opportunities emerged (Balchin 1995). Local authority provision of rented stock was no longer part of the national political agenda.

At the national level, these trends resulted in the following changes in the balance of tenure. In England, in 1979, owner-occupation made up 56 per cent of stock; council housing and New Town stock accounted for 29 per cent; the private rented sector amounted to 13 per cent; and housing associations held approximately 2 per cent of national housing stock. By 1997 owner-occupation accounted for 68 per cent, councils and New Towns held 17 per cent and private landlords and housing associations had 10 per cent and 5 per cent respectively.[6]

Urban divisions and crime

What are the implications of the recent, and continuing, transformations in housing in particular, and the urban environment more generally, for crime patterning and community safety? In addressing this question we must first consider the consequences of these processes for social and spatial polarization. For the gap between the most disadvantaged and most affluent areas in cities widened between the 1981 and 1991 censuses, and the most disadvantaged groups were more likely, but not exclusively, to be found concentrated in the council and social rented sector (Lee and Murie 1997). Of course, these changes were not simply a reflection of changes in tenure. They are also the product of wider social, economic and political shifts, which brought in their wake chronic shortages of employment opportunities for economically marginal groups. Changes in citizen's entitlement to and the value of welfare benefits, especially for young people, was also influential. Nevertheless, changes in housing tenure have meant that those suffering the most increasingly live in close proximity to each other, in the poorest quality stock. Second, we need to acknowledge that the concentration of crime reflects the concentration of poverty and disadvantage (Hope 1998).

Recent analysis of the British Crime Survey's data (Hope 1998), suggests that the highest crime communities are characterized by the following features: (1) Residents lack economic resources; (2) rental housing tenure predominates; and (3) their demographic composition tends to include a high proportion of young people (under 25), lone parent households, and single person households. Households living in areas characterized by these features are likely to face additional risks of victimization if they too possess these characteristics. Hope summarized that 'crime victimisation may be concentrating in residential areas alongside the concentration of poverty and disadvantage' (Hope 1998: 174; see also Hope 1996; 1997; Pitts and Hope 1997).

Beyond council housing

Most discussions of neighbourhood change and crime, in Britain, have focused on the council sector. Important though this is, researchers need to be mindful of the problems of disadvantage, crime and disorder in other kinds of neighbourhoods. Research by Lee and Murie (1997), for example, shows that patterns of deprivation do not match precisely those of council housing. Their findings demonstrated that polarization between affluent and poor neighbourhoods was taking place within the five local authority areas studied by these authors (Birmingham, Bradford, Edinburgh, Liverpool and Tower Hamlets), and that this is clearly related to unemployment. Though the most impoverished areas *tend* to be dominated by council housing, this is not the whole picture. Many of the most disadvantaged areas contain a mix of tenures. The relationship between council tenure and poverty is different in each local authority area. It is less strong when indexes of deprivation draw reference to limiting long-term illness and strongest for white populations (Lee and Murie 1997). Lee and Murie argue that simply focusing on council housing areas in policies to address deprivation in these cities would overlook the grave problems of deprivation in other tenures. They conclude that local strategies which are sensitive to the particulars of local circumstances are necessary.

Lee and Murie also noted that levels of deprivation may be greater in the private rented sector and in old owner-occupied stock in some areas in their study. Furthermore, there have been growing concerns about the residualization of housing association stock over recent years (Warrington 1994, in Balchin 1995). Observers noted that, because the role of local authorities in the provision of new housing has diminished, housing associations increasingly assumed the responsibility of accommodating homeless families and those with only very limited choice in the housing market. At the same time, associations experienced reductions in capital investment grants from the Housing

Corporation (see above). As a consequence, associations sought to develop economies of scale through acquisition and building larger estates; resulting in increasing concentrations of homeless, vulnerable and benefits-dependent residents in housing association accommodation. Many associations recognized that these processes can lead to residualization; as negative reputations of estates develop, those residents who can move do so, and those with the most meagre of choices in the housing market become concentrated in less popular localities. In response, some associations developed activities that go beyond the simple provision of housing to address the problems of estates at risk (see Joseph Rowntree Foundation, July 1997). 'Housing plus' or 'quality of life' functions were developed in efforts to ameliorate the problems faced by tenants. Nevertheless, these activities could be undermined by a range of factors beyond their control: cuts in grants from the Housing Corporation, pressure to achieve 'value for money' (often defined in housing terms) in their performance targets, and the problems of coordinating government departments and other agencies, which may affect their work, for example.[7]

New funding for housing investment to the tune of £4.4 billion pounds was announced in the Chancellor's Comprehensive Spending Review in July 1998. £3.6 billion of this was to be allocated from the capital receipts councils obtained from the sale of council properties, which had to be used to repay Treasury debts under the previous Conservative administration. Also, the government indicated its plans to develop more effective links between housing and regeneration, tackle social exclusion and strengthen local communities. As part of the Comprehensive Spending Review, the Home Office further indicated that £250 million would be spent over the following three years on a crime reduction strategy. This would include 'increasing informal social control and social cohesion in communities and institutions that are vulnerable to crime, criminality, drug usage and disorder'.[8] The report, 'Reducing Offending' (Goldblatt and Lewis 1998), that accompanied the strategy, was warmly welcomed by many commentators[9] and the Home Office, who proclaimed a new era of 'evidence-based' approaches to crime and criminal justice policy. For some writers, misgivings associated with these developments often remain associated with the kinds of 'evidence' that have been, and will be, used, and with the way central government's aims are translated into policy and action at local level. The recent HMIC (2000) report, *Calling Time on Crime*, for example, noted the tension between local priorities and centrally determined targets.

A number of authors (Donnison 1995, Pitts and Hope 1997, for example) had highlighted 'political will', at the local and national levels, as being of great significance in addressing crime and its root causes in declining and distressed neighbourhoods. As Donnison noted:

> purely technical solutions will not work. Initiatives which are to put these things right must be launched by political leaders who have the authority to change public priorities and focus resources in new and sustained ways on such areas. (1995: 1.73)

Without political commitment and strong leadership Donnison feared that some housing managers may continue to find it desirable to have undesirable housing where 'troublesome' tenants can be placed, for example (1995: 1.72; see also Gill 1977). Others noted that agencies involved in community safety may continue to regard inter-agency cooperation, the key means of delivering the strategy, as a means by which they can, as Pitts and Hope put it (1997: 48), 'discharge or displace their statutory responsibilities', practices promoted in a context of pseudo-market competition, declining local authority budgets and ever greater central government control (Pitts and Hope 1997; see also Crawford, 1997).

Community involvement

The importance of community group responses to crime and neighbourhood decline has been recognized in the American (see Skogan 1988a; 1990; Donnelly and Kimble 1997; Bennett 1995, Donnelly and Majka 1998, for example) and British literature (see Foster and Hope 1993, for example). In Britain, however, changes in housing service delivery and urban regeneration have affected community groups' capacity to mobilize and respond to urban problems. Precisely how these changes affect communities is complex and variable. Nevertheless, in general terms, as the 'market project' has been implemented in public services, 'exit' rather than 'voice' has been promoted (Pitts and Hope 1997: 51). Agencies and communities (especially those most lacking economic and political power) have become less able to address instability, crime and social dislocation (see Pitts and Hope, 1997).

Some agencies, the social landlords pursuing 'housing plus' for example, have been keen to involve residents and tenants in the improvement of their neighbourhoods. Indeed, central to 'quality of life' programmes is the involvement of tenants and residents. Others have accorded only token status to resident involvement, or, where commitment is present at the local level, extraneous factors have undermined community confidence in involvement processes. This is seen clearly in Power and Tunstall's (1997) study of 13 areas where serious disorder erupted between 1991 and 1992. The involvement of residents in regeneration initiatives, which had been present for many years in some localities, was not enough to protect areas from serious and violent disorder. Indeed, some residents felt that the manner in which regeneration had been pursued in their area had been 'directly provocative'. They described how physical improvements received greater priority than local jobs; outside contractors benefited rather than local, small businesses; short-term remedies (such as training) were favoured rather than long-term strategic action to address the deeply entrenched social and economic problems of these localities. Consequently, economically marginal young men's prospects failed to improve and their stake in the locality failed to be restored. Though residents had some involvement and, in some cases, influence in these programmes, many externally funded initiatives were 'driven' by external constraints. They were insensitive to the complexity of local problems (Power and Tunstall 1997; Kyprianou 1997).

In his review of community crime prevention initiatives and research in the USA and Britain, Hope (1995) argues the importance of strengthening both the horizontal and vertical dimensions of social relations in high crime communities. Both sets of social relations affect the capacity of communities to regulate crime. The horizontal dimension 'refers to the often complex expressions of affection, loyalty, reciprocity, or dominance amongst residents, whether expressed through informal relationships or organised activities.' The vertical dimension refers to 'relations that connect local institutions to sources of power and resources in the wider civil society of which the locality is acknowledged to be a part' (1995: 24). Hope suggests that many community-based initiatives have failed to address both of these dimensions. Instead, the dominant social, economic and political context in which such programmes arise has often meant that the vertical dimension has been neglected or inadequately supported. Where both dimensions of social relations are strengthened, such as in 'the French model' (see Pitts and Hope 1997), positive results are evident.

The crime and disorder act

The Crime and Disorder Act (1998) placed a duty on local authorities and chief police officers to develop and coordinate local plans for community safety in their areas. Inter-agency relationships are central to the success of the legislation. The Act provided government with the power to designate specific agencies who are to be involved in an audit of crime and disorder in each local authority's area, the establishment of a Community Safety Plan, and the delivery of its objectives. These provisions indicate government determination to develop inter-agency approaches for crime prevention and community safety and limit the ability of agencies to displace their responsibilities. However, a number of important questions remained. For example, what powers, if any, would be used to compel agencies (such as health authorities or local schools) to become involved in such partnerships should they question the relevance of their involvement or their capacity to participate (in the context of other demands upon their services)?[10] How can agencies be persuaded to provide a service they do not currently provide if it is deemed necessary by the inter-agency group? (The new statutory role for local authorities and police forces was not accompanied by additional core funding; see HMIC 2000.) Furthermore, the government intended that funding should follow only successful programmes.

Despite a lack of clarity regarding these issues, central government holds a range of powers designed to ensure efficiency and effectiveness in efforts to address crime and disorder in local authority areas. The Home Secretary may call for reports on any aspect of lead agencies' duties, and reserves the power to intervene in partnerships. (Though how, and under what circumstances, remains unclear; Home Office guidance suggests that such action will be relatively rare.) Devising performance indicators and assessing these against targeted outputs and outcomes is another key part of the monitoring process. Though the Audit Commission had noted in 1999 that few crime and disorder audits had used 'bench-marking' as an aid to the audit process, and many had relied on a limited range of data sources (HMIC 2000). Partnership agencies are accountable through their various inspectorates (including the Audit Commission, Her Majesty's Inspector of Constabulary, the Social Services Inspectorate, Ofsted and so on). Performance targets bestriding institutional boundaries, and the effectiveness of the work carried out by the lead agencies, are subject to central scrutiny through separate mechanisms by HMIC and the Audit

Commission. These procedures ensure accountability upwards, to the political centre.

These structures differ markedly to those established by the French government in the 1980s, when 'direct, vertical links, organisations, and communication mechanisms were established from the grassroots to the centre of national politics' (Pitts and Hope 1997: 44). Pitts and Hope noted that

> For a time, at least, the institutional infrastructure of the French Model provided a two-way conduit of power and resources along the vertical dimension linking the citizen, the community and the State. And, although local agencies were central to the process of delivering community safety, they were also held accountable to the task through a two-way conduit of democratic power – through the downward transmission of power from the central State, and through the upward expression of political 'voice' from the social margins. (1997: 52)

These authors convincingly argue that these structures, the vertical dimension of social relations, was key to understanding reductions in recorded crime in the poorest areas in France during the 1980s. Can the measures in the Crime and Disorder Act achieve a reduction in crime and disorder without such strong links between 'citizen, community and the State'? At present it is too early to say. To be fair, local communities are not absent from the government's thinking; the Act provides for, and its guidance strongly encourages, 'community consultation' in the establishment of Community Safety Plans and local peoples' 'involvement' in their implementation. Though, in general, it seems that the government expects communities to benefit, principally, through improvements to services and their coordination, and at the end of the process, though the reduction in crime that is expected to follow.

The research discussed in the following chapters offers insights into the complex ways members of high-crime communities perceive, respond, and aspire to resolve neighbourhood problems, including crime and disorder. Furthermore, it examines the contradictory and fragmented nature of urban services and community safety strategies in localities where such strategies and multi-agency coordination have been in place for several years. This will provide information about, and insights into, some of the obstacles authorities are likely to face discharging their responsibilities under the Crime and Disorder Act (1998).

The criminalization of social policy debate

Writers such as Crawford (1997) and Gilling and Barton (1997) have expressed concern about the way welfare agencies have become involved in community safety, particularly under current urban policy frameworks. They have been worried that, in these circumstances, social exclusion and disadvantage become less important in their own right. Rather, they become the focus of intervention because of their implications for social disorder and crime. These writers note that while this has offered some scope for welfare agencies to acquire scarce resources, the opportunities for developing welfare oriented programmes remain limited by this environment. Those seeking funding under urban policy initiatives are required to form partnerships with the private sector (seek private finance); it is a competitive rather than a needs-based process; and the initiative is time-limited (Gilling and Barton, 1997). In this context, not only do powerful organizations such as the police (who are able to claim expertise and play a pivotal gate-keeping role) but the very structure of urban regeneration operations – characterized by short-termism and led by performance indicators – shape crime prevention policy (Crawford, 1997). As Crawford puts it, this

> can serve to extend a particular vision of crime control . . . [which tends] largely to be pragmatic and managerial. The forms of intervention tend to be short-term and situational. Those interventions which are more amenable to simple evaluation so beloved of funding bodies, the commercial sector and the media are consequently accorded priority. As such, they tend to focus on target hardening, 'designing out' crime, and other 'technological fixes' at the expense of interventions which question the social causes of crime. (Crawford 1997: 232)

They also point out that the metamorphosis from community crime prevention to community safety has been disquieting for the following reasons. First, 'community safety' has become part of a bid for legitimacy on behalf of government in general and the criminal justice system in particular. Second, its aims are presentational. Third, it is a strategy for managing 'the underclass' and maintaining 'safe' areas (Gilling and Barton 1997). The current author sees no reason to disagree with these arguments, though it could be argued that some aspects of the criminalization of social policy debate raise the potential danger of defending a version of 'welfarism' that, historically, has constituted part of the problem in high crime communities. In this sense, it seems hazardous to assume that welfarism, as presently conceived, can play a role defending against, as Gilling and Barton put it, the 'excesses of a crime control philosophy' (1997: 81).

For successive pieces of research have demonstrated that policies and practices in housing and planning have had profound implications for crime and disorder (see Bottoms and Xanthos 1981; Bottoms et al. 1989; Bottoms et al. 1992; Foster and Hope 1993; and Gill 1977, for examples). Dee Cook has drawn attention, more generally, to the ways in which 'social policies may have perverse effects, in making both crime and punishment more likely for vulnerable individuals and social groups' (1997: 132). Indeed, social policies over the past quarter of a century have probably done more to stigmatize, exclude and polarize marginal groups than recent developments in community safety. Welfare, as it has taken shape in Britain, cannot simply be defended as 'good'. Instead, analysts need to scrutinize urban, social and, indeed, community safety policies for their criminogenic and/or, social exclusionary potential (see Crawford 1998) and open them up to public scrutiny.

Furthermore, rather than being a recent phenomenon, ushered in by changing forms of urban governance and crime prevention's metamorphosis to community safety, urban and social policies have often originated against a *backdrop* of concern about crime and disorder. They have long been regarded as part of a bid for legitimacy on behalf of the state. Bridges noted how some critics regarded the initiatives emerging from the Home Office-funded Urban Programme from the late 1960s as an effort 'to absorb, contain and divert the emerging protest of the urban poor, both black and white' (1975: 376). Radical observers said that

> The function of the Urban Aid Programme was to buy out community-based organisations by giving them relatively small sums of money for 'safe' activities such as adventure playgrounds and legal advice centres. The Community Development Projects had the same function on a larger and more concentrated scale. Of course, the Home Office hoped for some feedback from these projects in terms of research and intelligence on the urban poor, and, in the case of the Community Development Projects, university-based research teams were appointed for this purpose. But it was important that this feedback should be contained, that these projects should not be allowed to develop into truly effective

channels of political protest, thus the location of these projects in the Home Office, away from the main centres of administrative responsibility for housing, education, employment and the economy. (Bridges 1975: 376–7)

Bridges correctly regarded views such as these as too simplistic; they depicted a rigid view of urban policy that failed to recognize both the internal and external contradictions that have shaped urban social policy. But he nevertheless argued that, in the context of the deepening economic crisis of the mid-1970s, urban social policy took on an 'economic buffering function' (1975: 385) in addition to 'social and political buffering'. Developments in urban policy during the early 1970s, in Bridges' view, were 'an integral part of a co-ordinated and centralised programme of internal control and repression' (1975: 377). Seen in this way, it is questionable whether the welfare state addressed problems of inequality and social exclusion as issues in their own right before the New Right's re-commodification agenda. Indeed, the government's agenda, post-1979, was able to draw upon criticisms from left academics and pressure groups in its arguments to reform welfare, for the latter regarded the welfare state as insensitive (particularly to minority ethnic groups), inefficient and ineffectual in its redistributive task. This is not to support the welfare reforms that have taken place over recent years, far from it; rather it is to acknowledge the limitations of 'welfarism' over recent decades.

Gilling and Barton acknowledge that there may be variations in policy outcomes, and that to some extent the nature of the polity in which community safety partnerships arise will be of importance. Similarly, the nature of the personnel involved and the type and orientation of the agencies engaged in partnerships, as well as other local contingencies, will have an impact upon the form community safety takes – though these may be structured by wider political and economic conditions. It remains to be seen whether local political traditions within the UK will give rise to significant variations in community safety strategies following the Crime and Disorder Act. What is clear is that local and national political cultures need to be given due regard in studies of community safety policies (see Pitts and Hope 1997).

This introduction has raised a number of questions that are explored in detail in later chapters. Implicitly it has also established the need for interdisciplinary approaches to explore each of these questions fully. Interdisciplinary accounts have been relatively infrequent over recent years. However, Bottoms and Wiles (1995) have made strong pleas to the criminological community to employ social theory from a range of disciplines in their work.[11]

An interdisciplinary approach

The links between urban sociology and criminology, or, more specifically, between analyses of crime and theories of urban change, were central in the work of the Chicago School of Sociology in the 1930s (Shaw and McKay 1942). However, the concern to employ the theoretical insights of urban sociology in general has diminished. There are some exceptions. Baldwin and Bottoms' seminal Introduction to *The Urban Criminal* (1976) is a notable one. They recognized the importance of 'old urban sociological traditions' (1976: 18) for their study of Sheffield. In particular, they argued the importance of theories of urban change (which are immediately foregrounded in the work of the early Chicagoan theorists, even if other aspects of their model are rejected) and the significance of the methodological insights generated by their areal epidemiology, and they acknowledged the contribution made by their descriptive accounts of neighbourhoods. These authors also recognized the importance of John Rex's idea of 'housing classes'; Pahl's attention to the constraints (socially, politically, economically and spatially) on human choices; the idea of micro level 'social space', including notions of territoriality; and anthropological ideas about 'social networks' for criminological analysis. They concluded that

> one must begin with a careful review of the available stock of theories, their links and complementarity, and then go into the field searching for basic data on which to begin the task of progressive generation of higher order empirical generalisations. (Baldwin and Bottoms 1976: 35)

Some early urban sociology retains utility. The 'housing class model' highlighted the importance of differential ability of groups to gain access to desired housing (Rex and Moore 1967). Rex and Moore recognized the significance of this for peoples' lifestyles, associations, interests and their position in the urban social structure. Though these authors may have overstated their case in some respects (Hancock 1995), they nevertheless provide insights that are germane to aspects of

contemporary debates about neighbourhood change, crime and disorder. Indeed, their critics, Lambert and Filkin (1971) for example,
reminded us of the need to be familiar with the variety of meanings
people hold about their housing situation and to be aware of different
patterns of constraint upon housing mobility. They argue the importance of considering the effects of these on social relations, and how
they are mediated through power structures (Lambert and Filkin 1971:
2.11; see also Bassett and Short 1980). Some of these concerns are
found in modern accounts, such as Taub, Taylor and Dunham's (1984)
Paths of Neighbourhood Change. But some of the work urban sociology
has generated over the past 30 or so years is likely to offer important
lessons still.

More recently, Bottoms and Wiles (1992) have been keen to highlight the importance of Giddens' theory of 'structuration' for understanding the spatial dimensions of crime and offending (see Bottoms
and Wiles 1992). However, there have been surprisingly few attempts
to apply these theoretical frameworks to the study of neighbourhood
change, crime and disorder. Equally, few urban sociology or urban
studies texts foreground or, perhaps more importantly, 'place' analyses
of crime and disorder in their fields of inquiry. Susan J. Smith's (1986)
Crime, Space and Society is another notable exception. Smith integrates
analyses of crime and victimization with those of social theory
informed by a geographical perspective, though the data drawn upon
is now quite dated. *Britain's Cities: Geographies of Division in Urban
Britain*, edited by Michael Pacione, usefully brings together essays on
global restructuring, uneven economic development, social policy and
the impact of these on socio-spatial divisions in modern British cities.
In later chapters the collection includes work examining the impact of
these divisions, and responses to them, in a variety of spheres including crime. The chapter (by Nicholas Fyfe) on crime examines the intra-
urban spatial distribution of crime, draws attention to the impact of
crime and fear of crime on the quality of urban life and peoples'
lifestyles, and outlines some measures to address crime in residential
areas. However, the limited space available means that a full exploration of the connections between these phenomena and the early part
of the book cannot be made.

The research upon which this volume is based sought to develop a
'holistic' analysis informed by a range of theoretical insights and
current debates within the disciplines of criminology, urban sociology,
urban politics and policy-making, political science, human and economic geography. The aims of the research, its methods of data collec-

tion and other methodological issues are discussed in the following chapter. The following section provides necessary background information about its regional setting.

Merseyside

Located in the north-west of England, Merseyside contains five local authority areas, with their own local government, within its administrative boundary: Knowsley, Sefton, Wirral, St Helens and Liverpool. Approximately 1.4 million people live there. The area has witnessed long-term economic decline and, as such, contains high levels of poverty. Following a long trend, the 1991 Census showed Merseyside's residents to have declined in number by nearly 9 per cent in the preceding decade. The number of economically active males declined by over 16 per cent in the same period. (Liverpool and Knowsley experienced the highest rates of population loss for any major urban area during the 1970s and 1980s.) Unemployment in Liverpool, according to the 1991 Census, was more than twice the national average and much higher in the inner cities and outer housing estates. During the decade 1981–91, the increase in the number of unemployed was relatively slight, but this needs to be read in the context of the decade before (1971–81), when unemployment doubled to a fifth of the workforce. The inner areas have suffered the greatest population loss, partly because of slum clearance in the early 1970s, and in part the result of employment-led migration.[12] Youth unemployment averaged 31.2 per cent across Liverpool City in 1991, though the figures are much higher in the inner wards, where unemployment is generally higher, especially among black people.

Merseyside's economic problems are well known within and outside of the region. The flight of industrial, financial and commercial capital from the Mersey and its hinterland is well documented and need not be rehearsed here. Suffice it to note that despite the succession of regeneration initiatives that have been introduced over recent years, there remains a considerable distance to travel. The 1996 Merseyside Economic Assessment, for example, drew attention to the following:

- Despite improvements in performance Merseyside still lacked competitiveness compared to other UK regions.
- Though employment and GDP were expected to grow in the years after 1995, they were expected to remain at a lower rate than north-west and the UK as a whole.

- Lasting economic recovery and convergence were regarded as being possible only if the region's firms could secure and maintain competitive advantage, both within local and wider markets and if new inward investment were attracted.
- If the competitiveness of the region is to be maximized, those who are currently economically excluded must be reintegrated into the labour market and society.[13]

Indeed, full-time male employment was expected to continue to fall until 2005, but at a lower rate compared to the 1980s and 1990s. The report drew attention to the growing divide between those without jobs and those in employment, and the marginalization of those in the lowest paid jobs. Merseyside TEC drew attention in the report to growing social exclusion and polarization within Merseyside, which is partly accounted for by the lack of good-quality job opportunities, but also by the relative decline in benefit payments compared to other incomes. The report concluded that 'social cohesion will be undermined unless those without work can gain access to good quality employment opportunities' (section 3.26). Efforts to increase skill levels are acknowledged in the report; though, as another commentator noted,

> Merseyside looks like ending up with the best trained dole queues in Europe – unless more is done to create real jobs and help business. (MEP Ken Stewart, cited in Kyprianou, 1997: 33).

The Merseyside Economic Assessment report makes the worrisome observation that those who are more highly qualified are often the most mobile, and that unless local employment opportunities are provided, out-migration is likely to continue. An improvement in the national economy is therefore likely to be detrimental to some areas in Merseyside. A Liverpool City Council report noted, for example, that 'any upturn in economic activity nationally is likely to lead to people leaving Liverpool in even greater numbers unless employment opportunities on a large scale are available locally'.[14]

This situation is more stark when it is seen against the backdrop of renewal schemes, regeneration initiatives and anti-poverty programmes that have taken place in the inner areas and the most disadvantaged localities, including the study areas, over the past 30 or so years. Over recent years, these have included Merseyside Urban Development Corporation (established in March 1981), a Task Force (in Granby/ Toxteth, in Liverpool), Liverpool Housing Action Trust,

Estate Action programmes and three City Challenges. Each has tried to bring about economic regeneration and housing improvement in Merseyside during the 1980s and 1990s. Many of these initiatives have been incorporated into the Single Regeneration Budget (SRB) since 1994 to better coordinate regeneration efforts, and there are a number of SRB-funded, area-based and thematic projects around the region. In addition, European Union monies from Structural Funds, Objectives One and Two (targeted towards areas substantially lagging behind in their economic development) have also been utilized. Merseyside held Objective Two status before it received Objective One status in July 1993. (This brought with it £630 million – to be matched pound for pound by government, the public and private sectors.) Central to the Objective One programme is 'Pathways to integration', which aims to reintegrate the poorest communities through education, training and employment. Neighbourhoods identified as 'Driver 5.1' areas for European grant assistance, known as 'Pathways' areas, are identified as being particularly vulnerable to crime and victimization and are the focus of SRB and Safer Merseyside Partnership policies.[15] In 1996 about a third of Merseyside's residents lived in a Driver 5.1 area (SMP, 1996).

Surveys of residents indicate a high level of concern about becoming a victim of crime. For example, Merseyside Police's Public Perception Survey (1996) showed that 74 per cent of respondents were particularly worried about becoming a victim of burglary. But, as elsewhere, it is the most disadvantaged communities that face the greatest risk. The poorest neighbourhoods have a disproportionate level of all crimes, despite under-reporting (SMP 1996). However, factors additional to disadvantage need to be taken into account when explaining the variations in crime rates and reporting in different localities; social heterogeneity, population turnover and levels of guardianship are of particular importance (Hirschfield 1995).

Merseyside's local authorities are keen to attract inward investment to address the economic problems facing the region. At the local level, too, residents have not been passive in their response to the difficulties facing their communities. In many neighbourhoods across Merseyside, tenants and residents have been organized in community groups and residents' organizations for many years, even in some of the most disadvantaged localities. There are long traditions of self-help and mutual assistance in the region. The large proportion of community-based housing association and cooperatively provided housing,[16] voluntary sector education and social services are witness to the importance of the community as a site of activism and politics, and for the provision of welfare services.

Many community groups have been concerned with housing provision and have sought to influence housing policy and service delivery in a variety of sectors, though there are also a number of multi-tenure residents' groups. In such cases housing is often an important local issue. This is not surprising. In Liverpool, for example, of the 46,700 properties managed by the council, over 25,000 were considered to be in need of major repair in 1996. The estimated cost to achieve reasonable repair across the council's stock was £800 million, a figure well beyond the means of the local authority.[17] In the private sector, the Merseyside House Condition Survey indicated that more than 67,000 properties were either unfit or in need of major and urgent repairs. It also showed that 'the low relative income level of owners is an important variable which affects the ability of owners to invest in the repair or replacement of their homes'.[18] Consequently the demand for improvement grants is overwhelming. Liverpool City Council has considered a number of options to improve its stock: the transfer of stock to housing companies that can raise capital to refurbish the stock; Challenge Fund bids in partnership with housing associations; and the transfer of stock to the Liverpool Housing Action Trust, housing associations and the private sector. Between 1991 and 1996 over 10,000 properties were transferred to bodies such as these.

Reflecting the national trend, housing associations have become the main providers of new social housing. As elsewhere, there have been concerns about rent levels in the new developments, and, in turn, about how these may reinforce benefits dependency, limiting the ability of some low-income residents to take up employment. Similarly, housing associations have been troubled about the condition of some of their (older) rehabilitated stock.

Housing associations have had a long history in Liverpool, becoming major providers of social housing long before the 1974 Housing Act in some localities, which ushered in the modern movement. Associations were promoted by the Liberal administration in the 1970s as part of their housing regeneration strategy, and the former have evolved as the major players in areas where private landlords were withdrawing. They are the main landlords in some wards, though this tends to be overlooked when city-wide figues are examined. In Liverpool, for example, the balance of tenure in the 1991 census was as follows: 59.01 per cent private; 30.36 per cent local authority; 10.53 per cent housing association and 0.08 per cent 'other' stock.[19] Much of the housing association sectors' oldest property requires modernization, and in the light of the constraints upon capital investment (see above), associations have been seeking a variety of ways of improving the stock. Similarly, the borough-wide statistics for housing tenure in the Wirral also tend to downplay the importance of housing associations in the area. Here, 73 per cent of housing stock was owner-occupied, council property accounted for 15 per cent of stock, 8 per cent was privately rented, and 4 per cent controlled by housing associations. Yet associations are regarded as 'consolidating their role as the main providers of new social housing';[20] there are more than 20 associations providing new and older properties for rent and shared ownership, and many associations have developed partnership arrangements with the local authority to improve its stock. As in Liverpool, the older housing association stock is deteriorating and major improvement to the stock is imperative. The council's own stock has undergone considerable improvement over recent years, yet there remains a great deal of work to be done to improve its pre-war, high rise and maisonette style dwellings. Private sector stock in Wirral in the late 1990s was regarded as some of the worst in Merseyside. Almost 18 per cent of that stock (21,100 properties) was regarded as 'unfit', and over 20,000 required repairs to restore them to modern standards. But by far the worst living conditions were found in 'houses in multiple occupation', the majority of these are considered unfit.[21] Many of these features are found in the study areas.

Chapter 2 provides further information about the neighbourhoods that were studied, which is elaborated in later chapters. It describes how the study areas were selected, discusses the methods used to collect data, and examines a variety of methodological issues associated with investigating neighbourhood change, crime and disorder in the localities. Chapter 3 examines how neighbourhood decline, crime and disorder have been explained in British and American studies. That chapter illustrates the need to examine neighbourhood decline (and regeneration), and the place of crime and disorder in these processes, in *mixed housing areas* in Britain. It is longer than most of the other chapters because it has the additional aim of demonstrating the necessity of linking analyses of crime to those of urban change, and urban and social policies, and as such forms part of the background to the chapters that follow.

Chapter 4 argues that there are a number of contradictions evident in the implementation of community safety and urban (and other social) policies in the British context, through its examination of local government and other agencies' responses to decline, crime and disorder in the study areas. Chapter 5 examines how neighbourhood decline, crime and disorder were responded to in some mixed-tenure areas, including the study areas. Housing agencies' and policing responses are evaluated and discussed. Chapter 6 highlights the importance of community group responses to neighbourhood change, crime and disorder and the value and place of communities in community safety strategies. It argues that policy-makers often make unwarranted assumptions about community responses. In so doing, it illustrates some of the methodological issues associated with making sense of community responses (discussed in more detail in Chapter 2).

2
Researching Neighbourhood Change, Crime and Disorder

This chapter explores the process of researching neighbourhood change, crime and disorder in the study areas. It begins with an examination of the relationship between the study's theoretical concerns and empirical questions. A discussion of the way the study areas were selected and data was gathered then follows. Since the 'experience' of data collection in the two main study sites is worthy of discussion, the practical, political and ethical issues met during the research process are considered. The chapter may be of particular interest to academic researchers and policy-makers planning to undertake locality-based research following the Crime and Disorder Act, and some emphasis is therefore placed upon the factors that facilitated, and those that frustrated, the research, and the strategies employed by the author to overcome them.

The aim of the research, for most of its duration, was to investigate the processes involved in neighbourhood change (decline and regeneration), and the place of crime and disorder in these processes.[1] In so doing, the study sought to add to, and comment upon, debates around the 'community crime career' idea (discussed in Chapter 3) and the 'Broken Windows' thesis, for example. The following objectives were pursued: (1) To investigate the role of the 'new urban governance'[2] in relation to policies for high crime neighbourhoods; (2) To consider how housing market, labour market and other (for example, population and urban policy) changes impact upon residential communities, neighbourhood perceptions of change and various policy responses. The study areas exhibited relatively high levels of transience, housed heterogeneous populations and, as a consequence, were perceived locally to be lacking stability. In this context, the study aimed to furnish information that could add to, and advance, discussions about 'social disorganization' (particularly in the context of (2) above), which have recently regained popularity in environmental criminology.

There were a number of changes made to these objectives during the early stages of the research. In part, because of academic, political and public (especially policing) policy debates during 1995 and 1996, the nature and place of 'disorder' in neighbourhoods experiencing change became more important than originally envisaged. Some research attention was focused on 'policing' incivilities in this context. Likewise, at the onset of the research I had prepared for community-based respondents, perhaps a little naively, to report a greater amount of 'change'; regeneration initiatives had been present in or near to the neighbourhoods selected for study for a number of years. Early investigations revealed that some urban policies were undermined by the contradictory aims of other urban or social policies or by conditions that remained unresolved. This led to more complicated ideas about 'neighbourhood change', and the decision to investigate the nature of these contradictory processes in the study areas. As in most research of this nature, the research questions evolved as data were collected and analysed; ideas were clarified, some avenues of investigation were widened and others diminished in importance. Further research questions were generated when different kinds of methods generated data that suggested potentially contrasting findings.

These developments, typical of the ways in which data works on theory, show how the process of empirical research clarifies theoretical ideas. Research that is sensitive to its own needs cannot avoid this pressure for conceptual clarification. 'For a basic requirement of research is that the concepts, the variables, be defined with sufficient clarity to enable the research to proceed' (Merton 1970: 25). As the research developed, unexpected observations, which were surprising because they were inconsistent with prevailing theories or established 'facts', helped to shape theoretical developments. Likewise, the discovery of variables that have not hitherto been systematically included in analyses was important for reformulating theory (Merton 1970). These are discussed further in the chapters that follow.

The comparative approach

The study adopted a comparative approach involving two high-crime areas in the Merseyside conurbation, for the reasons outlined in Chapter 1, and because some of the most important work in this field has been achieved as a result of this approach. (See Bottoms and

Xanthos 1981; Bottoms et al. 1989; Bottoms et al. 1992; and Foster and Hope 1993, for example.) Furthermore, previous research carried out by the author had already illustrated the value of comparative work for illuminating some of the processes at work in participation relationships in the sphere of local politics. That said, the comparative approach requires that researchers be able to identify the variables to be present, to compare, so that the research questions can be investigated.

The study areas selected were both high-crime areas (though not neces-sarily the *highest* crime areas in the region). Economic, physical and social regeneration projects were ongoing in each area at the time of the research. Each neighbourhood had features that arguably indicate 'social disorganization' (Bursik 1988; Bursik and Grasmick 1993) and each exhibited social and physical disorder, which have often been linked with high rates of crime. Each area had the following social and spatial characteristics: a heterogeneous population (for example, regarding social class and/or ethnicity), living in relatively high densities (for example, multiple occupation), and in a mix of housing and tenure types. Each was located in an area controlled by a different local authority (Liverpool or Wirral), but sharing the same regional administrative boundaries. Both were close to their respective town centres. A number of community groups (involved in a range of activities) were present in each area, and the author has carried out research with some of the community groups prior to this research (during 1991–3). The neighbourhoods are to remain anonymous. They have been given pseudonyms, Earleschurch and Edgebank, for reasons that are discussed below.

Of course some of these characteristics were more amenable to identification and therefore inclusion in the selection criteria than others, despite recent developments in new technology (such as GIS). Nevertheless, this research benefited from the assistance of colleagues at the Urban Research and Policy Evaluation Regional Research Laboratory (URPERRL), at the University of Liverpool: their Social, Demographic and Land Use Profiler was an important tool for identifying some of the key features pertinent to the study. The 'profiler' was not only able to identify crime patterns across the region but also was able to discern, with clarity and precision, many of the social, demographic and spatial features indicated above (see Hirschfield, Bowers and Brown 1995; Hirschfield, Brown and Todd 1995). However, it is not able to identify actual 'neighbourhoods', rather it uses enumeration districts, police beats and associated categories of households and spaces. So, the author sought to identify, through the qualitative work, the 'character' and 'boundaries' of the neighbourhoods. By way of these methods the study was able to offer insights that would have been missed had it relied upon the quantified data alone, important though that was. The profiler was, of course, unable to identify community associations (though it was able to identify social meeting places). In this respect, the ability to select areas where community groups were active relied on the local knowledge and experience of the author. As the research progressed from the selection of the research sites to the collection of data, a number of issues germane to the collection and interpretation of data were raised; these are discussed below. Nonetheless, in the context of discussing the comparative approach, one further point is noteworthy. One of the research sites, Earleschurch, had a more developed community group infrastructure: there were more tenants', residents' and other associations and they had a longer history of organization compared to those in Edgebank. In this environment, pursuing a depth ethnography using community groups as the main points of access, as the author had in the early 1990s, would have resulted in unacceptable disparities in access and research attention in each locality. To some extent, uneven access is unavoidable. However, by using interviews, drawing on the 'snowball method', and supplementing this data with observation activity, some of its injurious effects could be limited. The decision to glean data in this way was justified early in the study, on appreciating the considerable demands that the current urban policy frameworks place on community groups. Urban policy partnerships need to involve local community groups in their activities, not only for information and to secure legitimacy, but because it is often a condition of funding bodies. In a context where local organizations depend upon volunteers, and most in this study did, the demands upon them are considerable. Consequently, the ability to work with them on a day-to-day basis is limited – it is too intrusive. This represented a notable change in the urban environment over the five or so years since the author had last carried out ethnographic work in the region.

In response to a concern that some of the processes detected in Earleschurch and Edgebank may be exceptional, observations and interviews were conducted with community groups in areas where:

- the housing was controlled by the local council and the area was undergoing or had undergone improvement (in some cases funded by non-local-government sources);

- regeneration project(s) were present at that time or had been operating in the vicinity over recent years;
- community groups were, or had been, concerned with crime and/or disorder and/or other neighbourhood problems.

This activity helped to clarify a number of processes. The two comparative neighbourhoods remained the most important priority, but the wider approach yielded valuable results, which more than offset the additional demands (particularly in terms of time) that accompanied it.

Data collection methods

The data needed to address the research questions were bound up with obtaining:

1. A profile of crime and disorder in the study areas together with information regarding their changes over time.
2. Material sufficient to enable an assessment of long-and short-term movements in the housing and labour markets.
3. Information about urban policies and their impact upon people and institutions in the comparative neighbourhoods.
4. Data regarding the kind of regeneration projects that were present at the time of research, and information concerning those that have existed in the past, where available.
5. Data concerning the nature of population change in the localities, and the ways in which residents regarded such changes.
6. Data regarding the ways in which individuals, community groups, businesses, policy-makers, planners, housing agencies, the police, regeneration initiatives, and other agencies with interests in the neighbourhoods, regarded the neighbourhoods and changes in the phenomena noted above.
7. Information about residents groups' responses in each area.

The principal research methods adopted for gathering these data are summarized in Table 1.

The fieldwork was conducted between October 1996 and September 1997. Interviews (mostly semi-structured) were carried out with community group members – usually in their homes. These were followed up with further interviews at three-month intervals. Community groups' newsletter advertisements and a 'snowball method' (respondents introducing me to a friend or neighbour) were employed to identify further respondents, who were then interviewed. This enabled contact with those who may not be involved in organized activities. This method also made it possible to capture more of the process of change than would be possible using single interviews, though single interviews could have facilitated a larger sample; 110 such interviews were carried out during the research. Incalculable hours were spent observing in a number of settings.

Crime-incidence and victimization data, and data regarding their geographical distribution, were gathered from Merseyside Police and other sources (notably URPERRL). Police command and control data (for example, spatially referenced calls to the police) were generated through the Geographical Information System developed at URPERRL. Data relating to housing market, labour market and population changes were gathered using existing data. Census information, in part generated through the Geographical Information System at URPERRL, and documents from a range of agencies operating at the local and regional levels – including regeneration projects, local authorities, housing associations, and so on – were key sources of data. Documents such as yearbooks, minutes of meetings and reports (in some cases, actual survey material) were obtained from a variety of sources. These data were supplemented with interviews with a range of policy-making, service-delivering and other agencies at regional and local levels (regeneration project managers, police officers, community safety coordinators, and housing managers, for example).

Table 1: A summary of data collection methods

Data to be collected	Main and supplementary methods
1	Official or officially derived sources. Interviews, observations, other secondary materials
2	Census, documents, interviews
3	Documents and interviews
4	Interviews and documents
5	Census and interviews
6	Interviews, documents, observation
7	Interviews, observation, documents

Data collection: some practical issues

In his discussion of methodological problems of field research, Zelditch suggested that there are two main criteria for judging the 'goodness' of a procedure used for gathering data. The first refers to 'informational adequacy, meaning accuracy, precision, and completeness of data'; and the second to 'efficiency, meaning cost per added input of information' (Zelditch 1970: 250). In some cases the methods chosen by researchers are arrived at straightforwardly. In other research the reasons for choosing certain techniques over others are not obvious. Some generalizations can be made: if the researcher is interested in describing a population, making generalizations, and commenting on frequency distributions, then sample surveys are efficient and adequate methods. Should a researcher require data about phenomena and behaviours considered to be 'natural', which may not be described, or about the dynamics of behaviour in an organization or social institution, qualitative methods will be more appropriate (Zelditch 1970). The type of method will be determined by the type of data the researcher is aiming to generate.

There was no intention to carry out a household survey; it would have been of insufficient depth to illuminate the sort of processes the study was principally concerned with: residents' understanding of and responses to neighbourhood change, for example. These phenomena are not easily amenable to measurement. Yet, the generation of quantifiable data can be said to be the most important advantage of survey methods. Furthermore, a number of urban sociologists have questioned the utility of survey methods for examining the related areas of housing preferences, race relations, and urban politics, for example (Rex 1971; Saunders 1983). Urban meanings and values, as they are expressed through associations, can be more useful for understanding social interaction in the city (Rex 1971; Hancock 1995). For we can expect members of a community to react to significant changes in their locality, and to endorse or object to urban policies, including community safety and policing strategies, through their existing organizations. To recognize this is to properly locate their actions and responses in the sphere of local politics.

Documents including minutes of meetings, organizational yearbooks, reports and so on were valuable resources in this research, as I have indicated. However, it is important to recognize the problems associated with their use: 'they are the "concrete" manifestations of a prior process of social construction in which "facts" have been created within a common-sense framework of interpretation' (Saunders 1983: 347). Data are arranged according to priorities other than those of the researcher, and some may not contain serviceable information (Saunders 1983). In many cases, in this research, data from interviews was necessary to supplement information derived from these sources.

Interviews were a principal part of the data collection process. Technically speaking, semi-structured and unstructured interviews are attractive because of the opportunity they provide to 'probe deeply, uncover new clues, open up new dimensions of a problem and to secure accurate, inclusive accounts from informants based on personal experience' (Palmer 1928 in Burgess 1982a: 107). Informal interviews are flexible but controlled, and non-directive interviews allow informants to take the subject of discussion in whichever way they prefer (Burgess 1982a). The importance of this aspect is discussed later. For our present purposes, we can summarize some of the problems associated with these techniques: detailed preparation is required; researchers must listen carefully, and be able to keep the conversation on a relevant topic, especially with informal interviews, or interviews as 'conversations'. In these instances, researchers must be able to recall the information so that it can be recorded in fieldnotes afterwards, and consider problems of comparability and ethics. They must think about the credibility of informants and reflect upon the 'truthfulness' of the information (Burgess 1982a). Even so, many types of interviews can produce a rather formalized impression of events and activities; and interviewees need only tell researchers what they wish to impart (Saunders 1983: 348). They sometimes portray only 'snapshots' of events where time and perceptions become distorted as they are reinterpreted and presented to the researcher. That said, the practice of returning to respondents after a time meant that information could be checked, and because relationships with respondents were developed in the process, some of these problems were diminished in this research.

We must also consider the problems of interviewing in a group context, since a fair amount of data from community groups was obtained in this way. Members of groups may raise only those issues that can be stated publicly, and the data generated from the questions posed may be difficult to compare. Nevertheless, the dynamic nature of social relationships between informants can be discovered with this method (Burgess 1982a). They also have the advantage of 'allowing informants to discuss their world and to argue over the situations in which they are involved. These interviews may afford glimpses of competing views and how consensus or difference is arrived at' (Burgess 1982a: 109).

Likewise, observation methods have many drawbacks, which can result in data that fails to justify the enormous amount of time and effort required when using this method: they can be inefficient. So, in this research, observation was used in specific settings and alongside other data collection methods, for the reasons already suggested. Nevertheless, there are considerable problems associated with 'participant-observation techniques',[3] which have been discussed in the expansive research methodology literature. Suffice it here to note that these may be amplified in a context where the research involves questions of a political character (Saunders 1983). The precise nature of these may not be known until observation is in progress. Other issues to be considered when using this method may include: the task of analysing vast quantities of data; problems of evidence, such as the credibility of informants; and concerns about the impact of the researcher's presence (Becker 1970). Participant observers and observant participants should also occupy themselves with the problem of ethics, the inevitably partial picture, dependency on sponsors, uneven access, and problems of over-identification, for example (Burgess 1982b; Gans 1982; Jarvie 1982), which accompany the employment of this method. None the less, observation methods can promote a deeper understanding of the issues from the point of view of the respondents than may be the case with interviews; and links built with groups can lead to introductions and meetings with significant other groups or individuals. In this way participant observation can be pivotal to the 'snowball' method. Still, its efficiency must be evaluated by considering the extent to which usable data is produced.

The problems with drawing upon official crime (and other) data has been discussed in many criminological texts and need not be rehearsed here (see Jupp 1989 for a summary). What is important, for our purposes, is that while the project benefited from data produced using GIS at the University of Liverpool, some of it was quite dated, even at the beginning of the research. Command and control data (calls to the police) referred to the period 1992–4, and recorded crime to 1994–5. These data required updating so that changes could be assessed. However, recorded crime data from the police was not until very recently spatially referenced. It is also important to note that the police beats, which cross-cut Earleschurch, were reorganized in 1994, and the police stations responsible for policing Earlesthurch changed. It is possible that the different stations had divergent reporting cultures. To overcome some of these problems, these data were supplemented with information gleaned from local beat officers, and compared with information from other sources, such as Victim Support, residents' organizations (some of whom had carried out small-scale surveys), and housing associations.[4] By using these methods, though not ideal, strong impressions regarding the scale and nature of crime and disorder and about changes over time could be obtained.

Up-to-date economic activity data were also not unproblematic. Again, figures derived from the census can map changes over time (in this case between 1971, 1981 and 1991), but more recent information is difficult to acquire. Regeneration partnerships record or estimate the number of jobs they have created both directly and indirectly, but at the time of the research (1996–8) there was no central database and there is the potential, at least, for employment outputs to be counted more than once. Indeed, a DETR-commissioned evaluation of the impact of City Challenge at national level identified 'some over estimation of outputs (and more importantly, outcomes)' and argued the need to put in place a system of verification for such programmes in a context where these are regarded with such importance (DETR 1999: 8). Regeneration activity (as alluded to in the previous chapter) is a political issue and, in some contexts, employment figures, though they may seem innocuous, can be a sensitive issue. Moreover, there is little data available to assess the *quality of jobs*; though a number of actors involved in the management and monitoring of regeneration activity felt this desirable. Many local people, throughout the study, said that there had been limited improvement in the employment prospects of local people – though the baseline for improvement is relatively low (as we saw in Chapter 1). They indicated that young peoples' prospects remained poor: the jobs on offer are often part-time, low paid, of low status, and temporary. Observations in job centres serving the study areas, for example, corroborated these views.

Sampling

Although 'sampling' is commonly associated with survey research, it is an essential part of field research (Burgess 1982c). Sampling refers to *where* to observe, *when* to observe and *what* to observe, in this context. Researchers are, therefore, interested in the selection of research sites, the times when observations will take place, and the people and events to be studied. These decisions will affect the data (Burgess, 1982c), its completeness as well as the efficiency with which the research task is undertaken. Having identified 'what' is to be studied, and having recorded the rationale applied to the question of 'where' (at the regional level), it is necessary now to consider other aspects of sampling.

The issue of 'where' and 'when' at the micro and meso levels was, to a large extent, determined by respondents or by the events to be studied. The following examples illustrate how data influenced where and when observations and interviews would take place as the research developed. First, what were considered to be relatively high levels of 'toleration' towards some forms of social 'disorder', notably prostitution, became evident from residents' accounts in Earleschurch (discussed further in Chapter 6). To establish if this was reflected in the experience of prostitute women, a small number of interviews were conducted with street prostitutes working in the locality and nearby. Accompanied by a colleague experienced in researching sex work, we interviewed women on the kerb-side during their working hours – late evening and nights, excluding Saturdays. (Saturday was regarded by some to be 'Wife's night'!) Very often women were content to participate in interviews between clients. If business was slow we were able to talk at length. In so doing, the geographical and temporal limits of toleration became more evident (though the topic deserves more detailed exploration). Second, observation techniques were employed with community beat officers in Edgebank and with a team of officers during the early stages of an initiative to address disorder in the town centre, according to shift patterns. Further interviews with police officers took place in their stations, usually during the working day, most community group members were interviewed in their homes, and most organization-based representatives were interviewed in their respective workplaces. What is important is that the research was not trying to observe 'everything', or to obtain information about all aspects of the social life of the eighbourhood, and of the agencies who operated there.

Access

Access is always uneven, as I have indicated. Interesting happenings may be going on away from the researcher's gaze and it is difficult to gain access across all social divisions operating in a community (Bell and Newby 1971). In this research, greater access to young men's and women's first-hand accounts (they often lack representation in community organizations) would have benefited the research, but regrettably they remained largely absent. Attempts were made to reach their views though other mechanisms, such as through youth workers. Nevertheless, it was interesting and pertinent to observe the way young people and their problems were regarded by their wider communities.

As a resident in Merseyside, access was perhaps easier than would be the case for other researchers, not only because of proximity, but also because of the importance of 'local perspectives' in the local culture (particularly in 'Earleschurch'). My residence of six or seven years at the start of the research, and previous studies carried out in the region, helped to establish trust. This was important because some respondents, during my previous research, noted the existence of a seemingly wide-spread view that researchers cannot be trusted. According to this view, university, government and other researchers have carried out studies either as a policy-oriented or academic exercise, and expectations were raised that improvements would result. Indeed, Gifford, Brown and Bundey (1989: 19) note that Liverpool is 'one of the most reported on cities in the country'. Yet few reports and studies have resulted in visible change for black (Gifford et al. 1989) and other marginalized residents. There is a view that people build academic or other careers out of their research, but they contribute little in return. Consequently, some people are reluctant to open themselves up to research, from which, they believe, they will gain little. That said, local knowledge and existing contacts were also invaluable in this research because, logically, the first issue raised by the question of access is the problem of identification (Saunders 1983): How can we identify likely organizations and individuals who may be approached for interview?

In Edgebank, where the author had no previous experience of researching, interesting and noteworthy data emerged during the process of identifying resident organizations in and close to the proposed study sites. My first points of reference were organizations in the locality: libraries, the local authority, and regeneration projects (who are identifiable through the Government Office for Merseyside, other regeneration initiatives and by way of local authority departments), for example. Given that community consultation is now a prerequisite for the transfer of funding under many urban policy programmes, regeneration initiatives were envisaged to be a fruitful source of information. (Library information was notoriously out of date because tenants and residents groups go through cycles of activity.) The following is an extract from fieldnotes written during the process of following these links; it clearly illustrates the role of gate-keepers who are central to the question of access. Furthermore, it demonstrates the interesting information that can be gleaned as a consequence.

Phoned [respondent's name] of [a regeneration project]. She has responsibility for involving community groups in the area. She said that there are two community groups that she has had contact with in [the vicinity] and that she would approach them before passing their contact addresses to me. She phoned one of them [community group name] for me just after our conversation on the phone – then she phoned back and said that the secretary has suggested that I write to her. I should inform her about my project and indicate what kind of involvement this would mean for her and the group. She said that they are very busy. I will do this over the next few days. She said that she would speak to the other group the following week and then inform me of their decision. She also gave me contact numbers of another initiative she was connected with and another contact who may be useful. She indicated that in her discussions with the two community groups the issue of crime had not arisen in her recollection.

This episode provided information about how little some of the agencies knew about the communities in their area. To illustrate, what follows is an extract of the first group interview that I conducted later with the first residents group that my contact had telephoned on my behalf.

People actually call it Beruit or the Bronx round here you know. There have been drugs raids and drug-related family feuds . . . where windows were smashed and cars were dumped. One time, all the windows were smashed in the flat above. I phoned the police because I was terrified.

My contact's insistence that she be the one who approached community groups in the first instance was disconcerting and worrisome; there was very little opportunity to exercise control over the way my research would be presented to potential respondents. This was important because, as the aims of the research suggest, a key concern was to examine the 'place of crime and disorder in perceptions of change in the neighbourhoods, that is, in the context of other neighbourhood problems (and perceived advantages of living in the neighbourhood compared with other areas). As such, it was important that crime and disorder were not highlighted in the presentation of the research task, in case community-based respondents responded by adjusting their replies accordingly. In other instances, to overcome these problems respondents would be informed that the aim of the project was to investigate the changes that are taking place in the region and the locality. The first question would usually be: 'Could you start by telling me about living in Earleschurch/Edgebank'? Such a strategy was significant for 'informational adequacy' and the efficiency of the data.

The data benefited from allowing respondents to 'tell their own stories' (a point I return to later). Nevertheless, this routine brings with it attendant ethical concerns, since the respondents have not been *fully* informed about the nature of the research. However, the ethical ideal to inform *all* individuals about the research project is complicated in the field. As Burgess (1984) observed, there is a tendency to posit overt and covert research as *alternatives*, which in practice is unrealistic. It is impossible for all individuals to know, understand and anticipate their roles in the research in exactly the same way as others, despite best efforts to present the research in a meaningful way to respondents. At the very least, the researcher has relatively little control over the way individuals interpret such information. Furthermore, at the practical level, it is not *possible* to tell the researched 'everything', as Roth (1962, in Burgess 1982b: 46) indicated. And, in public settings it is *impossible* to indicate to all the participants that research is being conducted. Details about the research project in these environments are left out to avoid disrupting the research process, or because there is good reason to believe that full disclosure will result in a significant change of behaviour or response.

The way that one presents the research task depends upon a number of factors, including existing relationships with respondents (and between them) and the nature of the research questions. Where different respondents were approached to elicit data that would illuminate, in some cases, different aspects of the research questions, it is not surprising that the research was presented in contrasting ways to some respondents, say, the police, regeneration projects, housing associations and community groups. Respondents need to be able to anticipate their role in the research. The interesting, sometimes disconcerting and perhaps unique feature of a 'community study' is that respondents frequently know each other, often talk to each other and, in so doing, sometimes talk about research projects in which they have participated and about the researchers! In this environment there are a number of problems to be confronted by researchers. For example, concerns about confidentiality must be remembered, and care needs to be taken regarding how the research task is presented. Indeed, it may sometimes be necessary to explain not only the research task but also the rationale for approaching respondents in a particular order. Quite often during the fieldwork I would telephone a potential respondent to set up an interview and be greeted with 'I was wondering when you would be contacting me . . . I was talking to [whoever] and they said they had been talking to you.' In some instances, respondents were disappointed that they had not been contacted at an earlier stage. Having prior experience of community-based research provided a degree of preparedness; in previous research carried out in Merseyside some respondents wanted to participate in the research precisely so that they could put a different point of view to that of other respondents they knew had been interviewed!

Gaining access requires that researchers can be categorized by their research community, as Bell and Newby (1971) noted in their classic text *Community Studies*. One's background, status or position can be a benefit or a handicap when seeking to obtain this acceptance (Burgess 1982b; Gans 1982; Easterday et al. 1982). There are benefits associated with having a similar status to the research participants. A number of writers have discussed the importance of gender divisions on data collection and have drawn attention to the implications of gender for the validity and reliability of data (see Bell and Newby 1971; Easterday et al. 1982). They point out that the ability of women to collect data on some male activities is limited, and vice versa. Others have noted that while respondents are influenced by gender (Silverman 1993), gender influences can be negotiated, and other variables may be more, less or equally important (McKeganey and Bloor 1991 in Silverman 1993). Nevertheless, the practice of sitting in public places to observe local interactions, as documented by male field-workers (see Moore 1977 for example), *can* be problematic for women; though such instances can come to represent interesting data in a context where fear of crime and incivility are part of the research questions. Still, the influence of one's status upon access is difficult to assess. Sometimes, engaging insights can be gleaned from its consideration. For example, after observations carried out with the police one Friday night, during a 'zero-tolerance' style policing initiative in one of the localities, the following comments were recorded in the field research diary.

> We went into several night clubs. Before entering one of them one of the officers told me that it was 'the worst club in [the locality], the clientele is awful'. He said that I would see what he meant. We went in and walked around (on each occasion the officers told the

people on the door that I was with them). Almost immediately we came across a number of off duty officers. I thought this was very funny after his comments about the clientele! Later, while we sat in the van, waiting for an officer who had gone to explain some requirements that needed to be addressed by the licensee, some of the off duty officers emerged from the club. They saw me in the van and they asked their colleagues – seemingly quite concerned about me – '. . . Why are you locking the lass up?'. The reply was much laughter; those accompanying me did not tell them the reasons for my presence in the van! They thought it was amusing.

The officers complaining about my presence in the van said that I 'looked OK'. They protested about my being 'locked up', and the officers with me continued to laugh and said they were taking me down to the Bridewell because I had 'been a naughty girl'. They thought that the 'wind-up' was great fun. It indicated clearly how I was perceived as being 'respectable' by the officers. On another occasion, I arrived at a police station for an interview where I was asked if I was there to make a complaint! The way the police responded to my appearance and demeanour, not surprisingly, contrasted with those responses reported by prostitute women during the interviews referred to earlier.

Kinds of access

While the kinds of access that researchers need will be determined by the research questions, other writers' discussions of similar research projects can offer interesting ideas. However, the research methodology employed by others may not always be applicable because of the nature of the locality. For example, in this research, Xanthos's (1981) methodology would have not been adequate. Polii Xanthos[5] worked as a taxi driver for two local firms, as a football pools collector and as a helper at a youth club to reach people on the estates she wished to study. However, in this study, because the research sites were relatively close to town centres, few people used cabs regularly. Furthermore, some respondents, when asked about the 'reputation' of their area, spontaneously indicated that they tell taxi drivers (on the rare occasions they used them) to drop them off nearby, but not in the neighbourhood, because they are 'ashamed' to tell them their addresses[6]. Also, in this research respondents indicated that there had been conflicts over the 'ownership' of youth clubs (in each study area); and many young people are self-, or otherwise, excluded from youth centres. The well-developed community group infrastructure in Merseyside meant that access through these organizations was more appropriate for this study. These observations illustrate the importance of Massey's discussion of the 'uniqueness of place' (see Chapter 1), which needs to be remembered when drawing lessons from other research and selecting points of access. Also in recognizing the special features of the study areas, its spatial and temporal specificity is fore-grounded and, in turn, questions over the ability to generalize from the research are raised.

By locating the study in Merseyside, limits *may* be placed on the type and number of generalizations that can be made. However, it could equally be argued that all cities are in some senses unique, despite their setting in an advanced capitalist urban society. Merseyside has a social, economic and political history that may differ markedly to that of other regions, and *some* observations made here cannot be held to be generally applicable. Nevertheless, some urban processes (changes in housing policy and the balance of tenure, attempts to regenerate declining regions, for example) are reflected in other cities, as I indicated in Chapter 1, and observations made in Merseyside can help to formulate hypotheses for studies elsewhere. That said, we must consider the importance of temporal specificity. In particular, it should be noted that the present system of local governance, and the mode and distribution of urban resources, are very distinctive features of the modern city and very specific to a particular period in the UK – one that is still evolving.

Checking data and findings

These issues raise questions about the ways in which we conduct validity[7] tests. While we may seek to test validity through a comparison with data gained from other sources, in some cases comparative data may not exist. The use of replication as a tool for assessing a study's validity (and reliability) is also difficult in studies of this kind because, as Bell and Newby (1971) suggested, communities will (and researchers may) have changed since the first study. Lacking other ways of evaluating the validity of findings arising from qualitative work of this kind, it is essential to check data for its internal consistency and ensure that the indicators used to provide information about more difficult to observe phenomena are appropriate to the task.

Field-work diaries are an invaluable tool for examining data in this way. In this study they were used to reflect on the data both during and after the fieldwork period. Here I documented where, when, what and of whom observations were made. Ideas of other writers were commented upon, tentative propositions were noted, and their usefulness or abandonment during the fieldwork period was recorded. As Burgess notes, 'the recording of field data raises questions about the relationships between data collection, formal and informal theorising, data analysis and the final research report' (1982d: 191). For, as Becker (1970) notes, tentative conclusions in the form of statements about a set of complicated inter-relationships among many variables are often made by researchers during this process. Searches are then made for alternative hypotheses and negative cases. Observers may indicate the kinds of evidence that would be likely to support or challenge the model and should actively pursue such evidence. Evidence that does not fit earlier formulations can then be used to refine the model, though it is important to acknowledge that some theoretical criteria are used to decide what to record and what to leave out (Burgess 1982d). Indeed, Burgess suggests that the ways in which fieldnotes are recorded, in practice, will depend upon individual researchers, the research context, the objectives of the research and relationships with informants.

Respondent validation has been found wanting by a number of authors (see Silverman 1993). The practice can be problematic. Some respondents may not understand a report written for a specialist audience; they may lack interest in what is essentially a social science project; or respondent validation may not be possible because the analysis runs counter to the self-image of respondents (see Abrams 1984 in Silverman 1993). Even though respondents may have additional knowledge, researchers cannot presuppose that they are able to comment upon their actions. Respondent validation may afford another source of data and insight but the fact that respondents confirm the researcher's findings cannot be accepted as direct validation (Fielding and Fielding 1986 in Silverman 1993). Nevertheless, once relationships had been established with key respondents, ideas and informal theories were sometimes discussed with them in this study. (In such cases, where alternative views were expressed these could be investigated as 'alternative hypotheses'.) Occasionally opinion was obtained on early drafts of papers produced during the research. Though this did not necessarily validate the findings, their confirmatory responses could be added to the overall picture that was being created.

The relative importance of crime and disorder *vis-à-vis* other neighbourhood problems could be ascertained by allowing respondents to talk freely about their neighbourhoods in response to questions framed at a more general level. At this point we can now note that, by allowing respondents to 'tell their stories' in this way, the study was strengthened in a number of other ways. It served as a useful check on other data drawn upon during the research. In many cases cross-method triangulation produced data that were mutually confirming, in others anomalies became evident between what *could* be inferred from one set of data when compared to what could be inferred from another data set, and further investigations were necessary to examine the reasons for these disparities. While we may agree with Silverman that data triangulation is inappropriate for 'adjudicating' between accounts (1993: 158), since it ignores how accounts arise in different contexts, there are insights to be gleaned from such a process, not least for the validity of some inferences that may be made about some data. The following example is illustrative.

Command and control data (calls to the police) from Merseyside Police were compiled according to the small area Enumeration Districts in the study areas, using the GIS facility at URPERRL, as indicated above. These data in the Earleschurch neighbourhood showed relatively high levels of calls about sexual offences. In Earleschurch as a whole, rates of reporting were 21 times the regional average, and higher rates (up to 89 times the regional average) were recorded in some subsections. (Other data indicated that these were mainly associated with prostitution-related activities.) It may be inferred that the disproportionate level of reporting indicated intolerance of prostitution in Earleschurch, or in sections of it. The validity of such a claim is questionable because the most we can glean from these data is that an unknown number of people report sexual offences, which are likely to be prostitution-related. We do not know how many people report, only the number of calls within a locality. Most importantly, we do not know why calls are made. We cannot assume that there is widespread support for a law-and-order response to prostitution. In short, we cannot assume that the indicator (calls to the police) is appropriate for shedding light onto more difficult to observe phenomena (intolerance).

Qualitative data: interviews with community groups, business pressure groups, victim support, and so on, throughout Earleschurch (see Chapter 6), suggested, on the contrary, that the community as a whole displayed a relatively high level of toleration towards street prostitution. Moreover, by asking quite general, open-ended questions, and allowing the respondents to take their answers in whichever ways they chose, and by adding 'anything else?' when they came to a halt, yielded very interesting data indeed. To illustrate, the following extracts indicate the responses from representatives from four community groups in Earleschurch, who were interviewed separately. They were responding to a question that asked them to talk about the problems they faced, and the irritations they felt, about living in their neighbourhood.

There is a lot of litter from the clubs – discarded curry and chip papers and other takeaway food. There are also problems with bottles and people urinating in the gardens because of the pubs and clubs around the area. The street lights are fine now. They didn't use to be but because of the new [. . .] buildings and the pressure from the [institution] there have been improvements. Occasionally there are streetlights knocked over and that is a mess because it takes ages for the council to repair them. Prostitution mainly takes place on [. . .] Street, not in this street, but I feel safer with the women walking around. I feel safe when there are lots of people about. I feel comfortable with the prostitutes, not a problem. That does not mean to say that the sex trade does not cause some problems for some people. There is a school down the road, a primary school [School's name]. There is a problem with condoms being left outside the school. There are also other problems with the school; absenteeism is a problem. (Professional woman in her fifties representing a mixed group of renters and owner-occupiers.)

Drugs are prevalent in the area, as they are elsewhere. Prostitution used to be more of a problem, say about 5 years ago, but it has declined in the last 5 years, the women have moved over towards [street name]. Most of the girls are on drugs, they were a bit of a nuisance but they didn't, don't bother me that much, more the people who are associated with them, the men. (Middle-aged white male professional representing a group mainly made up of professional people.)

Bottles are quite often broken on the outside wall [of the house]. The cars have been scratched as I said before. 'People hate success.' People like to bitch about things and complain – they like to blame. It is OK if you don't show success. There are people down the road who are very middle class but the outside of their house looks quite run down – they are OK – they try to blend in. The business next door has been targeted, they have a lot of problems. Other problems? There was someone recently who was pissing on the doorstep! The street-lighting is inadequate . . . The council came round with people from the home-watch and improved those that were felt to be inadequate but things have got bad again. Some in the home-watch scheme feel that the street-lighting is very inadequate, but some of the 'arty' people in the area like the Victorian look and don't want too many improvements. We get a lot of litter, especially glass bottles left on the window [there are several pubs in the vicinity]. I don't really mind myself but it does give the area a sense of neglect. There are abandoned buildings – there is one down the road with a nice patio, garden space with it. I thought that I would like to do something with it but there are soiled mattresses in that space. Things deteriorate when neglect gets a hold. (Woman aged 20–30, ex-student, representing a group, which includes a mix of owners, social and private renters and a mix of social classes.)

I have seen quite a lot of vandalism, gangs and the abuse that they have given us. The kids have nothing else to do and they have low self-esteem. As far as prostitution is concerned people are tolerant . . . because they know the women. People inter-relate. But some people have a nostalgic view of prostitutes. Many women are desperate for the next fix – desperate. It is awful to see, for our kids to see women like that. But we don't want to see the women more marginalized. There are more women than ever out at the moment. Some women are dealing. There are, it should be said, different levels of tolerance. People, in general, want the worst effects 'packaged' so that they feel safe. . . . Also, [prostitute] women tell people in the community about what they have seen, they tell people about neighbourhood or people problems. (Woman representing the community-wide residents' group)

These data make evident something of the complexity of community perceptions of, and responses to, disorder in Earleschurch, discussed further in Chapter 6. But in this context, further questions are raised: Who, then, is reporting prostitution-related activities, and why? How can we best account for the relative toleration displayed toward street prostitutes? These are some of the questions that were investigated in subsequent interviews. In so doing, further anomalies emerged and more questions were generated. For example, as the second extract indicates, some respondents regarded prostitution to have declined over recent years, while others, such as the respondent in the last extract, regarded the number of street-walkers to be on the increase (though relatively tolerant responses remained evident). Further inquiries revealed that the geography of prostitution had changed, and though there still appeared to be a perceived decline in the numbers of prostitute women on the whole, from the late 1980s, some residents had noticed an increase in numbers in their immediate area.

This discussion illustrates the importance of cross-method triangulation for testing *some* inferences, in some contexts. It also shows the importance of allowing respondents the freedom to elaborate their responses in a relatively unstructured way, in response to a carefully constructed question, and in a context where the research task has been presented in such a way that it should not influence respondents' answers. Of course, other studies have illustrated the importance of using a mixture of research methods. Janet Foster (in Foster and Hope's 1993 study of the impact of the Priority Estate Project on crime) noted, for example, that

> There is little doubt that the use of mixed methods in this evaluation was very important. Percentages are frequently given more credence than in-depth observations, but without the contextual information, survey data can be open to distortion and misinterpretation. Similarly ethnographic work will always be open to criticisms if observations cannot be supported with numerical and more generalisable data. (Foster and Hope 1993: 100)

The experience discussed here brings the importance of the eclectic approach into sharp relief. Moreover, it offers a cautionary tale for UK policy-makers who may consider (or who have) drawn upon command and control data as indicators of community perceptions of crime and disorder in their audits, and subsequently when developing their community safety plans under the Crime and Disorder Act (1998). It confirms the need to use other data to validate their conclusions. The remainder of this chapter discusses further issues to be considered by policy-making and academic researchers when conducting a research project such as this one. It deals with problems of intervention and identification, values in field research and, finally, those associated with 'writing up' the research.

Identifications and interventions

Because respondents were interviewed over a period of time, often at three-month intervals, relationships were established with respondents, which probably helped to put both them and me at ease. This

allowed for a style of interviewing that suited the particular respondent, the context and me. Sometimes, where appropriate, challenges to
points raised by some respondents were made and their reactions
helped to validate, contest or complicate earlier ideas. The way that
such interviews were managed relied on judgement, which in turn
relied upon having built up relationships with the respondents
concerned.

In building relationships with residents, one inevitably begins to
identify with many of the groups and individuals in the study. In these
communities, which are some of the most economically marginal in
Europe, it was difficult not to be moved by the ways in which people
manage to contend with difficulties. The poor conditions in which
people lived often made me angry, while witnessing people organizing
and taking action to overcome obstacles to improve their community
was inspirational. In these contexts, one can begin to understand why
people prioritize their (mail-order) 'catalogue' (if they can obtain one)
over other outgoings that may be prioritized by the debt counselling or
welfare rights advisers. For this is the only way to obtain 'luxuries' like
clothing and household appliances. In identifying with some of the
groups, however, a number of ethical and political dilemmas were
raised and interventions provoked. And, on a practical level, over-
identifying with a group may close off avenues of inquiry that may
otherwise be open. Though researchers are, after all, human beings
(Gans 1982)!

The issues associated with moving from observer to participant are
important ones since they have implications for the data collection
process, the data itself and the conclusions that may be drawn. One
may feel compelled to intervene for a number of reasons (see also Gans
1982). For example, field researchers are more or less dependent upon
sponsors to gain and maintain access to certain groups and areas of
social life that would otherwise be very difficult, if not impossible.
Such dependency can promote movement from observer to participant, despite intentions to the contrary. It was fairly common to be
asked 'What do you think?' during meetings with policy-makers and
community groups alike. Whilst 'The questions that the fieldworker is
asked are sometimes more important than the questions he himself
asks' (Bell and Newby 1971: 65), researchers need to be aware that
responses can influence the data itself. The pressure to do so can be
very strong, especially once a relationship has been established with a
sponsor (who believes the researcher possesses important knowledge or
a particular set of skills), or if a sponsor has developed an expectation

that the researcher will give support to their argument. This is not to suggest that 'participation' is not occurring in any case.

I follow Bell and Newby (1971), who suggested that researchers should report their interventions and activities as an actor, because the field of study has as a result been altered. There may be some advantages for the data in the sense that new insights may as a result of an intervention be gained into the social processes under observation, but new difficulties arise in the form of reduced levels of observation (Bell and Newby, 1971). I intervened occasionally – and reported them in my fieldnotes. For example, the possible negative implications of the 'zero-tolerance' initiative (referred to above) were brought to the attention of some of the officers involved in the operation. Two other instances stand out – both of which were reported on in my field-work diary. The first arose in relation to the group mentioned earlier in this chapter, who said people referred to their community as 'the Bronx or Beruit'. The tenants there had been campaigning for the redevelopment of the site. At first the tenants association wanted the maisonette flats converted into family houses. However, in November 1996 the council agreed that the maisonettes would be demolished and the area redeveloped by a housing association. The redevelopment would be put out to tender under the council's supervision; tenants were to be given the right to be involved in the negotiations and would have the right to return if they chose to do so. Later, I interviewed a representative of one of the regeneration initiatives, who informed me that it would be funding half of the redevelopment and the project was *not* going to be put out to tender. Instead, a [named] housing association would redevelop the site; it had an allocation from the Housing Corporation, which needed to be 'spent'. Later the housing association was contacted in the course of the project, though not specifically about this issue. During the subsequent meeting representatives indicated that a decision had been made that the area would be redeveloped on a mixed-tenure basis, which would include some rented accommodation, some housing provided on a co-ownership basis and some 'staircased' co-ownership units. (This is a scheme whereby people can buy increasing proportions, or all, of their dwelling if they can afford it, but if their circumstances change then the association can take back some or all of the property; the resident pays rent on the non-owned proportion. The scheme allows residents to remain living in the same dwelling.)

It was clear that many tenants of the pre-redevelopment scheme would not be able to gain access to these types of tenures. It was also apparent that tenants (who had campaigned for redevelopment) were now becoming increasingly marginal in the policy process. In this context, I mentioned that an active tenants association had been operating in the area. My respondents said they were unaware of the association, and added that all the tenants had now been 'decanted' (rehoused). My response affirmed that the tenants had been rehoused and I added that the tenants' association was maintaining contact with members nevertheless, and that they should be consulted.

In the second instance, my intervention came in the context where I was increasingly aware that housing associations were considering the disposal of some of their uneconomic, rehabilitated stock. Moreover, residents in properties managed by one housing association in particular reported that it was responding to emergency and urgent repairs only, and their cyclical maintenance programme was being cut. This fuelled the suspicions of tenants in one area where they were particularly concerned about the future of their housing; though it should be added that while some officers of their association had talked about disposals in interviews, they had not discussed it specifically with this area in mind. Nevertheless, the cost of maintenance and management was particularly high in the locality and this was understood by organized residents. In the context of my questions about changes in their locality, where housing had been a key aspect of my inquiries, tenants and residents asked about my thoughts on the matter of the maintenance cuts and what it may mean. They asked if I had any advice for them. I suggested in response that, following my analysis of some of the data collected to date, there may be a number of questions that they may wish to pose to the housing authorities in the area. For example, what do they consider to be the future of the rehabilitated stock? How do they propose to respond to the problems of the older properties? How do they envisage involving tenants in an area strategy that will secure the viability of the property and achieve stability in the area?

The issue of intervention raises another important issue, that of being perceived as being part of an organization. For example, if one goes out to observe the interaction between the police and community, one does not want to be thought of as a police officer, because the danger of being perceived in this way is that it may close off access to other groups or means of accessing data. In this research I tried to make sure that such observations took place towards the end of my fieldwork in each study area.

Values

As many commentators have argued, everyone brings their values and expectations to the field, and interventions indicate that they became manifest periodically. Furthermore, as Saunders suggested, problems found generally in social science research are likely to be exacerbated in contexts where differential power is part of the research project. 'The problem of values, for example, is likely to arise in particularly acute form when the subject matter of research is itself political' (Saunders 1983: 327). And, indeed, the subject matter is political, though not necessarily in the party-political sense. I do not intend to debate the desirability or otherwise of value-freedom in social science. Rather, my concern is to acknowledge that values and expectations can influence not only the data gathering process, but the writing of field-notes, the analysis of data and the conclusions drawn from it. Clearly values and expectations can have an impact on the objectivity of the research, and the difficulties associated with 'objectivity' must be recognized. Reflection on the data and the pursuit of alternative explanations and theories is the only practical way of moving forward with this issue (see Becker 1970). Nevertheless, it is not always possible to be self-consciously aware of one's own theories and expectations. Similarly, because this research was dependent upon information from informants and respondents, we need to be aware not only of our own biases and how they may effect the data, but also informants' own interests, which may be reflected in the way that data is transferred to the researcher (Becker 1970).

Leaving the field and writing up

Problems resulting from the way that some field researchers conducted fieldwork in Liverpool were raised earlier in this chapter. At this stage, we can note that the way researchers leave the field has implications not only for the collective expectations of the people with whom a researcher has had contact, but also for other field researchers who follow. Researchers must be aware of the unintended as well as the intended consequences of their activities (Solomos 1989; BSA 1992). I have tried to be aware of the issues associated with withdrawal from the field, the expectations of the respondents in terms of the way the project is written and could be disseminated, and what this may mean for the groups and individuals who have participated.[8]

Nevertheless, a number of concerns associated with these matters arose during the writing of this research and in earlier dissemination of its findings (Hancock 1996b, 1996c, 1997) that, despite best efforts, are not easily resolved. Throughout the project, I have considered it appropriate to maintain the anonymity[9] of the neighbourhoods where the research was conducted, because the stigma associated with high-crime areas, and those who live there, can have profound and lasting effects. To avoid contributing to this process, the author chose to use pseudonyms and, very occasionally, some features have been omitted. (It is hoped that, should the areas be recognized by any academic or other 'Sherlock Holmeses' (Parker 1974: 17), they will understand the rationale for this action and support my attempt to maintain anonymity for the localities.) However, the task of maintaining anonymity for research sites is difficult in community studies. As I have indicated, community members and agencies are apt to talk to each other and others. And, though I have made my desire to protect anonymity for the study sites known to all respondents, periodically they have sometimes forgotten and disclosed this information to other parties, albeit rarely. These problems are difficult to resolve and sometimes they lie beyond a researcher's control. They are made more arduous because some features of the research sites make them stand out, and in some instances they cannot be disregarded as a result of their importance to the research questions.

The professional traditions in sociology provide good practice guidance for researchers' relationships with informants and respondents and on attendant ethical considerations (BSA 1992). In practice, and certainly in the 'community study', managing ethical questions is not uncomplicated. As other authors have commented, the convention of ensuring that individuals are not recognizable, and the commitments to confidentiality and anonymity, are rather less easy to maintain than could be anticipated. Some individuals and organizations are, by their very position in the community social structure, recognizable by those with even a limited knowledge of the community under study (see for example Bell and Newby 1971). Changing the names of respondents is not enough in this context; it is difficult to disguise the identity of some informants or organizations without changing the meaning of their roles. Some measures can and have been taken in this work, but we necessarily fall back upon the additional need to render anonymous the research sites, and are forced to grapple with the problems accompanying this process, noted earlier. And, given the difficulties with this procedure, we need to acknowledge that the work may offend some respondents or organizations who *may* sense that they able to self-identify. As other writers have noted, in studies where power, class and status are principal parts of the research, it is likely that someone will be displeased with their portrayal (Bell and Newby 1971). It is my hope that those who are disappointed with their representation will not simply reject the study's findings and arguments. Rather, I hope that they will regard the ideas and arguments contained in the book as opening up the opportunity to debate some of its main concerns.

Conclusion

In this chapter I have tried to offer an honest account of the processes involved in researching neighbourhood change, crime and disorder in the main study sites. The chapter has examined the technical issues associated with collecting data in the research sites and their relationship to the theoretical issues that are explored in this book. It has explored some of the main obstacles to the gathering (and checking) of these data. Some of ways in which difficulties were resolved or not, as the case may be, have been described. In this way, the discussion has raised some of the key practical, political and ethical issues accompanying a study of this nature. Furthermore, it has illustrated some of the unique features of a 'community study' in the contemporary context. Consideration of some of the issues raised in this chapter may offer insights that may be of use to future researchers and policy-makers. None the less, it provides important background to the chapters that follow. The next, rather lengthy, chapter explores how neighbourhood decline, crime and disorder have been interpreted in studies in the UK and the USA before examining neighbourhood decline (and regeneration), and the place of crime and disorder, in the mixed housing areas that were the focus of this study.

3
Crime and the Urban Area: Explaining Neighbourhood Change and Crime

The aim of this chapter is to examine the connections between neighbourhood decline, crime and disorder. Since space limitations preclude an examination of all the literature in this burgeoning area, the chapter has two subsidiary aims. First, to weave analyses of crime and urban change (outlined in Chapter 1) more closely together. Second, to demonstrate the importance of this approach in a specific context, that of the mixed housing areas in Merseyside, which because of recent housing policies are becoming a feature of the contemporary urban landscape in Britain. The chapter is divided into three main sections. The first examines how changes in, and differences between, neighbourhood crime and offender rates have been explained in selected British studies. The second discusses insights from research in the USA on community change and crime. The third reflects upon sections one and two and synthesizes some of the key insights that find utility in the mixed housing areas in this study.

First we must be clear about the terms we are using. The concepts of 'neighbourhood change', 'neighbourhood decline' and 'gentrification' are introduced below.

Neighbourhood change

Skogan (1986; 1990) has usefully described how stable neighbourhoods reproduce themselves as social systems. Put simply, populations replicate themselves and the housing stock is regenerated. Threats to the stability of their social systems (including social and physical disorder) are averted – for example, by property owners maintaining and renewing their housing, or by the conscious or unconscious efforts of individuals and organizations (internal or external to the neighbourhood) who ensure that the neighbourhood is defended against destabilizing conditions.

Neighbourhood decline

Processes internal or external to neighbourhoods can 'trigger' change, disrupt their regeneration (Skogan 1986: 206) and result in decline. In the USA, Skogan has summarized some of these processes as follows:

1. *Disinvestment* by landlords and home-owners, and following the decisions of institutional actors such as mortgage and insurance companies.
2. *Construction and demolition* and nearby changes in land-use patterns, such as the building of freeways through neighbourhoods.
3. *Demagoguery*, by which Skogan is referring to the phenomenon of estate agents profiteering from the panic selling of white residents' property, who fear racial change in their locality, and sell (at inflated prices) to black and Hispanic residents seeking improvements to their housing situation.
4. *Deindustrialization*, loss of jobs, declining skill and wage levels; each diminishes community wealth. (Skogan 1986)

These categories are not exclusive, or exhaustive, and some of these processes may be found to be more useful than others in the UK context. The importance of demagoguery, for example, as Skogan described it, would seem to be less in contemporary Britain, where the provision of housing relies less on the operation of a 'free market' (though this is *not* to say that 'race' is not regarded as an indicator of urban deterioration). Moreover, the extent of local and national state intervention in the British context, reflected in the still relatively extensive social housing sector, for example, requires that we give due weight to the direct and indirect influence of public policies. Furthermore, the impact of the First and Second World Wars, both directly (through bomb damage) and indirectly (by promoting state intervention), is particularly germane in the UK context, as I show below.

What is important, however, is that the processes described by Skogan, some of which may be more prolonged than others, affect the status and number of people seeking to move in and out of neighbourhoods (Skogan 1986; 1990). Studies in Chicago have shown that those moving out tend to be more affluent, better educated nuclear families (Skogan and Maxfield 1981 in Skogan 1986). Those lacking such resources, and sometimes the more fearful, are left behind. The spiral of decline may continue as the housing market is destabilized in both the home-owner and rented sectors as the neighbourhood begins to attract those with only limited power in the market. Buildings may be abandoned as maintenance becomes uneconomic and, where demand remains for housing, its use may change to accommodate the new population. Skogan notes, for example, how large family units may be broken up for multiple occupation, with further implications for the ways in which an area's future demography will be structured (1986: 209). Once the destabilizing factors have established themselves the process of decline may accelerate.

Gentrification

On the other hand, neighbourhoods may undergo rapid change and destabilization and improve as part of a gentrification process, once investment has reached a sustainable level (Skogan 1990). Skogan argues that poorer neighbourhoods are not necessarily threatened by such processes, since it is disinvestment not investment that threatens them. Moreover, he suggests that, on the whole, few people are forced to move because of rising house prices; it affects only a small part of the housing market. Far more important, in his view, are the political decisions made by powerful institutions such as local governments, banks, insurance companies and so on. In the following section of this chapter we see, indeed, that decisions made by powerful institutions, particularly local authorities, are especially pertinent in the British context. Some of the implications of 'gentrification' for the study areas in Merseyside are discussed in Chapters 5 and 6.

1. Residential community crime careers: British studies

The studies drawn upon in this section highlight the importance of housing policies and practices for understanding variations in crime at the local level and changes thereof over time. At the onset we need to acknowledge that some of these studies refer to *offender rates*, while the present author's research was concerned with victimization rates. Furthermore, as Bottoms (1994) has noted, we cannot assume that areas with high offence rates and areas with high numbers of resident offenders are the same, though there is some interconnectedness (see also Bottoms and Wiles 1986; Bottoms et al. 1992; Herbert 1982). The role of housing markets in offender-based residential community crime careers have been the subject of more research in the UK; and the processes, as we shall see, are easier to distinguish. While the role of the housing market in 'offence-based' community crime careers in the UK are less striking, as Bottoms et al. (1992) have argued (and demonstrated – see Bottoms and Wiles 1986), it is significant. What is important, at this stage, is to note that certain kinds of areas, particularly city centres and other 'offence attracting areas', need to be approached slightly differently (Bottoms and Wiles 1986).

It is also important to recognize that the housing market does not operate independently. As Bottoms et al. (1992: 123) note, the housing market 'interacts with a range of other aspects of social life to create the relevant social effects'. These include *social networks, socialization processes, social control agencies, reputations and labels, economic development* and the *physical form* of the locality; each plays a part in creating conditions in which offender-based community crime careers can flourish. These processes, of course, take place in the context of wider changes in the political economy; though while national trends (changes in housing policy for example), regional or sub-regional conditions (fluctuations in the labour market for example) may influence social life and crime in neighbourhoods, the process is not mechanical. Herbert put it thus:

> In the same way as traditional criminological theory has identified poverty and disadvantage as conditions which *may* lead to criminal behaviour, so the forces which in turn produce poverty and disadvantages have influential but not mechanistic roles. Between 'the system' and its outcomes are many mediating factors, the effects of these need to be considered and give the question of understanding crime both its complexity and elusiveness. Areal analyses of crime and offenders must work in these terms. (Herbert 1982: 103)

Thus, we need to take account of the variability of responses (Herbert 1982): as Massey's (1995) analysis informs us (see Chapter 1), the effects will vary between cities and localities within them. In the UK, the role of local government will be important for structuring and mediating wider, societal-level processes, particularly in the areas of resource allocation, where councils have some autonomy from central government. This is clearly seen in Bottoms et al.'s (1992; 1986) research where they have shown how the 'housing market' in Sheffield is composed differently compared with those of other cities in England and Wales. Its larger proportion of council properties for rent contrasts with many other UK cities (excepting Scotland) – and can be seen as a reflection of the interests and power of organized labour in the local council. The allocation of these properties was also somewhat different to practices employed elsewhere (Bottoms and Wiles 1986).

It is significant that these authors draw attention to the political complexion of the city council, in their case the role of the Labour Party in promoting public ownership of housing. There may be variations in tenure composition, quality, and possibly allocation policies in localities where powerful interests, promoting particular housing services and modes of delivery, have been able to exert their will over local housing policies at particular times (see Smith and Whysall 1991, for example). These may have implications for the configuration of residential community crime careers. In turn, such considerations require that we recognize changing relationships between national and local government: the extent to which local policy-makers have been constrained by national legislation or have been able to resist aspects of its implementation. In housing this is particularly significant. Many early housing policies were permissive, and over recent years the scope for determining housing policies locally has diminished (see Chapter 1). Nevertheless, even though housing policies have been brought ever closer into line with central government, local conditions have a considerable mediating effect.

The importance of local housing 'market' conditions and allocation processes are evident in Foster and Hope's (1993) study of the impact of the Priority Estates Project on crime in local authority housing estates in Hull and London. Very briefly, they found that the PEP model's ability to reduce crime through strengthening residents' capacity to exercise informal social control was partial. Degrees of transience and population heterogeneity were principal components influencing its success. These were shaped variously by the social mix of the estates, councils' allocation policies and the nature and degree of 'market' demand. Not surprisingly these were different in each urban setting. For example, as a result of pressure on the housing market, the London (control and experimental) estates did not house large numbers of young single people in their own flats. By contrast, in Hull, where the housing market was much more fluid, large numbers of poor, vulnerable, single homeless people were accommodated in high-rise blocks on the experimental estate, which were experiencing low demand. These facilitated the development of a 'subterranean culture' in which crime and victimization often flourished unchecked. In contrast, other aspects of the PEP programme, such as environmental design, tenant involvement and improvements in housing management, served to increase stability in other sectors of the estate. The effect was an increasing concentration of crime and victimization in the area occupied by the young poor on the estate.

Studies in local authority controlled housing

One of the first attempts to investigate areal dimensions of crime in a systematic way was Baldwin and Bottoms' study in Sheffield. Since the publication of *The Urban Criminal* in 1976, several localities in the city have been examined by Bottoms and his colleagues. Their task was (1) to explain why seemingly similar areas consistently support markedly different levels of criminality and (2) to explain how the 'community crime careers' of these areas change over time. In a number of papers (Bottoms and Xanthos 1981; Bottoms and Wiles 1986; Bottoms et al. 1989; Bottoms et al. 1992) that analyse the various pairs of estates or housing areas, they emphasize the primary, if unintended, role of the housing and planning policies (housing allocation processes in particular) in their explanations. 'Gardenia' and 'Stonewall', for example, two similar pre-Second World War council estates, had very different offender rates in the early stages of their study. In Gardenia, offences against residents were more than three times higher than in Stonewall (Bottoms et al. 1989), despite the fact that they contained similar populations with regard to social class and gender composition. Both estates had relatively well-settled populations.

The authors draw attention to a number of events and phenomena in their explanation of the difference in offender rates between Gardenia and Stonewall, and the development of Gardenia's crime career. They note how, during the 1930s, Gardenia was beginning to lose its standing as a desirable estate (built to house the artisan working classes in the 1920s) as modern estates were developed; this process accelerated during the early post-war period. A number of families who were labelled 'rough' moved onto the estate in the 1940s and the number of 'respectable' families leaving increased. Gardenia began to obtain a reputation that, once acquired, was difficult to eradicate. Gardenia's reputation interacted with the housing allocation system to consolidate the process of decline; like other unpopular estates, Gardenia attracted people in acute housing need who are likely to face more problems of a material and social nature than those housed via the General Waiting List. Other incoming residents were more likely to have strong connections (family ties, for example) with people on the estate, and this helped to nurture a strong subculture on (the south-eastern part of)

Gardenia. The subculture, supported by long tenancies, was significant for understanding crime in Gardenia; it tended to accentuate the separate leisure time of adults (in pubs, bingo halls and clubs) and children, which meant that children were often left to their own devices. Moreover, the subculture tolerated and sometimes encouraged offending, since most members were involved in offending behaviour to some degree (Bottoms et al. 1989).

Bottoms and his colleagues do not suggest that tenants were 'dumped' on Gardenia. Rather they 'self-selected' themselves for housing in the locality, sometimes out of dire housing need (having been advised of waiting periods for the different estates in Sheffield by housing officers) and sometimes because they already had strong connections with the area (relatives on the estate for example). The authors show very clearly how significant it is to understand:

1. The direct and indirect effects of the housing allocation system on an estate with Gardenia's history, including the effect of the estate's negative reputation on the residents themselves.
2. The indirect social effects of the rather unusual geographical features of Gardenia, especially the south-east corner, which tended to 'cut it off', and with the long tenancies facilitated the development of a subculture.
3. Various issues associated with the socialization of children.
4. It is possible that the schools serving the estates had a differential impact upon them.

In their replication of the study in 1988 (Bottoms et al. 1992), Gardenia and Stonewall were found to have similar offence rates, though differential police reporting in each locality indicated that, officially at least, Stonewall was not as crime prone as Gardenia (see Bottoms et al. 1992). Gardenia's offender rate remained higher, but the difference between the estates had diminished compared to rates during the mid-1970s. In their explanation for the convergence, Bottoms and his colleagues point to changes in housing and social policy. As in their earlier paper (Bottoms and Wiles 1986), they recognize the importance of seeing changes in housing at the local level in the context of the changing political economy of housing in the UK. The authors also argue the significance of formal and informal attempts by the local authority to mediate such changes. For example, they note how some high-demand estates were insulated from pressures to accommodate homeless families.

Many components of their explanation for the convergence of crime rates reflect national trends. For example, Stonewall not only found itself accommodating high proportions of slum clearance tenants in the 1970s, whose stigmatization was commonplace in the UK, but also an increasing number of homeless families, following the Housing Act (Homeless Persons) 1977. These groups were often regarded in the same stigmatized way in public discourses during the late 1970s and early 1980s. In Stonewall's case, these also included a number of travellers, who have traditionally been regarded as 'undesirable'; residents clearly saw the estate's status to be plummeting. Gardenia, on the other hand, saw marginal improvements between the mid-1970s and 1988. Its standing in the housing hierarchy in Sheffield was elevated as estates containing high-rise flats were seen to be increasingly unattractive and unpopular. In part because of a modernization process and the 'decanting' of tenants, the strong subculture that characterized the south-eastern part of the estate was, to some extent, broken up. Bottoms et al. (1992) also suggest that improvements in the local school and the long-term impact of a crime reduction initiative, which may have had a positive impact on the estate by strengthening the organizational capacity of residents, may have been influential in the convergence. Reductions in child density may have been important too. Nevertheless, the role of the housing market was as central to their explanation of community crime careers in 1988 as it had been in 1976 – an argument reflected in many other studies, notably that of Owen Gill.

Shortly after the publication of Baldwin and Bottoms' *The Urban Criminal*, Owen Gill published *Luke Street* (1977). Like the Sheffield study, it emphasized the importance of housing market and its interaction with area reputation in understanding the community's crime career. The study, located in the Merseyside region, acknowledges the significance of the local economy and culture for understanding crime patterns and forms, though not in isolation: the author places the development of these in Luke Street's socio-spatial and historical context. In his explanation of Luke Street's decline, Gill notes that the small area (a few streets) contains almost half of the very large council houses (four and five bedrooms) put up in the whole of the town before 1946. Until the 1950s it was regarded as some of the better publicly owned housing. However, new estates of a higher standard were built outside the town in the early post-war period, and slum clearance began. Gradually the West End became the centre of the town. Luke Street's desirability fell to the point that it was at or near the bottom of the local housing area hierarchy. Housing records indicated that those deemed the 'worst' applicants were offered accommodation in the West End, and Luke Street in particular. From the 1950s, Luke Street increasingly housed families facing problems of a material nature 'resulting from the combined effect of large families [those sent to Luke Street had, on average, nine members], low paid, insecure work and possible ill health and unemployment' (Gill 1977: 29). But it was the families themselves, rather than the difficulties they faced, that were regarded as problematic by official agencies. Many of the tenants who had moved there when it was regarded as 'select' wanted to move out of the area, while few wished to move in. Vacant properties and vandalism became more prominent, which attracted the interest of the press (thus promoting its damaging reputation). Gill clearly shows how a large number of young people growing up together helped to form a strong subculture. The boys and young men in particular were regarded as trouble-makers and, lacking other identities, identified with the label (Gill 1977).

Like Bottoms et al., Gill describes a situation in Luke Street in which the unintended consequences of housing and planning policies are fundamentally important for understanding the creation of an area with a high offender rate. The housing department had to contend with the implications of a planning policy that had located a large pro-portion of the town's largest public housing stock in one place. Once its reputation had become established, as in Gardenia, the housing department was limited in its capacity to end the stigmatization of Luke Street; 'better' tenants refused to be rehoused in the area (Gill 1977: 40).

Barke and Turnbull's (1992) study of Meadowell also has as its central concern the way that Meadowell (an estate that received national media attention during disturbances in the north-east of England and elsewhere during September 1991) emerged as a so-called 'problem estate'. Similarly, these authors argue the need to locate Meadowell in its socio-political and historical context, within the city-region (and beyond), to understand its problems and reputation. To illustrate, the change from housing artisan workers in the early inter-war period to providing subsidies for housing slum clearance tenants (in estates such as Meadowell) under the Housing Act (1930) promoted the idea that the 'least deserving' would benefit from public subsidy. Furthermore, the undesirable image of the estate and those who occu-pied it must have been confirmed for many as the official disinfesta-tion policy, directed at new slum-clearance tenants, was implemented. The labelling process had begun.

Meadowell was used to rehouse slum clearance and overcrowded families. Priority was given to those households living four or more to a room, despite Meadowell's relatively small properties (the majority having three or four rooms). As a consequence large families were concentrated on Meadowell. This added to the reputation of the estate, as larger families had increasingly been associated with irresponsibility and lack of intelligence from the Victorian and Edwardian periods (Barke and Turnbull 1992). In the post-war period Meadowell's problems began to grow. By the 1970s population turnover increased and the downward spiral became more firmly established. The building of other estates in the post-war period may have lowered Meadowell's standing and, like Luke Street and Gardenia, a number of large, low-income families were concentrated in a section of the estate. The number of one-parent families also increased during the 1960s and 1970s so that this group constituted a third by 1979 (Barke and Turnbull 1992: 55). Relative deprivation became more severe,[1] fertility increased, and unemployment grew throughout the 1970s.[2] The number of people wishing to leave the estate multiplied and Meadowell increasingly housed those with little power in the housing market, including many young people allocated though the 'homeless' route. Voids on Meadowell increased rapidly and became the target for arson attacks and vandalism, according to these authors.

In this study we can see, very clearly, reflections of national trends: special attention to slum clearance tenants, the socio-spatial consequences of the economic downturn of the 1970s, and the growing presence of homeless people on estates during the 1980s, for example. We can also appreciate how particular social relations, practices and persistent ideologies can affect an estate many years (or decades later). In some localities, like Meadowell, the notion that a local authority housing estate is 'problematic' in some way has been present soon after its completion. Similar processes were observed in Merseyside and have been recorded elsewhere (see Damer 1974; Herbert 1982).

One of the local authority controlled housing estates in this research (see Chapter 2), like Meadowell, was built under legislation developed to rehouse those affected by slum clearance in the 1930s. The original inhabitants had resided in several streets of unsanitary houses, built during the mid-nineteenth century, whose names were synonymous with crime and dangerousness in local folklore. More often than not they were poor, large families who worked, often on a casual basis, in port-related work. After the slums were scheduled for demolition the tenants were accommodated in the new properties. But the stigma associated with their previous locality moved with them. According to local people and officials the estate 'always' had a bad reputation. Nowadays, those housed there have either no housing choice or are relatives of those living on the estate who wish to live near their families and friends. Indeed, housing officers say family names can be traced, in their records, to the 1930s. Though tenants' local connections are important for understanding the ways in which the estate reproduces itself, some housing officials privately acknowledged that once people are housed there they cannot easily transfer out, even if they wish to; the housing department prevents it. The department knows that the properties are unlikely to be re-let; and the prospect of more empty properties is resisted. Like Meadowell, it is an area with a (relatively) high offender rate and, like Meadowell, economic deprivation is endemic; two-thirds of all residents over 16 years of age are economically inactive. Set against this background it is not surprising that recent attempts to improve the area's reputation and standing by improving the housing (in local parlance, 'tarting up the housing') has met with little success. But it has not been without some benefits: residents have seen improvements to the condition of their properties.

Studies in non-local authority controlled housing areas

Though a great deal of the British research has been very much concerned with local authority provision, Bottoms and his colleagues included two private rental areas in their study in Sheffield between the mid-1970s and mid-1980s. They were interested in the implications of changing tenure patterns for community 'crime careers'. Also, Herbert conducted studies in Cardiff and Swansea in the 1970s which, though city-wide, included a number of areas where the housing was not controlled by the local authority (see Herbert 1982). But these are exceptions. They are also quite dated (see Chapter 1). Nevertheless, these studies are significant for generating insights that may assist our understanding of mixed housing areas in the current context. In Bottoms and Wiles' study (1986), 'Havelock' is the most interesting of the two areas (the other is referred to as 'Graybridge'), and the following section concentrates on the Havelock area.

'Havelock' was developed in the mid-nineteenth century as housing for the merchant class; it is located quite near to Sheffield's city centre. In the early decades of the twentieth century this class moved out and multiple occupation became widespread, although some owner-occupation remained. The relatively small residential area is described as being bounded by many public buildings; within its distinctive boundaries a mix of social classes inhabited the area. Havelock was known as the main 'red-light' district in Sheffield and as an area where drug use was high. It had the highest recorded notifiable offender and offence rate of any residential district in the city (Bottoms and Wiles 1986). Part of the reason for the high crime rate was found in an examination of the opportunities available in the area for the commission of crimes, such as those presented by multiple occupation for burglaries (Bottoms and Wiles 1986). Bottoms and Wiles also suggested that the area allowed for a degree of socialization into deviant behaviour and that, to an extent, the deviant status of Havelock was accommodated by its inhabitants. Older residents complained about problems, such as prostitution, but the authorities were reluctant to intervene in less serious incidents because the area was scheduled for redevelopment.

Subsequent changes in housing policy, however, had a significant impact upon social life and crime in Havelock over the decade from the mid-1970s to the mid-1980s. In particular, it benefited from the shift from clearance to rehabilitation and the use of improvement grants and area-based improvement initiatives, especially as it was regarded locally as being desirable and worth preserving. Middle-class professionals, especially home-owners, in the area were instrumental in organizing for improvement policies to be implemented in Havelock, and in 1978 it was declared a Housing Action Area. As a consequence, planning blight was removed and the private rented stock declined as a small number of properties moved into owner-occupation and others were taken over by housing associations. These factors combined to show evidence of gentrification in the area, although in many ways it remained a poor area (Bottoms and Wiles 1986). Some of the newcomers added their voices in opposition to the deviant status of the neighbourhood, prostitution in particular. The authorities responded to their concerns with traffic management schemes to disrupt the clients of prostitutes, as well as other physical crime reduction strategies (Bottoms and Wiles 1986). But the authors could find no evidence of prostitution declining as a result of the intense political pressure that emerged in the early 1980s. The important point is that housing policy caused changes in the social composition of the area and transformed the locality into a desirable residential district in spite of its reputation. Nevertheless, Bottoms and Wiles note that Havelock continued to have one of the highest offender and offence rates in Sheffield; burglary and drugs were seen as being particular problems for the area.

The emergence and impact of a neighbourhood reputation are, perhaps, more complex in mixed housing areas compared with local authority controlled sites. Note, for example, Bottoms and Wiles' point that Havelock was seen as a desirable district despite its reputation. In considering this, it is necessary to reflect on the role of the local authority in the emergence of reputations in such areas, along with those of other powerful bodies. Evidently the local authority is important despite its lack of, or more limited, involvement in housing management. It is likely that planning decisions made by the council, the funding possibilities that these create, and the ideological messages such policies convey are of importance in this matter. In the Sheffield study, the council's decision to clear the area under its slum clearance programme, with its attendant implications for 'red-lining' by building societies and, later, its decision to grant Housing Action Area status under the 1974 Housing Act, were pivotal processes in Havelock's status career. Nevertheless, the precise role played by the local authority and by other powerful city institutions in the creation or diminution of reputations in mixed housing areas of British cities is unclear. These issues need further research. We also need to remember that people do not accept labels unquestioningly (see Damer 1974); though whether communities in non-local-authority controlled areas are more able to resist such labels remains an interesting question. In Edgebank, for example, an area with an offence rate that was usually in the top three crime-prone police beats in the town, residents invariably named other areas (mainly local authority estates) as being more crime prone, often incorrectly as far as official figures were concerned. In Earleschurch the picture was more complicated. Community organizations challenged the reputation of the area on one hand, and on the other said that they were 'unconcerned' about it, while some *used* it, and the presence of social disorder that helps to sustain it, when they campaigned for more resources of one kind or another. These practices reflect the limited number of campaigning options open to community groups in inner-city areas when attempting to obtain scarce resources. These issues are explored further in Chapter 6.

Housing policy, ideology and reputations

Through an examination of many British studies of residential community crime careers it is possible to trace some of the main changes in housing policy over the last century. Changing political attitudes towards council housing, in particular, are evident, though they are not always explicit in the various texts (for a summary of political attitudes towards council housing see Darke 1991). For example, we can trace the building of dwellings for better off, respectable, working-class people in the 1920s (Gardenia, for example), which followed the shortages left in the wake of the First World War and the need to appease organized labour in a context of political unrest (Lowe 1991; Darke 1991). The poor and 'undeserving' were expected to benefit from the 'trickle-down' effect. In contrast, in the 1930s policy often focused upon slum clearance; standards were poorer and rents more affordable for less well off tenants (Meadowell, for example). Malpass and Murie noted that one of the considerations underpinning the lowering of standards 'was probably to make council housing less attractive to those who could afford to secure private accommodation' (in Lowe 1991: 6). Following the Second World War, Bevan (Minister of Health) ushered in a period where council housing was to be seen as a high-quality good, for *all* social classes (Darke 1991). This is reflected in the lowering of Luke Street and Meadowell's standing in the housing hierarchy, in Gill's and Barke and Turnbull's studies respectively. In both cases, their status fell as new estates were built to much better standards. Bevan's approach was short lived: a more residual role was envisaged for council housing from the mid-1950s (Darke 1991). High-rise building was supported by both Labour and Conservatives in this period (Darke 1991). But the impact of these policies on local communities, once the worst slums had been demolished, was reflected in the protests that emerged around slum clearance in the 1970s (Darke 1991; Lowe 1991).

The shift in policy from slum clearance to rehabilitation in the 1970s, which benefited Havelock (Bottoms and Wiles 1986), followed in part because of the financial crisis in this period (Lowe 1991). Housing associations were envisaged to play a major role in the Housing Action Areas declared under the auspices of the 1974 Housing Act (Balchin 1995). The importance of this was seen in Havelock (Bottoms and Wiles 1986), and their role will be seen to an even greater extent later in this chapter. During the 1970s, the number of homeless people increased, as it did throughout the 1980s and 1990s, particularly among the young (Balchin 1995), when the sector was shrinking (the number of good-quality dwellings in particular, because of the 'right to buy'). The impact of these national-level trends was reflected in the Stonewall and Meadowell studies.

The significance of all this lies in the 'messages' that various pieces of legislation have transmitted about the status of public housing in particular. First, we should note that one of the main issues that have traditionally divided Labour and Conservative parties has tended to be associated with the 'quantity, quality and pricing' of public housing, derived from different ideologies about its role (Darke 1991: 159). Conservatives have traditionally supported minimalist provision in periods of chronic housing shortages; for specific groups, or those on low incomes who could not afford decent housing in the private market; and, during the 1980s, for the most economically marginal, if at all (Darke 1991). By comparison, Labour governments have *traditionally* sought to develop council housing as a major part of overall housing provision, 'catering for a broad section of the working class or even potentially for almost the whole population (1945–50)' (Darke 1991: 160). The importance of public housing in Labour's manifesto commitments has diminished over recent years.

Despite party ideologies, inevitably there have been compromises. The exigencies of war (1914–18, 1939–45), political pressures and economic imperatives have variously constrained ideology-driven housing policies of Liberal, wartime Coalition, Conservative and Labour governments in the UK (see also Darke 1991; Lowe 1991; Harloe 1995). The housing forms that have resulted from trade-offs struck over housing policies, locally and nationally, in these contexts have in large part shaped urban Britain.

'Messages' conveyed by various national housing policies, the funding following them, and the rhetoric surrounding them, have influenced the status of public housing and its tenants in public discourses during the last 80 or so years. At particular periods, council housing has been portrayed as a desirable commodity for the fortunate and respectable. In others, such as in the contemporary phase in the UK, the sector has been viewed as a problem rather than a solution; a stigmatized tenure for the unfortunate few. Against this, home ownership has been regarded as the standard to which all should aspire. In short, national housing policies have played a significant part in the labelling of council housing estates. Policies at the local level, of course, can ameliorate or exacerbate the labelling process (policies to disinfest slum clearance tenants, for example). In this way, some national housing policies may have, in part, contributed to the development of community crime careers in British cities, through the role it has played in the creation of area reputations. Nor is the process confined to council housing. Over recent years, housing associations have been concerned about following local authorities down a path of stigmatization. As Dow put it

> For me, the greatest task that faces associations is to create a dramatically improved image of renting as a housing tenure. That includes

changing the social and economic image of those who rent. To do this, we *must* stop our housing becoming the exclusive preserve of the poor. We must do this, not because we have lost any commitment to those in the greatest need, but because we have to recognise that the society around us is unsympathetic to those it believes have failed.[3]

He adds,

But ask any man or woman in the street what they now think of council housing. They think it has failed. For many the most powerful totem of this failure is the inner city tower block, synonymous with rotten living conditions, social decay and eventually, public housing as a whole.[4]

Despite these warnings, many housing associations have found that much of their stock is occupied by welfare dependent tenants; their older stock is deteriorating, and some housing association estates have begun to develop problems akin to those in the council rented sector.

There is, of course, nothing new in arguing the importance of connecting societal-level processes with those operating at city and local levels. Such an argument is reflected in Herbert's 'framework for a geography of crime' (1982: 26). Here the interactions between macro (including ideologies, power and resources), meso (for instance, the allocation and management of resources) and micro level social processes (patterns of local, social behaviour and responses, for example) are emphasized (see also Bottoms and Wiles 1997). Nevertheless, there is a tendency to make our arguments at a particular level often between two of the three levels, without recognizing the *nature* of the *interactions* that take place between each. Moreover, the way in which actors and institutions operating at each level mediate the processes that occur between them, in different urban spaces and times, remains under-researched, in part because of an absence of appropriate data.

2. Residential community crime careers: some insights from the USA

This section explores some of the insights that can be gleaned from American studies of residential community crime careers. Here, researchers have benefited from access to longitudinal data for particular cities (notably Chicago). Longitudinal studies are, as Reiss (1986) notes, essential if we are to map changes over time, though they are expensive to conduct. To be most effective, studies should be replicated at relatively short intervals, since communities often undergo rapid change. Crime rates need to be studied in the context of residents' behaviour, community organization and structural properties. Study designs should recognize the place and order of communities within the city region, if we are to fully understand the variability of communities (Reiss 1986). Unfortunately, such studies, excepting those in Sheffield, are rare in the UK context.

As I indicated in Chapter 1, the links between urban change and crime were central to the work of the Chicago School in the second quarter of the twentieth century; and much urban criminology can be traced back to their work. It is appropriate, then, to begin with Park, Burgess, and MacKenzie's theory of urban change, known as the 'human ecology approach' developed in the School of Sociology at the University of Chicago. Chicago, the site of the study, was then a centre of population growth fuelled by migration from the South and from overseas.

Clifford Shaw and Henry McKay, in their famous study *Juvenile Delinquency and Urban Areas* (1942), drew upon Park et al.'s theory of urban change. In their model, the city is composed of a number of zones. A 'zone in transition' (of old subdivided houses) encircles the Central Business District (the 'loop' in Chicago) and the zone of factories. This zone is 'invaded' by the expansion of businesses and manufacturing. In zone three are the workers, who have escaped from the deteriorating conditions found in the 'zone in transition', but who remain in proximity to the CBD and factories because of their need to be near their place of work. In residential zone four are the high-class apartment buildings and single family dwellings. Beyond this is a commuter zone (zone five), a suburban zone of single family dwellings. The CBD is the dominant zone. As it expands, it pushes the other zones further and further out (Shaw and McKay 1942; Bassett and Short 1980).

Migrants entering the city could afford only the cheap rented accommodation in the zone in transition. In the model, as the CBD expands, the housing stock is reduced and people are forced to 'invade' the other residential areas, eventually 'succeeding' the previous population. The competition for space, the process of urban change, for Park and Burgess, is characterized as a series of invasions and successions (Park et al. 1923; Bassett and Short 1980).

There have been a number of extensions to, modifications of (Hoyt argued the importance of 'sectors' rather than 'zones', for example, in 1939, in Bassett and Short 1980) and criticisms made of the model (see Bassett and Short 1980 and Saunders 1986 for useful summaries). Space precludes a thorough examination of these. However, before examining Shaw and McKay's insights, we should note that in the British context many writers have referred to a 'zone of transition' rather than a 'zone in transition' (Haddon 1970). Analyses have centred upon changes in the *use* of housing. Typically these have focused on changes in use from Victorian town houses built for the middle classes to subdivided dwellings occupied by lower-status groups (Haddon 1970: 123; see also Rex and Moore 1967). In Park et al.s model, their emphasis was on the expansion of the central business district, which led to 'both a change of land use and a change in the resident population within the same land use type' (Haddon 1970: 120). This is not to say, in making this observation, that the expansion of the CBD is not important in the UK context; it is. However, by focusing on changes in the use of residential housing, analyses have been more rooted in the political economy of housing. Moreover, they have taken place in a context where economic pressures to expand the CBD have been more constrained by planning regulations (Haddon, 1970). Thus, in Britain, analyses more readily rejected the notion that urban change was a 'natural' process that would result in equilibrium. Writers such as Pahl (1970) emphasized that individuals are not autonomous decision-making units. Rather, decisions take place in a context where power and knowledge are not evenly distributed; land and housing are managed by 'agents', who operate in a context where conflicts between different interests have to be resolved (Pahl 1970; Bassett and Short 1980). One further point about context is noteworthy: as I have indicated, Park et al. and Shaw and McKay worked in a setting characterized by rapid growth. In the Merseyside research, as in many other cities in the UK and North America, the context is one of decline (see Chapter 1). I return to this point and its importance below.

Many writers discuss the Chicago School's methodological contributions and there is no need to rehearse these here. Suffice it to note that data collected in Chicago from the 1920s and since has been an invaluable resource for subsequent generations of theorists. Shaw et al. collected, on an ongoing basis, masses of primary data. In addition to data collected through their ethnographic work in the neighbourhoods (Bursik and Grasmick 1993), they collected data from the courts, which included the home addresses, offences and the age and gender of offenders. They achieved a data set of male adolescents referred to the Cook County Juvenile Court from 1900 to 1965 (Bursik and Grasmick 1993). The residential address of each individual was plotted onto a base map of the city. Rates of delinquency were then computed on the basis of census tracts. What is significant is that Shaw and McKay observed how (1) juvenile delinquency had a definite spatial pattern; (2) the number of delinquents decreased as the distance from the city centre increased; (3) rates of delinquency in the inner areas were stable over time, even though the populations changed rapidly. Shaw and McKay concluded that the pattern of neighbourhood delinquency was related to the same processes that gave rise to the socio-economic structure of urban areas, noted above (Bursik and Grasmick 1993). Areas with high rates of economic deprivation (the inner areas) tended to have high rates of population turnover, because they were undesirable residential areas – people sought to leave when they could. They also contained heterogeneous populations. These factors, according to Shaw and McKay, created a context in which it was difficult for residents to achieve common goals (see also Bursik and Grasmick 1993): they were socially disorganized (Bursik and Grasmick 1993); rapid population turnover and heterogeneity thwarted neighbourhood-based social controls, necessary to provide an environment relatively free from crime. High rates of crime and delinquency, they argued, are more likely in such a context (see Bursik and Grasmick 1993).

The idea of 'social disorganization' has been the subject of considerable criticism. Critics have noted that delinquency may be a factor used to define social disorganization, as well as a consequence – resulting in analytical muddle (Bursik and Grasmick 1993; Bottoms and Wiles 1997). Others have noted that crime is often high in areas with dense family networks and kinship ties, which are very stable over time (Bottoms and Wiles 1997). Commentators have argued the need to recognize the links between neighbourhood communities and networks, and society at large, its power structures and economic context (Bursik and Grasmick 1993; Bottoms and Wiles 1997). Furthermore, it has been suggested that (1) it is deterministic – over-predictive of crime (Bottoms and Wiles 1997); (2) it implies a 'consensus view' of community (Bursik 1988), which suggests that there is agreement or a consensus about crime and signs of disorder; (3) it ignores how 'different types of social organization and disorganization can coexist in a neighbourhood' (Bottoms and Wiles 1997: 342). Despite these criticisms, as Bottoms and Wiles note, the concept has been resilient. Recent work has taken account of some of these criticisms, and the theory has been refined, and has been argued to have utility not least in the study of victimization (see Bursik 1988; Bursik and Grasmick 1993). For this reason I return to the concept below.

Following more recent observations that some neighbourhoods' crime rates exhibited change, rather than stability, a number of writers turned their attention to 'residential community crime careers' (Reiss 1986). Reiss, in his influential essay 'Why Are Communities Important for Understanding Crime?', noted that the driving forces behind change in residential community crime careers are (1) population shifts, which alter the social and organizational structure of a community and (2) and the 'ageing and evolution of a city's community configuration' (Reiss 1986: 19). He also noted that, for some theorists, crime itself is regarded as influential, as populations respond to changes in rates of crime in their locality (a point I return to below).

As in the UK literature, the housing market plays an influential role in these changes, but in general its place is as part of a loop involving the processes noted by Reiss (above) in the context of wider changes in the structure of the urban environment. These include, for example, economic decline, depopulation and consequent reduction in the demand for some housing types. This approach is reflected in Skogan's findings regarding disorder and decline (in the introductory sections in this chapter) and in the work of Taub et al. (1984).

Taub et al. highlight the importance of the following factors for understanding neighbourhood change in urban areas. First, *ecological facts* – such as the potential employment base, pressure on the housing market, age and quality of the housing stock, amenities; they determine the social and economic context of the area (1984: 182–3). Second, *corporate and institutional decisions* – such as those of banks, universities, insurance companies and so on, because they can 'buttress or abandon a neighbourhood' (1984: 183). They not only contribute to the ecological make-up of the locality but can play other important roles, for example as a lobby of government, or as supporters of community organizations. Conversely, decisions to move away from a neighbourhood can have a devastating, negative multiplier effect.

Taub et al. discuss the importance of community organizations in the process of neighbourhood change. Their importance lies in their capacity to influence levels of satisfaction in the neighbourhood, which in turn influences individual decisions: Taub et al.s third set of influences on neighbourhood change. Dissatisfaction, concerns about crime or fears of abandonment, for example, can set in train a series of events that can trigger further deterioration. These factors cannot be seen independently, however; they interact. Moreover, Taub et al. argue that the impact of crime is not a direct one. Rather, perceptions of safety play an important part in residents' evaluations about the likely future of their area – economically and socially, and in turn these affect investment decisions. The impact of crime can be offset or reduced by the presence of other conditions or amenities (ecological facts); they increase residents' tolerance levels (1984: 170). Corporate decisions can, in this context, play a symbolic, as well as material, role in determining the direction of neighbourhood change. They can signify that a locality is worthy of investment.

There has been a great deal of discussion about the relative importance of crime in neighbourhood change, particularly in the period since 1982 when Wilson and Kelling published their article, 'Broken Windows'. I return to this point shortly. However, Schuerman and Kobrin's (1986) study of neighbourhood transitions and crime in Los Angeles County is noteworthy at the present stage of discussion. These authors examined Los Angeles County's highest crime areas using longitudinal data spanning 20 years to 1970. Their task was to explain the process involved in the movement from low-crime to high-crime status. Three key stages were identified: emerging, transitional and enduring (1986: 68). Of particular importance was their observation that deterioration was evident *before* rises in crime in the early stages of an area's 'crime career', though during the enduring stage crime rates lead further and faster rates of decline. These authors put it thus:

When a neighborhood moves from a low – to a high-crime state, there occurs an earlier change in the ecological factors of land use and population composition and a later predominance of prior change in their socioeconomic and subcultural character. As neighborhood deterioration advances and crime rises, the sequence of change in the components of neighborhood social structure begins with shifts in land use. These involve principally an increase in multiplex dwellings and in renter-occupied housing. Changes in population composition then occur, marked by rising proportions in the minority ethnic groups, of single-parent families, and of unattached individuals. The structural component that then moves into predominance is that of socioeconomic status, to be replaced finally by subcultural change. Thus, initial limited changes in land use induce a larger number of demographic changes, in turn fostering a still larger number of changes in the socioeconomic features of the resident population. (Schuerman and Kobrin 1986: 97)

These insights are useful for understanding the development of community crime careers in the contemporary mixed housing areas in the UK, though not without some modification. It is also helpful to note that these authors highlight the velocity of change, particularly in socio-economic status and subculture, as being important for changes in crime rates in the earlier stages of the process. Though, perhaps in this context, it is relevant to draw attention to the wider urban context in which Schuerman and Kobrin were working: namely, that the population of the county doubled. Indeed, as Taub et al. (1984) have argued, many theorists concerned with urban change and crime have developed their work against a backdrop of urban growth (see also Reiss 1986). Yet, as Taub et al. show, while their assumptions hold in particular environments, we need to recognize the way cities have undergone tremendous change over the post-war era (see Chapter 1 in this volume). Moreover, in a context of urban *decline*, these transformations have considerable repercussions for the ability of local communities and governments to intervene to affect the conditions that foster crime in communities in the emergent, transitional or enduring stages. Different cities and neighbourhoods are, of course, affected by these processes in contrasting ways (see Taub et al. 1984; Massey 1995). Nevertheless, in urban areas that are losing population and employment, there are obvious ramifications for housing markets and tax revenues. And, in so far as these deteriorating areas are also high-crime areas (Taub et al. 1984), there are clear implications not only for the ability of communities to bear the social costs of crime, but also the economic costs. While Reiss (1986) has discussed the costs of crime for communities and its resource implications for municipal authorities, we need to recognize the limited capacity of such authorities to bear these costs where their resources are depleted by the costs of decline. Consequently, schools may continue to deteriorate, parks may become undesirable amenities, housing and street maintenance may be deferred and so on, with attendant implications for perpetuating decline as they impact on levels of satisfaction (see Taub et al. 1984, and Chapter 1).

Schuerman and Kobrin (1986) suggest that intervention is most profitably directed at emergent areas: policy should be directed towards retarding rates of population change and shifts in socio-economic status. More worrying, they note that 'Any neighborhood that has had a high level of crime over a period of several decades may be considered "lost" territory for purposes of effective crime reduction' (1986: 98). These authors' remarks are included here because they have important parallels with the views of Wilson and Kelling (1982) in 'Broken Windows', regarding their preferred sites for policy intervention. Schuerman and Kobrin's proposals differ in important ways: they regard the manipulation of urban settlement as being of primary importance, followed by interventions in education, social services and policing. Wilson and Kelling had a narrower focus: (policing) interventions directed toward incivilities, which (their view suggests) precede rises in crime; this is a reflection of their different interpretations of the place of disorder in the process of neighbourhood decline. More recently Kelling and Coles (1996) have argued for a wider interpretation of the thesis, though the earlier version received the most a-cademic and policy attention. Below, I turn to Wilson and Kelling's thesis in view of its importance not only to policies in the US but also because of its currency in UK policy-making. First it is useful to elaborate the notion of disorder.

Like the idea of 'order', the notion of 'disorder' is not easy to define (Skogan 1990). In general terms, writers have tended to split disorder into physical and social types (sometimes referred to as incivilities). For Skogan, social disorder refers to activities and behaviours such as public drinking, prostitution, vandalism and loitering, while physical disorder refers to signs of decay, such as abandoned or ill-kept buildings, broken streetlights and litter, for example (Skogan 1990: 4). These different types of disorder can be distinguished by their longevity. The former are seen as being 'episodic' while the latter are regarded as ongoing conditions. However, in many (but not all) cases they are seen to engender similar reactions – fear of crime and further decline (Skogan 1990). It is also useful to note that the role of the criminal law is ambiguous regarding these phenomena. Some activities and behaviours are clearly proscribed in law. For others it is less clear (Skogan 1990), though certainly in the British context there have been recent attempts to develop new sanctions and remedies (in the Crime and Disorder Act 1998) for some disorderly behaviours, such as neighbour nuisance and youths causing annoyance.

That said, and to put it briefly, in contrast to Schuerman and Kobrin, Wilson and Kelling claimed that there is a linear relationship between incivilities, crime and neighbourhood decline. They argued that by targeting policing toward order maintenance the possibility of crime control would be enhanced; disorderly behaviour would not be allowed to develop into more serious criminal acts. A number of authors critically evaluated the thesis. Skogan, for example, found that 'disorder' can be linked to fear of crime and *may* be causally related to crime (Skogan 1990); disorder can foster withdrawal from community affairs, undermining the capacity of communities to exercise social control. Local housing markets may deteriorate as peoples' satisfaction with the area declines, and as the reputation of an area grows (Skogan 1990; Hope and Hough 1988). Disorderly neighbourhoods are regarded as more likely to attract and admit people involved in crime and deviance (Stark 1987 in Skogan 1990: 79).

Hope and Hough (1988) examined some aspects of the thesis in the UK context using data derived from the 1984 British Crime Survey. They did not attempt to 'test' Wilson and Kelling's hypothesis conclusively. Rather, their study sought to take the debate forward a little. It is perhaps important to note also that their study did not examine actual areas. Rather, it drew upon data from types of areas, using ACORN classifications (see Hope and Hough 1988). In the present work actual neighbourhoods were studied (and community responses to disorder are discussed in Chapter 6). Hope and Hough's work is useful in that their findings are 'suggestive, at least of links between incivilities, crime and community life in different types of community' (1988: 32), in the British context. As such, it does not validate or refute it but provides qualified support for it. More recently, the British Crime Survey of 1998 shows those households in a locality with more physical disorder face greater risks from burglary (Mirrlees-Black et al. 1998).

However, the impact of disorder on neighbourhood decline (the housing market) depends, in part, upon the level of tolerance members of the community feel towards (various kinds of) disorder (Skogan 1990). People make all kinds of 'trade-offs' and weigh the risks and benefits (of moving or staying) when making decisions about whether to move out of disorderly or high crime areas. And, as we have seen, other conditions or amenities may compensate for the perceived risks of remaining in a neighbourhood (Taub et al. 1984). Second, crime and disorder may promote withdrawal from community life, and a reduction in the capacity for control (Bursik and Grasmick 1993), in areas with high levels of disorder and fear of crime. But 'middle ranging' levels of concern may not be destructive toward community group activities (Hope and Hough 1988 in Skogan 1990). Indeed, some neighbourhoods may have the economic or political resources to withstand or endure these 'signs of decline' (Matthews 1992: 32). There may be periods of resistance, followed by other periods when disorder may appear to grow more rapidly as community resources wane. Furthermore, there may be more of a relationship between some forms of disorder and fear of crime than with crime itself (Matthews 1992;

Skogan 1990). Maxfield (1987) found that there is a relationship between different types of incivilities and people's perceived risk of certain types of crime. Certain types of incivilities were found to have little or no impact on the fear of crime, 'and others only appear to have an influence on certain groups under certain conditions' (in Matthews 1992: 26). Moreover, considerations about risk are strongly related to 'vulnerability' in which age and gender are important variables (Matthews 1992). These qualifications suggest the need to examine actual neighbourhoods.

In a more recent contribution to the debate, Taylor (1997) examined not only the impact of disorder on peoples' responses to crime, through victim surveys, but also the impact of the setting (locality), through trained 'raters'. With this method he was able to assess differences between settings. His study also controlled for neighbourhood structure (ethnicity, stability and status). Taylor found that a significant and consistent predictor of fear or worry about crime was prior experience of victimization. Though he found some differences between neighbourhoods regarding responses to disorder, for example in terms of fear or social control activities, these were relatively modest. Such differences as there were flowed from differences in neighbourhood structure, and the most important factor generating fear and worry about safety in these cases was instability. Taylor found that 'the effects of crime and disorder on responses to disorder are operating largely at the psychological rather than ecological level' (1997: 71); variation in outcomes was most evident between different people in the same locality. Taylor drew attention to the implications of his findings for public policy. He suggested that addressing people's *perceptions* of disorder could affect residents' fear, for example, and reducing instability in neighbourhoods may indirectly have an impact on residents in this way.

Of course, when attempting to stabilize neighbourhoods policy-makers must consider the causes of instability. In contexts of urban growth or decline they will differ. And, as I have shown, a number of writers have paid particular attention to changes in the structure of cities in their analyses of neighbourhood decline and disorder (Skogan 1990; Taub et al., 1990). Wilson and Kelling's approach contrasts sharply in this respect. As Matthews notes, these authors are reticent about the role of economic restructuring, changes in the labour market and social and economic exclusion (1992: 30). The political-economy-of-disorder approach put forward by Skogan (1990), for example, on the other hand acknowledges how neighbourhood decline and disorder are related to the decline of cities; a product of cities losing out to others in the global market-place. It recognizes the importance of poverty; poor housing; political decisions made by governments and other powerful players; as well as individual housing market decisions (Skogan 1990).

Instability, transience and heterogeneity are central concepts, as we have seen, for those writers who have used and developed the idea of social disorganization to explain neighbourhood variations in offender rates. As I have indicated, social disorganization has remained a resilient concept in urban criminology (see Bottoms and Wiles 1997; Bursik 1988; Bursik and Grasmick 1993; Sampson, Raudenbush and Earls 1997), though more recently some writers have preferred the term 'collective efficacy' (Sampson, Raudenbush and Earls 1997). In part, this new concept has replaced that of social disorganization because socially heterogeneous communities are, in some circumstances, able to assert common goals. This aspect of the social disorganization approach has been downgraded as a consequence.[5]

Bursik and Grasmick (1993), building on the ideas of Hunter's approach to community-based social control, developed their 'systemic theory of neighbourhood organization'. This has three aspects to it.

1. The *private* level: such as within families and informal groups. Social control can be achieved (though the processes remain complex) by criticism, ridicule, ostracism, deprivation, taking the dispute to third parties, desertion, violence and so on.
2. The *parochial* level: relationships between neighbours and local institutions who may influence the control of crime in a locality: for example, schools, churches and voluntary organizations (Bursik and Grasmick 1993: 17). The ability of neighbourhood and volun- tary-based community groups to exert influence over their members may depend upon their ability to direct resources and interventions from agencies beyond the neighbourhood; that is, control may depend upon 'vertical relations' with agencies at the public level.
3. The *public* level: relations with external agencies may be pivotal to the ability of neighbourhood groups to obtain funding for welfare- oriented projects and other welfare provisions within the commu- nity. Relationships between communities and formal policing agencies beyond community boundaries, for example, may be critical for crime control.

Relationships at each of the three levels are generated over time, through interaction. In this sense, there is an inverse relationship between degrees of instability and the likelihood that such networks will be able to control crime.

These developments are important because they properly locate neighbourhoods within the wider social structure – a problem identified with the earlier Chicago model. Such an approach is reflected in Hope (1995) and Pitts and Hope's (1997) work discussed above in Chapter 1. However, as in the case of earlier formulations, 'the theory assumes a normative homogeneity across society which may not exist' (Bottoms and Wiles 1997: 341), which Bursik and Grasmick acknowledge (1993: 15). Indeed, Bursik (1988: 535) suggested that the framework may be unsuitable for the study of all crimes: there may be less of a consensus over less serious crimes, in which case common goals cannot be achieved because they are not evident. Moreover, Bottoms and Wiles noted that, though the revised model recognized the wider context in which neighbourhoods exist, the political level, proponents of the new social disorganization framework did not examine the problem of normative homogeneity at *this* level: that is, whether those institutions who can or do direct resources, particularly policing, into a community are considered legitimate or not. Furthermore, their work in Sheffield, and other recent studies, suggest communities may be both 'organized and disorganized' and in different ways each contribute to crime and its control.

Sampson[6] has recognized the need to examine variations in social and spatial structures, which enable or disable community crime control. Social and economic exclusion and segregation have been considered important in providing the conditions under which community controls are facilitated or inhibited (Sampson et al. 1997; McGabey 1986). Nevertheless, Sampson et al. (1997) have shown that *some* of the effects of socio-economic conditions can be offset by 'collective efficacy'. Moreover, collective efficacy, 'defined as social cohesion among neighbours combined with their willingness to intervene on behalf of the common good' (1997: 918), can be used to explain neighbourhood variations in rates of interpersonal violence. Nevertheless, as Bottoms has noted,[7] these considerations require that we examine further the following questions: What kinds of order do communities want? What kinds of conditions obstruct collective efficacy and community mobilization around neighbourhood problems? Some insights into these questions are provided in subsequent chapters.

What is of interest here are the ways in which 'collective efficacy' has been used to explain variations in neighbourhood rates of *victimization* over recent years (Sampson et al. 1997; 1998; Bursik 1988). In so doing writers have added aspects of the 'routine activities approach' (Bursik 1988; Bursik and Grasmick 1993). Put simply, routine activities and social disorganization approaches are argued to offer *complementary insights* into the offender/target/absence-of-capable-guardian convergence which is necessary if victimization is to occur. In this convergence (spatial) proximity and time are clearly significant. As Rengart and Wasilchick (1985) have noted, in relation to the latter,

> holding all else constant, one would expect the rates of criminal victimisation to be highest in those neighbourhoods in which a relatively significant portion of the population has predictable, non-discretionary time blocks outside of the home, thereby creating an absence of capable guardians. (in Bursik and Grasmick 1993: 69)

Few contemporary theorists using the 'social disorganization' or 'collective efficacy' model would agree with some of the assumptions made in Shaw and Mckay's model, notably that the configuration of urban populations is a 'natural' process (Bursik 1988: 537). The history and extent of national and local state interventions urban areas are, of course, evident to a much greater degree in British studies.[8] And here, as a consequence, a number of writers have demonstrated the limits of the concentric ring model for understanding of offender rates in British cities, as local authority housing provision has been shown to influence spatial patterns of offending (Bottoms and Wiles 1986). However, few British studies have demonstrated the ways in which, in the contemporary context of the *mixed economy* of housing consumption, planning (and planning failures) and housing policies have, in part, contributed to physical disorder, neighbourhood deterioration and destabilization. In the next section of this chapter, and in the chapters that follow, these processes are examined. The discussion shows that housing is not only important indirectly, because housing choices, policies and management practices shape the population make-up of a locality (see also Wikström 1991). It examines decline and crime in Earleschurch and Edgebank, the mixed tenure housing areas in the Merseyside study. These case studies offer particularly interesting insights because their 'mixed economies of housing' are relatively well established, and lessons may be drawn from their experience for localities that are at earlier stages in the trajectory of change.

Table 2: Housing types in Earleschurch

Description	*Approximate percentage[9]	Location quotient (Merseyside average = 100)
Detached houses	0.7	7
Semi-detached houses	0.4	1
Terraced houses	9.5	25
Purpose-built flats	23.0	166
Converted flats	65.4	1,584

3. Explaining victimization prevalence in the mixed housing areas in the Merseyside case study

Housing

Earleschurch is a small residential area containing approximately 2,000 households close to one of the town centres in the Merseyside conurbation. A number of public buildings lie within its boundaries and on its periphery. Large Victorian houses, in various states of repair, line the streets and give the area a sense of decayed elegance. Most of the houses are subdivided into small flats; some have been this way since the inter-war period, although most were converted after the Second World War. Table 2, drawing upon the 1991 Census, for example, shows patterns of housing composition for the area. Edgebank's housing types are summarised in Table 3.

However, the figures in Table 3 mask considerable variation within the Edgebank sub-area. In one of the sub-areas the number of converted flats is 15 times the Merseyside average (similar to the average for Earleschurch). Thus we skew the figures when we average census data across the whole of the neighbourhood.

Table 3: Housing types in Edgebank

Description	Approximate percentage	Location quotient (Merseyside average = 100)
Detached houses	3.6	38
Semi-detached houses	18.3	51
Terraced houses	26.9	72
Purpose-built flats	17.0	123
Converted flats	32.8	797

Table 4: Housing tenure in Earleschurch

Description	Approximate percentage (in 1981 Census)		Location quotient (Merseyside average = 100)
Owner-occupation	6.0	(11)	9
Council rented	11.0	(12)	48
Private rented (furnished)	12.3		502
Private rented (unfurnished)	8.2	(22 f & uf)	158
Other (mainly housing association)	62.5	(55)	967

Changes in the use of housing have, not surprisingly, resulted in physical and social changes in both areas. While some houses in multiple occupation are neatly presented, others display considerable neglect. And the subdivision of property has promoted transience. The 1991 Census, for example, indicated that 26.9 per cent of the population of Earleschurch had a different address the year before. Table 4 shows the tenure make-up of Earleschurch, one that is quite different from the national picture. Edgebank's tenure make-up is set out in Table 5. Thus, Edgebank is much more 'mixed' and has more privately rented properties.

The housing problems in Earleschurch and Edgebank have a number of dimensions. In Earleschurch, for example, those responsible for converting the property into multiple occupation failed to provide adequately for waste storage and disposal for the newly converted properties (which could be expected to accommodate up to 9 households). As a consequence, waste tends to spill out onto the streets and back alleys. Second, derelict properties blight the area, though the number has declined over recent years. Third, in the housing finance

Table 5: Housing tenure in Edgebank

Description	Approximate percentage	Location quotient (Merseyside average = 100)
Owner-occupation	41.2	74
Council rented	9.4	40
Private rented (furnished)	9.2	376
Private rented (unfurnished)	12.8	247
Other (mainly housing association)	21.3	330

climate that followed the Housing Act (1988), housing associations (the major sector) found housing improvement difficult to achieve. Furthermore, the type of housing provision available (mainly small flats) was regarded as a barrier to building a 'sense of community' because it inhibited population stability. It is not surprising, therefore, to find that rehabilitation of the housing stock in Earleschurch has been a major priority for local residents. Housing problems in Edgebank are explored below.

Population

There is a mix of social classes resident in Earleschurch. The area is attractive to professional people, largely because of its central location: nearly 34 per cent of residents were found in classes 1 and 2 in the Registrar General's classification in the 1991 Census. But it is also a very poor area in a number of ways. Forty-seven per cent of people were economically inactive and 35 per cent unemployed (nearly 51 per cent of 16–24-year-olds). That said, the area has seen the number of economically active people increase between the 1981 and 1991 Censuses. For males there was a total increase of 4.3 per cent (compared to a drop of 16.3 per cent for Merseyside) and the percentage of economically active female residents increased by nearly 23 per cent (compared to a drop of 2.5 per cent for the region as a whole). The demolition of a public housing scheme with a high proportion of unemployed people to the east of the locality (within the same enumeration district), during the 1980s, lowered the percentage of unemployed people in the area as a whole. Also, the increase in economic activity is spatially variable across the neighbourhood. In some subsections of the area there have been considerable reductions in the number of economically active people (see Chapter 5). The area also has a higher than average number of students, a higher than average mix of people from different ethnic backgrounds (33.7 per cent described themselves as 'non-white' in the 1991 Census), and a high number of adults but not old people. It also has a low number of children and juveniles, which has implications for the types of disorder reported by residents. These characteristics form the context in which the figures regarding rates of economic activity need to be understood. That said, excepting the employment profile of Earleschurch's population, many of these characteristics found in Earleschurch have been present for several decades; the declining number of people in employment over most of the post-war period is perhaps the most striking change.

Edgebank is also a mixed area, though not as ethnically mixed as Earleschurch. It has approximately the same number of households, but there are more individual residents (its population at the time of the fieldwork was approximately 3,800 people). Edgebank has undergone considerable change over the period from the mid-1970s. Though actual numbers of residents have remained relatively stable over the period between 1981 and 1991 across the neighbourhood, within its sub-areas there has been dramatic change, with some areas witnessing reductions of around a fifth of their number. The figures for economic activity show pronounced divergence between subsections of Edgebank. Again, averaging across the area tends to mask considerable variation. On the whole there has been a decline of about 10 per cent of economically active males. But 5 of the 9 census sub-areas have seen a decline of between 11 per cent and 17 per cent and some have seen declines of more than a quarter of all economically active men. The west side contains a high number of young adults and lone parents. But across the neighbourhood, Edgebank has a higher number of old people and a low number of students compared with Earleschurch.

Decline and regeneration

The merchant and commercial classes left Earleschurch before or during the inter-war period, as the economic fortunes of the town began to wane and new housing of a higher standard was built in the (then) suburban areas. Multiple occupation began to appear, along with prostitution and some other signs of social disorder. This is a familiar picture in cities in the USA and Britain. But key influences on the trajectory of change in Earleschurch were the direct and indirect impact of hostilities during the Second World War. Such experiences, of course, were not reflected in the same way in American cities (see Harloe 1995). In the UK context, air raids not only damaged housing stock, but pent-up demand, against the backdrop of a changed political and economic climate, had to be contended with in the period following 1945. Locally, in Merseyside, bomb damage on the docks and surrounding areas during the May 1941 Blitz took its toll on the housing stock and population. In Earleschurch, rapid change took place as a consequence of population shifts inwards (because of pressure on the housing market) and movement outwards from it. One respondent in research carried out by this author traced his origins in the locality to this time. He indicated that he knew many people from his previous locality who followed suit – but later left. The 1950s and early 1960s were a period of considerable transition as people were rehoused in the new public (and private) estates, but some professional people and (what older, local people refer to as 'arty types') remained.

However, many of these groups moved out during the 1960s, perhaps because of planning blight, though the town saw rapid popu-lation loss as a result of economic decline and slum clearance (includ-ing the building of New Towns and other slum clearance estates) in this period. Empty, derelict properties became more prominent. Other properties were taken over by the local authority and later passed to the growing portfolios of housing associations, which were beginning to expand, facilitated by the shift to renewal (see above). Small social housing units (mainly housing association controlled) were built on cleared spaces during the early 1970s, supported by the availability of funding through the Housing Corporation. During the early 1970s, as in Havelock (Bottoms and Wiles 1986), some professional households moved in, attracted by the proximity of the area to cultural amenities and encouraged by the removal of planning blight. Nevertheless, a large proportion of the houses were converted into flats, especially one-bedroom flats, and only a small proportion of dwellings remained in single family occupation. Transience became an established character-istic; families were not enabled by the nature of the property available in Earleschurch.

The evidence is unclear regarding its current status as a declining neighbourhood. While it has clearly been in a state of decline from its position as an affluent area built for the merchant class, it is by no means clear that, for the area as a whole, the path of its decline will continue. At the time of the research it was evident that subsections were experiencing a period of arrested decline, or regeneration. Other sections were clearly experiencing further decline (see Chapter 5). Over recent years monies from City Challenge, English Heritage, English Partnerships as well as a (reduced) amount of Housing Corporation funding has been spent in the area, and some parts of Earleschurch seem to be improving as a result. Some properties have improved and property developers have shown a growing interest in the area (though public funding remains important, not least for their confidence). There is evidence of a similar expansion in interest on behalf of owner-occupiers, and some improvement in employment prospects in the arts, culture, education and leisure sectors; though, as I discuss in Chapter 5, it is difficult to assess the quality of the employment oppor-tunities brought by growth in these sectors. Moreover, the spatial dis-tribution of poverty, victimization and political power seems to be being redrawn as a consequence of recent investment.

In Edgebank the decline of the neighbourhood appears more recent and gradual; the clearly *visible* signs of decline were less striking to the casual observer until the mid-1970s. Like Earleschurch, though occurring slightly later, the oldest parts of the area were built for the middle classes, close to the town centre and other amenities (parkland, for example) during the mid to late nineteenth century, when the town grew rapidly. After the Second World War, many affluent middle-class residents moved away (if they had not evacuated during it). Many of the large, single family houses, unlike those in Earleschurch, were bought by less wealthy but nevertheless upwardly mobile residents, for the most part from the local town, who regarded the locality as desirable. The properties were being sold relatively inexpensively and the post-war boom meant that some local people could afford them. The following story was not untypical.

I lived in a council house in [named neighbourhood] on being married. I was really lucky to get it. Unfortunately it was damaged by bombs during the war and we had to leave . . . We'd been in the air raid shelter! We moved to [present number of house and street name] and rented it at first. Then we bought it off the old lady who owned it – for £1,000 – using a mortgage from what was then the District Bank and is now the Midland. At that time my husband worked for the Co-op. He didn't go into the forces because of his eyesight and he always felt bad about this. Anyway . . . The houses are about 130–40 years old. It has ten rooms altogether, two downstairs living rooms, and a parlour and a kitchen, four bedrooms and a back yard . . .

It is convenient for the shops and the bus stops. The park is also handy. [The road nearby] used to be very posh – with nice, high-class shops. These have all gone now. Now there's so many charity shops taking over. The nice shops went when all the supermarkets started to grow – and some of the other shops went. The trade has gone to the shopping precinct. There used to be a high-class confectioners on [nearby road] but it has closed down. It is now a pub with people on the doors. They tell the customers to keep quiet, to avoid upsetting the residents. There are some people who have been here a long time, but when the houses become empty they get turned into flats and bedsits.

As this group of residents' children moved away, the occupants entered retirement, and some died, more visible changes in the use of housing occurred. Because of the town's growth from the mid-nineteenth century onwards and especially during the post-war period, the study area is close to the town centre and the houses are no longer attractive to families. More affluent families can find properties that are less expensive to maintain, for sale at reasonable prices, and located near to better schools in the suburbs. No longer desirable for single family owner-occupation, many dwellings were taken over by housing associations and private landlords. As a consequence of the market in private rented accommodation, houses have been subdivided and let (often as furnished property – seen as the least desirable housing type). Not surprisingly this has promoted transience as people move in, move within, and move out of it when circumstances allow. The longer-term residents are still mainly older owner- occupiers. Improvement to their properties is difficult perhaps in part because mandatory improvement grants are means-tested (Local Government and Housing Act 1989), and often a 'value gap' remains. Few older people are motivated or able to undergo large-scale improvements; instead they seek exit strategies.

These residents perceive a higher level of physical disorder (litter, poorly maintained houses, and graffiti, for example). Some residents attribute this, and the growing problem of social disorder (young people hanging around outside the pubs at the weekend, and people drinking on the streets, for example) and crime to the change in the nature of the population. The building of a local authority housing scheme nearby in the mid-1970s (during slum clearance) is for some linked with the decline of the area, though clearly a reduction in the demand for owner-occupation was taking effect before this time.

Between the oldest housing (built during the 1860 to 1880s) and the aforementioned council schemes, a small number of which were built in the area during the 1970s, there are a number of properties built at the end of the nineteenth and beginning of the twentieth centuries. These are owner-occupied, privately rented or let by housing associations to an increasingly impoverished clientele. These are laid out in traditional terraces without gardens.

The local authority has made efforts to improve its accommodation in the schemes it controls in and around Edgebank, often in partnership with housing associations and with the assistance of central government grants. And, like Earleschurch, the area has received a share of funding from a variety of central government urban initiatives, for example City Challenge. Grants from the European Union, during the 1990s, have also been drawn upon to regenerate the town and its hinterland.

Crime and disorder

Prostitution emerged in the inter-war period and is still found in Earleschurch. But it is worth emphasizing that in the current period residents show considerable compassion toward women working on the streets (I return to this phenomenon in later chapters). More generally, degrees of toleration are shown towards people pursuing so-called 'deviant' lifestyles, to such an extent that such dispositions can be described as widespread. In a survey carried out by this author in Spring 1992,[10] 70 per cent of the sample reported that they were aware of kerb-crawlers; 12.5 per cent were aware of brothels, and 35 per cent were aware of 'street alcoholics'. More than three-quarters of the sample (77.5 per cent) were aware of prostitutes working in the area, and another 37.5 per cent knew of illegal drug users and dealers. Considerably fewer reported being bothered by them. When asked, 'Are you troubled by any of the above?', 25 per cent replied that they were troubled by kerb-crawlers; 5 per cent were worried by the presence of brothels; and 7.5 per cent by street alcoholics. Only 10 per cent were troubled by prostitutes and 15 per cent by drug users and dealers.[11] This is supported by more recent research carried out in the area in 1995–6, which found 95 per cent of residents to be aware of street prostitution;[12] 39 per cent said that they felt 'indifferent', 24.5 per cent said that they felt 'concern for the women' or 'uncomfortable', 20.7 per cent reported that they felt 'mild or serious annoyance'. Clearly no consensus exists, but only 8.3 per cent said that they wanted prostitute women to be removed from the area.

Prostitution, drugs and other offences against the person or property are invoked in the minds of outsiders when they think of Earleschurch. Its reputation is blown out of proportion according to residents, workers and some police officers, but the area does have a crime problem. While there were approximately 90 to 100 recorded (cleared up) dwelling burglaries and 25 non-dwelling burglaries in the year from 1 July 1994 to 30 June 1995, these figures clearly underestimate the crime problem for residents in the neighbourhood. Command and control data from Merseyside Police for 1992–4, show that there were a disproportionately high number of calls to the police for a range of offences – excepting 'juvenile disturbance', where rates were considerably below the Merseyside average. (The nature of the population, which includes a high number of adults but not of old people,[13] at least in part explains this phenomenon.) Property offences made up over 13 per cent (13.4 per cent) of calls to the police in this period

(1314 calls). Calls regarding burglary totalled 446 in Earleschurch as a whole; that is, two and three-quarter times the regional average. However, as I discuss in Chapter 5, there are some subsections of the area where calls were made at a rate four and a half times the regional average, and as much as seven times the regional average in one of the areas. Robbery calls were four times the regional average in the neighbourhood as a whole. Though, again, averaging across the area tends to 'flatten' the picture. In some subsections it was more than double this figure. Calls to the police about neighbour disputes, minor and serious disorder are all disproportionately high. On average there are five calls a week regarding minor disorder (excluding juvenile disturbance). *Serious* disorder, according to official data, erupts about once a year. Even so, it is likely that these figures underestimate some of the problems confronted by residents in this area, as I show in Chapters 5 and 6. Suffice it to note that under-reporting is a large problem in Earleschurch, particularly in the eastern sections where the risk of victimization is greatest.

There have been reports of prostitution near the town centre adjoining Edgebank since the town grew rapidly during the second half of the nineteenth century, though working women have rarely, if ever, solicited on the streets of Edgebank, and the area cannot be said to have a 'reputation' in the same sense that Earleschurch does. Yet a glance at the recorded crime figures would suggest that the area has more of a problem with burglary. Between 1 July 1994 to 30 June 1995 there were 144 domestic burglaries recorded. Assaults are about double the number in Earleschurch, according to cleared up crime data. In both neighbourhoods, there were very few repeat domestic burglaries: 11 addresses in Edgebank and 9 in Earleschurch during this period. However, this finding may be questionable because of inadequacies in the data set; the time frame in the data referred to here was one year. The Crime and Disorder Audit, produced by the police and local authority to comply with the Crime and Disorder Act (1998), suggested that the ward in which Earleschurch is located did indeed have a high rate of repeat domestic burglaries, though these data too need to be treated with caution, and comparisons with the data above cannot be made, because: (A) those compiling the Audit used a different time frame (for the years 1995, 1996, 1997). (B) Data were gleaned from command and control data, and it is possible that addresses, particularly regarding houses in multiple occupation, may have been recorded differently, which could either inflate of deflate figures for repeat victimization. (C) The police beat areas changed in the mid-1990s when different police stations have taken over the responsibility of policing Earleschurch, and they may have divergent recording cultures. Recording practices and protocols have changed over recent years. (D) The Crime and Disorder Audit used ward-level analysis, a larger geographical area than that used in this research, which drew upon command and control data in units of approximately 200 households (see Chapter 2). Moreover, police and Victim Support representatives indicated in semi-structured interviews that, with a couple of notable exceptions, there did not appear to be a high level of repeat victimization in Earleschurch. We should also note that there seems to be more of a willingness to report neighbourhood problems to the police in Edgebank. This may result from having an older population and differences in the nature of their relations with the police, even amongst those who tend to come into contact with the police most frequently.

Activities related to prostitution, notably soliciting and kerb-crawling, account for the considerable over-representation of calls to the police regarding sexual offences in Earleschurch, but they cannot account for the relatively high number of calls to the police regarding sexual offences in Edgebank. (While this neighbourhood is not a soliciting area, it is likely that some 'business' is carried out in the locality.) An examination of command and control data in each of the sub-areas that makes up Edgebank shows that sexual offences are oncentrated in the vicinity around the parkland that borders the neighbourhood (a finding reflecting those of Herbert 1982). Here calls were more than 13 times the regional average. Burglary calls are nearly 3 times and robbery more than 3 times the regional average in this part of the Edgebank study area. Cleared up crime broadly reflected this picture.

More recent recorded crime data show Edgebank to have one of the highest crime rates in the town. It is in the police beat area that is consistently, on average, among the three highest crime areas for both personal and property crimes – the most problematic beat is, of course, the town centre. However, some residents, particularly older people, do not perceive the area to be more crime prone or disorderly than other areas. They name other neighbourhoods in the inner and outer city that they regard as befitting these descriptions. Some referred to council housing schemes close to Edgebank in this context (although official crime data tends to contradict such labelling; I return to a discussion of some of these localities in Chapter 6).

It could be that organized residents do not report the locality to be problematic because they wish to present the area in a particular way. The most organized residents are older owner-occupants who may have interests in preserving a more favourable view of Edgebank. Whatever the reason, most of the older residents, organized into residents' associations, do not view the area to have an established 'reputation'. Some have experienced or witnessed property crime, but they are not victimized to the same extent as the more recent new-comers to the area, who live in the private rented and housing association properties, who tend not to be involved in local organiza-tions to the same extent. Still, most respondents agree that the area is 'going downhill'. The following interview extract is typical of the organized owner-occupiers.

> It is not too bad, when you compare it with other places. It has gone down in the past few years. Out of the houses on this side of the road only four people have lived here any length of time. There is a quick turnover of people. The businesses have changed. There is a hamburger place on the corner and a lot of litter.

She continued:

> There are lots of young people hanging around at weekends. There are five pubs on the corner. It is awful at shutting time. There is a *lot* of litter. People throw their litter down as they walk past.[14] We have also had problems with broken windows. Buildings have dete-riorated. The newcomers [private renters] don't care; they don't take care of their properties. We have also had problems with people drinking on the benches at . . . [down the road]. People were exposing themselves to passers-by. Also, a 'porn' shop opened down the road – but after complaints to the police, and a cam-paign, it was shut down. Litter has increased and pride in the area has gone down. (Owner-occupier, elderly, female resident of Edgebank)

Key factors contributing to crime and disorder in Earleschurch and Edgebank

This following section discusses some of the key factors that explain the prevalence of crime and some types of disorder in the mixed-tenure areas of Edgebank and Earleschurch. It draws upon the insights gleaned from earlier sections of the chapter and begins with the impor-tance of the neighbourhoods' physical location.

i) Physical location

We saw in the introduction to this chapter that certain kinds of areas, particularly city centres and other 'offence attracting areas', need to be approached slightly differently to those of residential areas in the outer city (Bottoms and Wiles 1986). In these areas, as Bottoms and his colleagues have shown, crime is more likely to be self-contained. That is, crimes are likely to be committed by local people. In Earleschurch and Edgebank the available data is not sufficient to be able to say that crime is self-contained.[15] This is not surprising given their proximity to town centres. Moreover, the physical location of Earleschurch; its proximity to the town centre, appears to be of some importance to the explanation of the high level of kerb-crawling and soliciting; those selling sex will seek to locate themselves near to their potential market. In making this point, we should also note that this part of Merseyside has one of the lowest car ownership rates in the UK.

In his analysis of survey data from 40 neighbourhoods in 6 cities in the United States, Skogan (1990) argued that neighbourhoods hosting commercial sex differed in important ways to localities with other types of neighbourhood problem. These areas were unlikely to be either the 'best' or the 'worst' neighbourhoods in town. As Cohen (1985 in Skogan 1990) observed, prostitution could not flourish in dangerous neighbourhoods or where there was effective, organized resistance to it; the industry has to attract paying customers. Skogan found that prostitution was most common in racially heterogeneous areas with fairly low levels of threatening crime. He added that in these areas commercial sex was not seen as the most important problem facing the community. A number of these findings are reflected in Earleschurch. As I have noted, many residents are strongly attached to Earleschurch, including affluent groups with considerable housing choice, suggesting that the area has many benefits and is not seen as the 'worst' type of area, despite fairly high levels of crime. Like Skogan's study, residents did not see prostitution as the most worrying problem facing the community.

It may also be that the physical proximity of Earleschurch and Edgebank to their town centres is important for understanding other types of crime, such as burglary. For, as Patricia and Paul Brantingham (1984) have shown, offenders are unlikely to commit crime in areas that they do not know. Rather, offences occur where opportunities exist and where these overlap with offenders' routine use of space (daily journeys from home to school or work, shopping or in pursuit of leisure and entertainment). The Brantingham's conceptual scheme has been criticized for implying too much of a rational calculation of costs and benefits in offenders' decisions about neighbourhood targets (Bursik and Grasmick 1993), but in any case there is insufficient data to test the Brantinghams' hypothesis in the study areas. Nevertheless, the idea that certain neighbourhoods offer greater opportunities for criminal victimization is useful. For not only are the neighbourhoods *en route* from the respective town centres, but Edgebank in particular also contains a high number of social meeting places and pubs; physical location is intimately connected with land uses in cities. In one sub-area social meeting places and pubs are 29 times the regional average. It is in this area that the respondent, noted above, complained of the litter caused by the pub clientele. Moreover, while recorded crime data suggest *some* overlap between assault victim residence and offence locations, the pattern breaks down the closer one gets to the town centre. Police data suggests that most assaults take place in the evening and night-time. Therefore we need to recognize the space – time convergence. These findings are consistent with those noted by other writers (see Herbert 1982).

Physical location is likewise important for understanding the relatively high rates of sexual offences and robberies near the parkland in Edgebank, though ethnographic data also suggests that an explanation of these phenomena is also intertwined to some extent with social disorder, fear of crime and consequent social withdrawal from these localities (see Skogan 1990). In this way, respondents' routine activities go some way towards explaining the concentration of these offences in particular areas such as this, though, disentangling the primacy of each factor is difficult. Respondents, particularly older interviewees, in this part of Edgebank, indicated that they were afraid to go into the park on their own 'because of the 'druggies' and 'fear of sex attacks'. The official data suggest that there was indeed a greater risk of victimization in the area, and in some cases these responses were based on prior victimization (see Taylor 1997), or the direct experiences of people in their social circle. Of course, reluctance to use these spaces and places, as Skogan (1990) has argued, also creates the conditions in which incivilities and some crimes continue unchecked: guardianship and the interventions of others are less likely. I return to the utility of notions of disorder to understanding the prevalence of crime in Earleschurch and Edgebank below. What is important here is that fear of crime and disorder was closely connected to particular geographical locations within the study areas and, to some extent, to specific social groups. However, these conditions did not mean that respondents withdrew from these locations completely. Several respondents, including those who described fearfulness in the vicinity of the parkland, and their community organizations, were immensely proud of the amenity and they continued to play a role as part of local organization that promotes its use and upkeep.

ii) Physical design

Clearly the physical design of much of the housing in Earleschurch and Edgebank provides a number of opportunities for potential offenders. Few writers would agree wholeheartedly with the view that physical design actually *causes* anti-social behaviour and crime (Coleman 1985), though many writers would concur with Power (1989) that housing areas with poor design features (usually, but not necessarily, referring to deck access and high-rise developments) can give rise to feelings of insecurity, alienation, are likely to be unpopular, and can inhibit surveillance. As we saw above, these factors can result in other, unintended effects. As Power notes, however, this is only part of the explanation for high crime rates in certain areas. Few British writers, however, have looked at design and crime in non-local-authority controlled areas.

In Earleschurch, rented property provided on a non-profit basis by housing associations is the dominant tenure type. Converted flats are the most common property type; their prevalence is nearly 16 times the regional average. For many properties, the conversion from single family housing to flats (often up to 9 in each house) took place many years ago, before the 1974 Housing Act.[16] This legislation made funds available to housing associations to improve and let property, and as such many of these properties are, by modern standards, rather poor. The bias towards new-build in housing association subsidies over recent years has meant that many of these rehabilitated properties are likely to remain poor unless new funding can be found. Improvement is likely to be very piecemeal. The situation in Earleschurch is made worse because the property incurs high relative costs for the associations. Relatively high rates of tenant turnover[17] mean higher management costs; the poorer standard of housing results in proportionately higher maintenance costs. And since expenditure increasingly has to be met by rental income (among a tenancy highly dependent upon Housing Benefit) the likelihood of the situation changing in the current financial climate for housing associations seems low.

The survey of tenants in Earleschurch, referred to above, focused on tenants occupying properties acquired from private owners and the local authority. Forty-five per cent of respondents reported that they had experienced a break-in at their home; 35 per cent said that they needed burglar alarms, 20 per cent felt window locks were necessary, and a half of respondents said better door locks were needed. The communal areas raised a number of security-related concerns for the respondents. Forty-seven per cent, for example, said that they needed their own postbox. Indeed, 'security' was considered to be the highest priority for the tenants association for whom this survey was conducted. This is not surprising given the nature of some of the converted property. To illustrate, during a group discussion as part of a survey commissioned by one of the housing associations in the area some years earlier (1987), for example, one tenant commented:

> In the flat we've just moved into, the outside wall of the flat leading to the stairs is just plasterboard. I could put my foot through that myself. I know the people who live in no. 13 . . . they got broken into through the walls because it's just plasterboard. (Male, 20–30, flat/bedsit)

The housing association, in this case, began to provide a security package for its tenants some years ago, which was recently expanded, but clearly more capital funding is needed to rehabilitate the older stock.

Similar findings are evident in Edgebank, though not on the same scale; the acute problems are concentrated in specific areas and streets. Nevertheless, the quality of the rehabilitated housing-association controlled stock is deteriorating beyond these pockets, though the properties became part of housing association portfolios more recently than those in Earleschurch.

In Edgebank and Earleschurch, the privately rented properties are, for the most part, notorious for their poor quality. In both study areas, the worst living conditions are found in 'houses in multiple occupation'. Landlords in the private rented sectors are less likely to commit expenditure to providing security measures to their tenants. Moreover, if they were to do so, it would be of marginal benefit given the poor quality of the physical fabric. The following extract, from Earleschurch, is not untypical for this part of the housing market.

> We have bars on the windows at the rear, which were no good when we were broken into because they were knocked in – the plaster is very old. The landlady is reluctant to have bars on the windows at the front. (Private renter in a house in multiple occupation)

iii) Social disorganization

We may also note that the design of many of the dwellings in Earleschurch and Edgebank (the conversion of properties into small flats or multiple occupation) has encouraged a high degree of transience, and with it the sense that the areas lack social cohesion. The idea of social cohesion and the concept of social disorganization have been discussed above. For our present purposes we may note that the 'consensus view' of community (Bursik 1988; Bottoms and Wiles 1997) invoked by the model, which suggests agreement or a consensus about crime and signs of disorder, is questionable in the study areas. This is particularly the case in Earleschurch. Here some incivilities and 'less serious' crimes, notably the use of soft drugs and soliciting, are tolerated to some degree on a fairly widespread basis. In such a context, crime-centred common goals cannot be achieved because they are not evident. There is more agreement over the need to police 'more serious' crimes, and there is considerable evidence to suggest that residents do exercise informal social control on such occasions. As the respondent cited above noted,

On one occasion I found someone trying to get around the back of the building – I challenged him – he was very odd. He said that he was looking for [name] Street. I didn't believe him. I watched and found him trying to get down the area between two of the houses further down the road. He saw me and shouted all kinds of things to me. It was clear he was looking for opportunities – break-in opportunities. It was awful. He effed and blinded – there was no shame.

Likewise, some organized residents report incidents to the police on behalf of their more reluctant neighbours. However, because of the high turnover of residents, a large number of residents are unable to distinguish legitimate newcomers from others seeking criminal opportunities, and this was reported to moderate people's willingness to intervene (see also Shapland 1988).

Despite the high degree of transience, there are a core of people, mainly long-term residents in both areas, who are organized in informal and formal, locally based organizations. The idea of social disorganization implies that the locality as a whole is disorganized or that symptoms of social disorganization (for example, population turnover) are uniform throughout the community under study. Data from the case-study areas therefore support Bottoms and Wiles' (1997) criticism of the social disorganization model: communities can be both organized and disorganized and, in different ways, both can contribute to crime and its control.

There were community-based organizations of various kinds, including a number of residents' associations, in the study areas, as I indicated earlier (see also Chapter 2). The community-group infrastructure in Earleschurch was particularly strong; and this has been the case for many years. Yet, at the same time, there were lots of other indicators of social disorganization, as I have described. These localities, Earleschurch especially, exhibited a high level of population turnover *and* a stable community of residents some of whom were highly 'organized'. Indeed, it may be that the organizational structure of communities elsewhere is more complicated than some studies suggest. For most community groups go through cycles of activity: periods of intense energy and others when they lie dormant for a while (see Lowe 1986). Moreover, there was some evidence to suggest the involvement of relative newcomers in the community-group infrastructure in the Earleschurch locality – a well-supported and sometimes influential community group, which included crime prevention activities in its goals, was started by a woman who had recently migrated to the area. Residents talked of Earleschurch as being 'not one community but many' when they described the social networks that were supported in the neighbourhood. The important point is that the complex social and organizational structure of neighbourhoods and, indeed, the social histories that create them, need to be recognized in criminological accounts and crime prevention strategies. In this context, we cannot expect that community organizations will be successful at developing social control functions that regulate the behaviour of members and their neighbours, though they may direct police and other resources into the area and, in so doing, they may contribute to crime control. This is the case in Edgebank, for example, where the most organized section of the community are elderly owner-occupiers. They are more likely to report incidents to the police or the local authority community patrol, even if they are less likely to come into contact with some social disorderly behaviour and crime (assaults outside pubs late at night, for example). In Earleschurch there are considerably more problems with the legitimacy of police interventions, but even here community organizations have organized around crime and its underlying causes over recent years. I return to these issues in Chapter 6.

Despite these misgivings, the Merseyside study provides some support for the recent extensions of the social-disorganization or collective-efficacy model. As we have seen, this has been achieved by adding aspects of the 'routine activities approach' and by pushing the theory forward into the study of neighbourhood-based victimization (Bursik 1988; Bursik and Grasmick 1993). This approach offers insights into the offender target absence of capable guardian convergence, necessary if crimes are to be committed. The time – space convergence is clearly important. And, in this context, we can see how this mode of explanation, in addition to the land-use and physical location factors already discussed, helps us to explain the high levels of assault around the public houses around Edgebank. Similarly, it is useful, alongside the explanations already offered, for understanding the sexual offences and robberies near the parkland on the periphery of that neighbourhood. Put another way, fear of victimization associated with the physical cues, prior experience and some disorderly behaviour create a context in which there is an absence of capable guardians near the park-land for those who cannot or do not avoid the area.

Routine activities also aid our understanding of the prevalence of dwelling burglaries in the study areas. In this setting, we are interested in non-discretionary time periods away from home. And, against this backdrop, we can note that Earleschurch, for example, is located in the ward where, according to the 1991 Census, there was the highest rate of full-time employed females in the local authority. Of the number employed, no less than 71.7 per cent were employed on this basis. Similarly, in Earleschurch and Edgebank the number of people with no children and in employment was nearly three times the regional average. These groups, it could be argued, are less likely to spend their leisure time at home. In both study areas the number of employed females (full and part time) is increasing, suggesting an of absence of capable guardians.

We cannot be conclusive; this research did not examine offender motivations. However, in each neighbourhood there are plenty of attractive targets for burglaries and other property crimes. This is suggested by the population mix: a fair proportion of people in the higher social classes reside in both areas, but especially in Earleschuch. Some residents responded to their perceptions of themselves as potential targets by trying to 'blend in'.

> It is okay if you don't show success. There are people down the road who are very middle-class but the outside of their house looks quite run down – they are ok – they try to blend in. The business next door has been targeted. They have a lot of problems. (Woman aged

20–30, ex-student, representing a group which includes a mix of owners, social and private renters and a mix of social classes[18])

However, despite such attempts to reduce the risk, other characteristics contribute to the creation of available targets, as the main property type, converted flats, is attractive for 'break-ins' and *some* of the social disorganization features discussed above suggest an absence of other community-based controls in Earleschurch and sections of Edgebank. As I have indicated, offenders are less likely to be identified in a context where the population is in a state of flux and newcomers are commonplace. Against this background we can understand the prevalence of property crime in the communal areas of flats, and the theft of goods of low monetary value amongst the less well-off households, so frequently related in interviews with residents and community beat officers.

iv) Disorder

We must, in this context, briefly consider the role and level of 'disorder' when seeking an explanation for Edgebank's and Earleschurch's crime patterns. In Earleschurch and Edgebank we find ample evidence of social and physical disorder – excepting juvenile disturbance. Command and control data for the period 1992–4 show that calls to the police regarding juvenile disturbance were consistently below the Merseyside average in all the enumeration districts of Earleschurch and in most sections of Edgebank, though residents here tended to complain more about young people hanging around in the course of interviews. In Earleschurch, residents were aware of a range of 'disorderly' behaviours even if they were quite tolerant of or found ways to manage them. However, it is important to note that residents of both localities were, in general, less tolerant of physical disorder; litter, derelict buildings and the quality of the open spaces or parkland than some social disorder, notably prostitution-related activities, which I deal with separately in Chapter 6. Indeed, the open spaces and parkland were a focus for community-group lobbying.

That said, two important issues require some comment. The first concerns the impact of disorder on neighbourhood deterioration; the second refers to the impact of disorder on fear of crime. I return more fully to community-group responses to crime and disorder in Chapter 6, but here we may note that much depends upon how residents view the origins of these and other neighbourhood problems. Without pre-empting my later discussion, it is clear to many residents in

Earleschurch that litter and abandoned buildings and some other physical disorder is at least in part caused by the failure of housing and
planning policy over a number of years. The subdivision of property
took little account of the waste-disposal needs of the converted properties, resulting in waste (in easily damaged black plastic bags) often
being left on the streets, for example. And this too was a topic around
which residents and tenants, and housing association managers, had
lobbied and taken action in recent years. The conversion of privately
rented and housing association properties in Edgebank was also, for
some, linked to changes in the housing and labour markets both
locally and regionally. Though, others tended to lay a proportion of
the responsibility for Edgebank's decline on some of the newcomers
(see also above).

> The houses have been taken over by private landlords and they, and
> the tenants, don't care; they don't take care of their properties. The
> railings between the houses and pavement have been pulled off.
> The area has gone downhill . . . declined. (Retired woman, owner-
> occupier, residents group in Edgebank)

Nevertheless, in the course of semi-structured interviews such respondents often added further explanations for the decline of their area,
which were linked to changes in the economic fortunes of the city-
region and the locality.

The impact of disorder on the housing market depends in part upon
local people's willingness to tolerate (various kinds of) disorder (Skogan
1990). Levels of toleration have been shown to be high amongst a large
proportion of the population in Earleschurch in particular.
Furthermore, as Taub et al. (1984) noted, people make all kinds of
'trade-offs' and weigh the risks and benefits (of moving or staying)
when making decisions about whether or not to move out of disorderly and/or high-crime areas, for other amenities compensate for the
perceived risks involved when remaining in a neighbourhood. In all
cases, groups identified a number of benefits associated with living in
their locality. In Edgebank the proximity of their neighbourhood to
the town centre and its amenities was the most often-cited benefit. In
Earleschurch, these were supplemented with references to the architectural character and the cosmopolitan atmosphere – the mix of population and lifestyles in Earleschurch. There were no discernible
differences between residents' groups regarding this matter. Of course,
for potential incomers these arguments may be less easy to sustain.

Nevertheless, in the Earleschurch case study, the evidence is unclear regarding its current status as a neighbourhood continuing to decline. Whilst it has clearly been in a state of decline from its position as an affluent area built for the merchant class, it is by no means clear that its decline will continue along the same trajectory. As a whole, Earleschurch seems to be experiencing a period of arrested decline, and there is evidence of regeneration in sections of the area. Census data (1991) indicates that Earleschurch has seen the percentages of economically active residents, especially those in non-manual groups, increase between 1981 and 1991. But this evidence is not straightforward. Part of this change is explained by the demolition of a large block of publicly owned housing to the east of the locality during the 1981–91 period. Moreover, it seems that the neighbourhood is becoming increasingly divided; some subsections have witnessed rates of economic activity increase among residents over recent years, while other parts of the neighbourhood have experienced deterioration in their rates. Nevertheless, it remains an attractive area for professional people as I have shown. These issues, and their implications for crime patterns, are explored in Chapter 5.

Crime and disorder may promote withdrawal from community life, and as a consequence there may be a reduction in the capacity of the community to exercise control (Bursik and Grasmick 1993), particularly in areas with high levels of disorder and fear of crime. Nevertheless, there is some evidence to suggest that 'middle ranging' levels of concern are not necessarily destructive forces as far as some community-group activities are concerned (Hope and Hough 1988, in Skogan 1990). Such a view was reflected in this study. And, as we have seen, and as I discuss in Chapter 6, active community groups can play an indirect role in crime control by directing resources into their area. Still, it was evident that social disorder in particular geographical locations within the neighbourhoods invoked fear among some social groups (see above), though the role of 'disorder' in resident fearfulness was often entwined with other factors similar to those highlighted in Taylor's (1997) work: individual's perceptions and prior experiences. Even among these groups, however, no interviewees expressed degrees of concern that prevented them from engaging in community-group activities.

Of course, the main point of access in this research was via community organizations, and this may influence the conclusions that we may draw in this respect. Nevertheless, these findings illustrate the importance of understanding community sensibilities, and the conditions that underpin them, when considering their responses to neighbourhood change, crime and disorder. To understand the circumstances that help to forge community sensibilities, we need to consider a variety of interventions in local areas and their intended and unintended consequences, issues that are explored in the following chapter.

4
Regeneration, Community Safety and Local Governance

This chapter examines the development of community safety strategies in the study areas against the backcloth of inner-city economic regeneration initiatives and modes of urban governance. The findings complement those of other writers who have mapped some of the power relations, conflicts and compromises in crime prevention 'partnerships' (e.g. Crawford 1997; Hughes 1998; Edwards and Benyon 1999). The chapter focuses upon the predicaments and contradictions that emerge between community safety policies and other urban and social policies and existing conditions, under new forms of 'governance' (see also Edwards and Stenson 1999a, 1999b, Edwards and Benyon). It shows how *local* and *regional* approaches to crime and disorder in Merseyside have intended and unintended consequences for the study areas. Furthermore, it provides an important background against which the processes discussed in Chapter 5 need to be considered, and forms the backdrop against which community-group responses to crime, disorder, decline and regeneration need to be understood. These are discussed in Chapter 6.

Before further discussion, two related points arising from the previous chapter should be noted. First, while Schuerman and Kobrin (1986), like Wilson and Kelling, expressed the view that some high-crime areas may be effectively 'lost' as far as effective intervention is concerned, few policy-makers (or writers) in the UK would adopt such a perspective. Second, as Hope and Shaw observed, apart from the strategies advocated in 'Broken Windows', there are at least two other ways of intervening in neighbourhoods that are in danger of 'tipping' into a spiral of deterioration (1988: 16–17). Following the work of Taub et al. (1984), the first advocates 'broader economic investment in an area to increase its desirability, especially in keeping house prices buoyant, and neighbourhood facilities – schools, parks, shops – clean, safe and attractive' (Hope and Shaw 1988: 17) – though British circumstances, which include the relatively large social housing sector which allocates housing according to 'need' and current modes of urban governance and service delivery, can complicate efforts to employ this model in an undeviating fashion. Of course, investment in social housing and mixed-tenure neighbourhoods may enhance residents' satisfaction with the area, improving its desirability and, consequently, faciliting its stabilization. With this scenario in mind, this research explored the following question: Does the presence of economic and housing regeneration activities in a neighbourhood make an impression upon residents' commitment to, and perceptions of, the locality? Some of the findings were surprising. (They are discussed more fully in Chapter 5). Suffice it to note here that they illustrate the significance of Massey's analysis: new rounds of investment can produce unintended consequences, depending upon the existing nature of the locality and its economic and social history (see Chapter 1). The findings also demonstrate the importance of combining such approaches with the second 'alternative mode of intervention' outlined by Hope and Shaw. This 'involves the more concerted attempt to improve both environmental factors as well as community cohesion and confidence' (Hope and Shaw 1988: 17). This thinking underpinned the work of the Priority Estates Project, sponsored by the former Department of the Environment, and the Safe Neighbourhoods Unit, managed by the National Association for the Care and Resettlement of Offenders in the UK (Hope and Shaw 1988). This chapter provides evidence to support these modes of intervention. However Chapter 5 shows that community cohesion is sometimes difficult to achieve in a mixed-tenure environment, under the circumstances described in the introductory chapter.

| The Crime and Disorder Act (1998) placed a duty on police forces and local authorities to coordinate, draw up and implement local plans for community safety in a manner that is responsive to local needs.|As we saw in Chapter 1, local bodies have, at the time of writing, completed the early stages of this process; they have conducted Crime and Disorder Audits and established strategies and action plans to bring them to fruition. This chapter examines debates concerning the assessment of local needs and, in particular, makes manifest the problems of addressing them under current frameworks from the Merseyside experience, though the present research's fieldwork preceded these developments.

An Audit Commission report into crime and disorder reduction partnerships (*Safety in Numbers*, 1999) suggested that few lead agencies had
identified or evaluated existing activities to reduce crime in their plans
and strategies (in HMIC 2000: 2). In the Merseyside region a number of
initiatives were evaluated. However, this by no means indicated the
extent and nature of anti-crime activity pursued by local authorities
and other bodies in the study areas, as is illustrated in the following
section.

Responses to crime and disorder

The two local authorities where Edgebank and Earleschurch are located
are both partners in the Safer Merseyside Partnership (which covers the
5 local authority areas in the region). In addition, both have initiated
autonomous projects in their attempts to address crime and disorder
before the introduction of the new Act in September 1998. Some
initiatives were linked explicitly to efforts to regenerate poor areas;
others have been more broadly concerned with addressing poverty and
social exclusion, and can only loosely be described as anti-crime
activities. Crime diversion or reduction may be components, but are
not their defining purposes, which consist of formulating activities for
young people in Edgebank and Earleschurch, for example. Policies
aimed at addressing disorder have included the introduction of
'introductory tenancies' for new lettings in the local authority serving
Edgebank. This authority has also employed a uniformed 'community
patrol' for a number of years, as I discuss later. Both authorities, in
partnership with other agencies, such as housing associations and
urban regeneration initiatives, have been involved in a myriad of other
community safety projects: a neighbour disputes mediation service,
which was facilitated by funding for a development worker from Safer
Cities, for example.

Safer Cities[1] also funded in and around Edgebank an action research
project concerned with drug misuse and community development and
training initiatives with a community safety theme, in partnership
with local authorities and regeneration bodies such as City Challenge.
Indeed, the funding context of crime prevention projects is an appropriate starting-point for our analysis (see also Edwards and Benyon
1999). Current frameworks not only leave projects vulnerable when
time-limited funding ends, but they can also undermine project coordination and partnership durability.

i) Competition

Service providers made bids to funding bodies (local authorities and urban regeneration initiatives, for example) in the competitive environment outlined in Chapter 1. Respondents in this research noted that there were often a number of agencies providing similar services across the region, and sometimes within each local authority area, but often they knew little about each other and bids for funding were made against other service providers. Not surprisingly in this setting there was evidence to suggest that some agencies were reluctant to share ideas and information; agencies were therefore unable to learn from good practice (see also Edwards and Benyon 1999).

The problems of competition for multi-agency working were not confined to the 'qualgocracy'.[2] Nor were they limited to wasteful competition. Legislation aimed at disempowering local authorities during the 1980s (the Local Government Act of 1988) was regarded by a number of respondents as a hindrance to effective multi-agency working. As one respondent noted,

> The rules governing other aspects of local government activity have also made things difficult. For example, rules about CCT [Compulsory Competitive Tendering] meant that there were sometimes difficulties associated with involving both providers and suppliers on the same committees – since they may have interests in bids – this made multi-agency working quite difficult. Solutions were difficult to arrive at as a result.

The White Paper, *Modern Local Government: In Touch with the People*, presented to the House of Commons in 1998, elaborated government's proposals to replace the existing CCT regime with obligations to achieve 'best value'.[3] New national performance indicators would be developed to measure each local authority's ability to deliver quality, effective and efficient services; additional local indicators to reflect local conditions would be established following local consultation. The White Paper envisaged the establishment of a series of 'bench-marks', regular internal reviews of objectives and outcomes, and the extension of external audit and review procedures to ensure improvement. Comparing the services of other public, voluntary and private-sector bodies were important to the proposals. The government envisaged a more flexible approach to service delivery than that pursued under CCT, though the requirement to secure competitiveness was undiluted. Instead, the White Paper, rather incongruously, places 'partnerships' with the voluntary and private sectors at the heart of this competitive environment; and pledges to frame guidance on competition to reflect these conflicting ideals. While it is too early to assess the likely impact of the new regime on inter-agency community safety working practices, or the kinds of services discussed in Chapter 3, the evidence suggests that the opposing pressures of 'partnership' and 'competition' will challenge local authorities. It is unclear how promoting competitive pressure will encourage information sharing; and the proliferation of performance indicators (set by the government and relating to the activities of each principal service area) may promote pressures towards separation rather than partnership, despite the existence of performance indicators for 'partnership' activities. The government will reserve powers to intervene where an authority is deemed to be performing poorly in major service areas, and therefore it is likely that attention will be directed to these in the first instance. Furthermore, as Edwards and Benyon (1999) note, '[t]he "peripheral" status of crime prevention in the major statutory agencies involved in the partnerships – the police and local authorities – has been exacerbated by externally imposed performance criteria'.

ii) *Ad hoc* funding

In the Edgebank area, City Challenge developed a number of community safety projects during its lifetime (1992–7). Some projects were wholly funded from this source, others were funded through 'partnership' arrangements with the council and/or the Safer Merseyside Partnership (see below). Community development was a key focus and pursued in a number of ways. A residents' liaison officer, previously funded by Safer Cities, and a community drugs prevention worker were employed using City Challenge monies. In addition, there had been a number of target-hardening initiatives. A 'safe and warm' project (which provided heating and insulation improvements and personal alarms for vulnerable residents) aimed at older residents, for example. Security and street-lighting improvements were also made as part of its community safety brief. Earleschurch was also encompassed within a City Challenge area during the same period. Here, improvements to street-lighting and community development activities were also pursued.

A number of 'Partnerships'[4] also carry out community safety work as part of their remit in Earleschurch's local authority area. And in Edgebank's vicinity there were two other regeneration initiatives, funded from the Challenge Fund, during the fieldwork period. Both carry out community safety activity, though the funding of one was cut on the assumption that the Safer Merseyside Partnership would be funding some of its proposed projects. (A high-profile project to install CCTV in the town centre survived the resulting cut in funding.) These local agencies and bodies are not an exhaustive list; nevertheless the extent of community safety activity in and around the study areas, prior to the introduction of the Crime and Disorder Act, should be evident, and the need for coordination apparent. One could argue that a number of provisions made through these bodies are properly the responsibility of the local authority. Street-lighting improvements funded by regeneration initiatives reflect this most clearly. The ideological opposition to local authorities extending their functions during the 1980s and most of the 1990s prevented some courses of action. Still, the evidence cited above, and below, highlights the need for funding to be used to integrate work with offenders and community safety more generally into mainstream sources of funding, if *ad hoc* provision is to be avoided.

iii) *Ad hoc* provision

Edwards and Benyon (1999) discussed the implications of *ad hoc* funding on local projects in outer housing estates in Leicestershire and Nottingham. They showed how the myriad of local projects that made up the 'local strategy' often had different funding periods which impaired the coherence of the strategy itself. Moreover, they revealed how communities' prior experience of attempts to regenerate the locality impacts upon residents' dispositions towards crime prevention partnerships. They put it thus:

> Partnerships also encounter problems of credibility given the failures of former urban policy interventions – they often suffer from scepticism amongst local residents, whose expectations have been raised and then dashed by previous, unsuccessful, attempts at regeneration. A local government officer involved with the Nottingham partnership explained that when she began work on the estate people said 'well, yet again, another person is parachuting in'. (1999: 15)

Chapter 5 shows similar experiences in the Merseyside setting. The important point here is that time-limited funding, and the *ad hoc* provision it generates, exacerbates community scepticism; yet community involvement has been identified as an important indicator of the

likely success of community safety (HMIC 2000) and regeneration partnerships (DETR 1999). In this research the damaging implications of
short-term funding on communities in Edgebank's local authority area
were clear when City Challenge ended in March 1997; the community
development residents' liaison post (see above) concluded with it. The
immediate impact on local activists was marked. Roles such as these were
regarded as of considerable importance by local people; support was
considered essential if community groups were to obtain access to (the
complicated) structures of power in the city-region. City Challenge, like
most urban regeneration initiatives, expected social projects like this one
to be self-sustaining by the time its funding expired. Other commentators (not least community activists themselves) argued that few
communities enduring social and economic hardships can achieve self-
sufficiency. This may be especially so in those communities experiencing
rapid population change.

The need for continuous funding is confirmed by the existence of
projects funded on a *series* of short-term funding contracts, as the
residents' liaison post had been. Similarly, a project designed to work
with disaffected young people – especially those excluded from school
– was funded in a similar fashion: first by Safer Cities and then by City
Challenge in the Edgebank area. But the problems of discontinuity do
not dissolve when funding contracts are renewed; instability remains
(Edwards and Benyon 1999). Moreover, while a number of short-term
projects for young people were funded during this research, long-term
voluntary and local authority funded youth club provisions in
Edgebank and elsewhere were being cut back.

A recent evaluation of the City Challenge programme at the national
level (DETR 1999) highlighted the high level of staff turnover towards
the end of the initiative as having a disruptive impact upon the partnership and its work. To overcome these problems it suggested
ongoing roles or secondments as a way to avoid staff leaving as programmes near their end. Moreover, the research observed that 'In areas
of very high unemployment, it may not be realistic to expect to
achieve fundamental changes [as a consequence of the programme as a
whole] in the short term' and that 'the appropriate time scale should
be determined by local circumstances, not fixed, and in some cases in
may need to be 10–15 years or even longer' (DETR 1999: 2). The evaluation noted also that Challenge funded anti-crime initiatives were the
least successful as far as the delivery of their stated objectives were concerned. In part the researchers identified a lack of strategic direction as
a key reason for this finding, adding that the new crime and disorder

partnerships could help to overcome these problems, though core funding did not accompany the new statutory role for the lead agencies (HMIC 2000).

These recent developments, the Crime and Disorder Act and the introduction of 'best value' principles in local government services and tendering regimes, offer opportunities to avoid some of the problems generated by the (short-term) contract culture of the late 1980s and early 1990s. However, there remain a number of difficulties that may be encountered by community safety partnerships. The following section highlights some of the obstacles that may be faced.

The regional partnership

The Safer Merseyside Partnership was formed in 1994 by the five district councils in Merseyside, the police, and other statutory, private and voluntary organizations. In December 1994 the Partnership received £4.5 million following a competitive bid for Challenge Funding, under the provisions of the Single Regeneration Budget. During the fieldwork period, at each local authority level a Community Safety Coordinator was employed and a multi-agency Community Safety Forum established. Similar projects were pursued across Merseyside, although there was a policy, at the time of the research, to pilot new initiatives in one of the authorities. Chief among the initiatives was a range of target-hardening measures, particularly for those at risk from multiple victimization and for other vulnerable residents (elderly people, for example): For example, security grants for small businesses in vulnerable areas; support for victims of domestic violence; detached youth action work; drugs action teams; and action to tackle racial harassment in housing were pursued across the region. But in 1995–6, by far the greatest expenditure was allocated to target-hardening activity, focused on the most disadvantaged neighbourhoods, known as 'driver 5.1' areas for the purposes of Objective One (European) funding (see Chapter 1). The partnership focuses its activities in these areas because it recognizes (and its research shows) that the most disadvantaged communities experience the greatest risk of victimization. While it may be expected that this produces an approach that targets funding on the most disadvantaged communities, this was not always the case. Where funding had to be shared throughout the Partnership, and because levels of deprivation are not uniform, the aim to target the most needy had the potential to be compromised.

When the SMP was established it agreed that work would be focused on disadvantaged localities, defined as areas containing the poorest 20 per cent of the population. However, as one informant noted, one local authority area did not contain any specific, identifiable geographical communities using this criterion. Since the Partnership depended upon the capacity of its leaders to secure the interest and involvement of the 5 local authorities, criteria were relaxed to focus on the poorest 30 per cent. Even so, disadvantage was very much scattered across the authority's area. In Liverpool, in comparison, the 'pathways' areas (as they are known) cover over 50 per cent of the city. For some initiatives, at least, there were proposals that Liverpool should receive only a fifth of the Safer Merseyside Partnership funding.

Conflict is inevitably produced in such a context, but it manifests further when resources are scarce. Local authority representatives lobby for the development of flagship projects in their authority because they identify a particular need, or desire them as part of a public-spirited enterprise, for example. Some respondents understood that particular members and officers have sought to enhance their careers and standing in this way. Be that as it may, members and officers were keen for 'their projects' to succeed. The competition produced within the partnership inevitably brings about conflict, which need not necessarily be viewed negatively. However, discord was reported to be more than usually evident in early 1997 following the announcement of grant aid from another round of Challenge Funding. The SMP sought £11 million; half was allocated, £1.1 million for each authority. Projects had to be dropped; the budget had to be reduced. To manage these conflicts, each authority was provided with the means to develop a preferred project in their district – trade-offs are a necessary part of partnership activity. There also were different interests evident at the regional and local levels. Some local groups were more articulate in making their case for funding compared to others; while others were simply more demanding. Coordinators reported that they had to resist claims from small businesses from outside the pathways areas who were seeking funding for security, for example. On local forums, further divisions lay between agencies who support offenders and those who are more 'victim-oriented' (see also Crawford 1997).

Some Community Safety Coordinators were based in powerful local authority departments, giving them an advantage over colleagues in weaker ones. Coordinators with experience of local government's departmental cultures, bureaucracies and standing orders were regarded by some commentators as being better prepared than those new to local government: 'Managing conflicting interests is much easier when you know where people are coming from.' However, this view was opposed by another Coordinator who suggested that being a newcomer was preferable; they were not subject to departmental 'cultural conditioning'. In this context, it is not surprising that Community Safety Coordinators held different philosophies about the nature of their business. The Coordinators with responsibility for Edgebank and Earleschurch agreed that there was too much emphasis on target hardening. The Coordinator covering the Earleschurch study area at the time of my fieldwork felt that policy should be directed towards the 'causes' of crime (social and economic exclusion in this case) and community safety problems, rather than 'symptoms', and in this sense the respondent felt that the budget available was meagre. The Edgebank Coordinator's preferred focus was on community development, a focus that had something of a historical precedent in the local authority's area (see above), and this was pursued enthusiastically.

At the local level coordinators reported good working relationships with the police, but at higher levels some disunity was reported. Non-police respondents believed this derived from police representatives' limited understanding of local government affairs; and, in their view, some police officers seemed to assume that only they really knew how to deal with crime. In evidence they said academic research (a recognized basis for policy-making in the SMP) appeared to be 'downgraded' by some senior officers. That said, interviewees acknowledged that officers more recent to police policy-making were more open to new ideas compared with their longer-serving colleagues. This is to be expected given the extensive literature regarding cop-culture and the status of particular forms of knowledge in police work (Reiner 1992; Crawford 1997).

The policy arena

The notion of 'policy arena' is useful for making sense of these findings (and others discussed later in this volume). Through its use the analyst is able to envisage a fluid situation where actors emerge and disappear, relationships and outcomes arise out of negotiation and conflict, and are shaped by external demands. The concept may be more helpful than that of 'policy networks', which has proved difficult to apply in a context of perpetual change, in the nature of relationships and networks, and between local, national and global levels (Wilks 1995). The policy arena allows us to distinguish powerful actors in the arena (of an organizational and personal nature). However, an uncomplicated notion of competitive pluralism is rejected by Wilks, for,

> [w]ithin the policy arena only certain actors are able to gain inclusion in those games where key decisions are made and there are likely to be a number of actors which are excluded from taking part and therefore are forced to spectate. (Wilks 1995: 731–2)

Wider economic, political and ideological forces shape the 'policy arena'; but they should be comprehended through an understanding of how they mould policy interventions, which will vary over time and space (Wilks 1995). As such, the idea is valuable for understanding how sectional interests within communities have achieved access to the policy arena, and how others have found themselves excluded.

Regeneration and community safety

This section examines some of the principal elements which coalesced to produce particular policing responses in and around the main study areas during this research. It illustrates how the police exercised considerable power in the 'policy arena' and how regeneration, 'public opinion' and the need for measurable results blended to generate a special initiative. However, the main concern is to highlight its ramifications.

Managers of the regeneration initiatives in Edgebank's vicinity (like elsewhere in Merseyside) have been keen to improve the image of the locality; leisure-led regeneration was being hindered because people perceived the area to be a site of violent crime. They were willing to support police initiatives that could address crime and disorder (in their most visible manifestations) and fear of crime. During this research a special initiative was developed to address these concerns. It was a high-profile project; for senior police officers media attention was essential if fear of crime in the town centre was to be addressed. Though the initiative was in large part funded by Merseyside Police, as a special project, it was a multi-agency initiative involving not only the regeneration bodies but also the local authority, Merseytravel and the Transport Police, among others. Officers responsible for the project invoked the need to take tough action to reassure the public *in the interest of regeneration*. But they also drew on academic theories ('Broken Windows') and research (on repeat victimization, for example), and invoked public opinion in their rationale at the initiative's launch. 'There have been complaints from councillors and more importantly from residents who have been complaining about kerb-crawling and soliciting women.'

Indeed, the project fulfilled a number of police needs. As Walklate and Wardale (1997) have argued, in a context where there is increasing pressure for value for money and efficiency, measured by performance indicators, 'it is of no great surprise that a local police manager may decide that the best way to deploy their resources, and thus meet the goals set, is to choose the Zero Tolerance option'. Concerns about losing public support may also influence adoption of the zero-tolerance approach. Though other policing styles and initiatives may be preferred by 'consumers', it fits the 'crime fighting' ideal (Walklate and Wardale 1997), and in this instance the police were able to show a willing engagement with 'partnership' approaches, which in turn can legitimate action.

For our purposes, we should acknowledge that senior officers denied they were engaging in 'zero-tolerance' policing, though they talked about 'clamping down' on disorder and 'more serious crime'. 'Clamping down' did not end at the point of arrest: prostitute women were subject to curfew and other offenders found their bail conditions included exclusion orders (usually from the town centre). Although the initiative raises a number of issues, for the present purposes we may note two consequences of policing prostitution, in particular, in this way. First, spatial displacement became evident in two ways: (a) Evidence from interviews and observations showed that prostitute women were increasingly working from their flats, putting their tenancies at risk, because of the introduction of probationary tenancies and nuisance clauses. (b) Prostitute women moved to the neighbourhood I have called Earleschurch, in another local authority area and policing division, to carry out business. (Other offences are likely to have been displaced too.) Second, agencies working with prostitute women were limited in their ability to support them. Although senior officers recognized that women involved in prostitution needed help, and said that it would be provided, there was no evidence to suggest additional support was available, at least in the early months of the initiative.

The growing numbers of women working on the streets in Earleschurch had further repercussions. In late 1997 the police in this locality adopted what they described as a 'tactical change' towards street prostitution. Senior officers attributed it to a change in shift patterns. But the attachment of exclusion orders to bail conditions here were, according to one police respondent, a response to a perceived increase in the number of women working in the area because of the initiative above. In this way the orders were an attempt to demonstrate that they were 'not soft' on prostitution, and an effort to deter more women from coming to work in the area. Complaints from residents and other organizations in the area were also used to justify this action (Campbell and Hancock 1998).

Intensive policing in the area of displacement, in and around Earleschurch, resulted in later working patterns for prostitute women. In turn this meant greater isolation and concerns about safety for working women. Furthermore, the increasing visibility of working women led to worries among support agencies, and other local commentators, that this would test the tolerance of the community, especially given their visibility in the summer months, which follows from changes in clothing and light nights (Campbell and Hancock 1998).

As I have indicated, despite the police officers' claims noted above, Earleschurch's locals have a relatively high level of toleration towards working women, which, in part, derives from their experience over a long period. Many are aware that an aggressive policing policy simply moves the problem around and does not remove the underlying causes. I discuss community responses to crime and disorder in this and the other study areas in Chapter 6. Here we may simply note that this experience suggests that local authorities and police forces, when developing community safety strategies, need to be alive to the implications of policies for other authorities, and those directly and indirectly involved in crime and incivilities.

Whose order?

One of the distinguishing features of government rhetoric regarding 'partnership' and 'community consultation' is that it assumes, and seeks to create, a community of interest around the objectives of community safety policies, and the means of bringing them to fruition. The evidence presented in this volume challenges these assumptions: Chapter 6 shows how neighbourhood problems were conceptualized by tenants' and residents' groups and how they differed from local agencies. The evidence from other interest groups also shows divisions over the definition of local problems and appropriate measures to resolve them.

Businesses in the study areas, not surprisingly, experience relatively high levels of property crime. There are also the economic costs associated with fear of crime and area reputation, and high insurance premiums to contend with; each can affect business confidence and the prospects for regeneration. In the previous chapter we saw, in residents' accounts, how some local shops had seen their trade adversely affected by the arrival of new shopping centres nearby (in some cases these had been promoted by regeneration initiatives) and changes in the fortunes of their clientele. In most circumstances businesses and other organizations have clear interests in regeneration and community safety policies, though a consideration of these issues raises questions regarding the relative weight of business concerns and residents' views in consultation exercises, in instances where they differ. If we can anticipate that residents' views of crime and disorder (particularly those of a 'low-level' nature, as discussed in the previous chapter) and, perhaps more importantly, strategies to resolve local problems, may vary within and between neighbourhoods, we should acknowledge that there may be differences within and between the business communities. Though not conclusive, there was evidence to suggest an absence of shared perspectives regarding how to respond to local problems in these research sites. In some instances their views corresponded, in others they clashed, with those of residents (see Chapters 5 and 6). Like some groups of residents, one of the 'cultural industries' pressure groups in Earleschurch suggested that they play down the importance of crime in the area, though concern about the impact of car crime on custom was expressed to the author. Interestingly, this influential pressure group did not express a view on prostitution in the area; a 'position' reflected in opinion gathered in a survey of local businesses carried out by this organization. Those (few) businesses that were concerned about prostitution reported that they favoured different responses to women soliciting.

When there are divergent interests between groups, loud or more persistent voices are able to assert themselves in the policy arena. This is particularly so in conditions where national or extra-local-level rhetoric and ideologies around crime and disorder, and indeed other urban problems, are prominent. In the present period, political rhetoric supports authoritarian, populist responses to these problems. At national level,

> the new government wants to see a zero tolerance approach towards the kind of anti-social behaviour and petty crime which intimidates the public and damages business. (Mike O'Brien, Home Office Minister, press release, Central Office of Information, 18 June 1997)

Locally, Merseyside MP Frank Field was reported, in *The Daily Mail* on 3 December 1996, to have put forward a number of suggestions for 'taming the new barbarians', young people in this case. The action Field was reported to be promoting included harsher punishment and challenging activities; it was necessary to address 'the seemingly unstoppable rise of this underclass of brutish and almost unemployable young males who mature into anti-social, often criminal, adults'.[5]

The social groups that are the subject of pronouncements such as these are portrayed as a threat to, and 'apart from', the rest of the community. Some social policies and policing initiatives, for example zero-tolerance, reinforce these divisions. For those who make up the social groups subjected to demonization, feelings of social exclusion are exacerbated. In this way, political rhetoric and media sensationalism foster a context in which intolerant responses towards young people, prostitute women and drug-users (for example), exercised by other sections of the community, are at best left unchallenged. There was evidence, occasionally, of more violent reactions towards those who occupy or are perceived to belong to social groups such as these encountered in accounts in this research. One respondent, for example, recounted a story about a man who was regarded by his neighbours as a 'smack-head' (hard-drug user) because he was seen injecting a substance. He was allegedly hounded out of his home. Later, neighbours discovered he was a diabetic. Prostitute women have also been attacked in Merseyside, in one case because a prostitute woman was identified as being HIV positive in a national tabloid. Thankfully, these instances were infrequent. Nevertheless, what is clear is that central and local government efforts to promote social inclusion and cohesion are undermined by exclusionary discourses.

Contradictory forces

Some mechanisms put in place by the Crime and Disorder Act (1998) may, in themselves, usher in contradictory processes. In the early stages, for example, crime and disorder audits often indicate varying levels of crime and disorder in each ward in a borough or local authority area. And, while making this information public may not *necessarily* impact on the housing markets in these areas (see Chapter 3), there is a danger that for the more precariously placed neighbourhoods, particularly where housing and labour markets are fragile, highlighting crime and disorder problems may exacerbate decline (and, as a consequence, crime). Indeed, in recognition of the adverse implications for residents, that may result from identifying 'hot spots', some police forces have refused to name these localities.[6] According to the Home Office, other 'partnerships' maintain that it is 'only by highlighting blighted areas that the high levels of public support needed to turn them around would be won'.[7] The evidence presented in this volume (Chapter 6) suggests that the latter view is simplistic. Moreover, without measures to adequately address housing 'market' problems in distressed neighbourhoods, or those at risk of 'tipping', community safety measures are likely to be undermined by conditions that remain unresolved. Target-hardening, for example, was chief among the interventions pursued in Merseyside during the period of this research (1996–8). However, evidence presented in Chapter 3 has suggested that many properties in the study areas, particularly in the social and private rental sectors, are of such poor quality that 'burglar bars', for example, are little protection for some residents. While locks and other devices were fitted to some properties, the private and older housing association properties continued to deteriorate in both areas, and multiple occupation became more prominent in sections of Edgebank in particular.

One of the largest housing associations in Earleschurch, in response to tenants' concerns, in the early 1990s made a security package available to tenants which was later extended. The package largely consisted of physical anti-victimization measures (anti-burglar bars, for example). Though welcomed, it did not address what many regarded as the underlying problems. Instability was identified as a 'root cause' of the areas' problems, with the hopelessness and disaffection that results from poor employment prospects, particularly in the eastern side of the neighbourhood – the most disadvantaged section of the locality. Because the nature of the properties had a tendency to produce instability there had been pressure to reconvert the properties for family occupation. There have been some small sections where this was achieved by this association in particular, which was willing to invest some of its reserves in stock improvement. However, because of cuts to housing association capital spending, the ability to address housing problems on a large scale was not evident during the field research. Other associations in the area either lacked the resources or were unwilling to commit them to improve their properties. Indeed, some commentators reported that some *lowered* their standards because of the need to reduce costs. These issues are discussed further in the following chapter.

Addressing the 'root causes'

Evidence in this volume suggests that many community groups (and in some instances other local actors) in the study sites were primarily oriented towards supporting 'root solutions' invoked by consideration of the 'root causes' of neighbourhood decline and disorder (see Skogan 1990). The political-economy-of-disorder approach acknowledges how neighbourhood decline and disorder are related to the decline of cities; a product of cities losing out to others in the global market-place. This approach recognizes the importance of poverty; poor housing; political decisions made by governments, banks, insurance companies and other powerful players; as well as individual housing market decisions. While housing choices are conditioned by the available housing stock in an area, each of these factors affects disorderly neighbourhoods (Skogan 1990). Decisions regarding these conditions, however, lie in large part, but not exclusively, beyond the neighbourhood, though the approach sits easily with other more local strategies: for example, policing priorities that address the unequal nature of victimization; prevention of malign displacement; limitation of social injury for the vulnerable and least resourced groups, including support and compensation; and the development of 'intermediary agencies' (Matthews 1992). As Matthews notes, it is paradoxical that the value of these agencies is being increasingly acknowledged at a time when their prominence has declined markedly.

> Once-familiar regulatory bodies, park-keepers, station guards and social/political organisations which once acted as channels of political and social participation and as vehicles of expression and control within the public sphere, have either gone into decline or disappeared. (Habermas 1989, in Matthews 1992: 39)

Matthews draws attention to the need for a more imaginative use of resources, targeted towards those considered at risk, hostels, youth clubs, drop-in centres, clinics and so on. The cost of these services could be offset against expenses incurred processing individuals through the criminal and penal systems.

New 'policing' agencies could be included under the rubric of 'intermediary' agencies (Morgan and Newburn 1997). Many respondents in this research articulated their approval of the 'community patrol' in the local authority serving Edgebank, and all but a few had used the service. They distinguished between the kind of problems prompting a call to the police and those circumstances in which they would contact the community patrol: the police are called to incidents that residents consider 'serious' or as involving 'crime'. Some interviewees said that they intuitively knew when something was 'serious' or less so, but found it difficult to articulate the distinction. More research is needed to investigate the nature of their perceptions and experience of services like this. What is clear, however, is that in most cases residents did not want to invoke criminal sanctions. Calls to the community patrol are primarily a response to incivilities, especially youths causing annoyance. When 'more serious' incidents are reported to the patrol, they are referred to Merseyside Police, with whom managers say they enjoy good working relationships. Between January and October 1996, 21,342 incidents were reported to the community patrol. The patrol's managers suggested that complaints, when made by the public, concerned the 'service', not individual 'officers'. For, as some community respondents indicated, the 'community patrol' does not actually *patrol*; it responds to calls for service. Those who were dissatisfied said they received a better response from the police, especially from the community beat officers, who enjoy good reputations in and around Edgebank. The following chapter looks at community perceptions of policing more generally, and the impact of housing and economic regeneration on community cohesion and crime is examined more fully.

5
Interventions in the Mixed Housing Areas

This chapter examines how community groups perceive neighbourhood change and the agents and interventions associated with those changes. Regeneration initiatives, housing agencies and policing responses, in the mixed housing areas, are discussed. The argument is simple: the combination of housing and urban economic regeneration initiatives pursued in recent years has inadvertently resulted in further social exclusion and alienation for some and the betterment of others in the study areas, particularly in Earleschuch. Moreover, intra-neighbourhood inequalities in victimization data reflect these emerging social and spatial divisions.

Merseyside's economic problems were discussed in Chapter 1, and historical and contemporary attempts to regenerate the local economy have been alluded to in other chapters in this volume and in many studies elsewhere. They are not repeated here. What is important to note, however, is that despite these efforts Merseyside's economic performance continues to lag behind that of the north-west of England. For example, between 1981 and 1991 employment fell by 13 per cent in Merseyside, against a fall of 3.4 per cent in the north-west region.[1] That Merseyside continues to lag behind other regions in the UK and elsewhere in Europe is seen in the allocation of a further round of European Objective One funding for the period 2000–6. Objective One is the highest level of support granted to the regions.[2]

As we saw in the previous chapter, experience of urban programmes can have important consequences for local people's dispositions toward crime prevention and community safety partnerships (Edwards and Benyon 1999). Moreover, Chapter 3 illustrated the significance of residents' satisfaction and commitment to their locality for their capacity to withstand or resist neighbourhood decline. Economic investment can arrest decline and has the potential to set in train other positive multiplier effects, including greater community confidence (Taub et al. 1984). Chapter 3 also discussed the importance of external agencies' relations with neighbourhood groups for sustaining social control at local levels; directing resources into neighbourhoods was considered important for facilitating 'collective efficacy'. Yet few criminologists in the UK have combined studies of crime and urban renewal. Thus, in this chapter we look at how communities perceive and respond to neighbourhood change before examining the impact of neighbourhood transformations upon crime and victimization. The following section examines residents' responses to regeneration in Edgebank and Earleschurch.

Residents' responses to regeneration

Community activists in both study areas were aware of a number of regeneration projects that were, or had been, developed in their vicinity. In Earleschurch, those less involved in organized community activities were more likely to be familiar with the nature and extent of regenerative efforts compared to their less-informed counterparts in Edgebank. City Challenge programmes in Edgebank were an exception to this rule (funding ended 1997; see Chapter 4). It was the most highly regarded of all the initiatives cited in interviews with community-group members throughout this research. The following comments are characteristic of their views in Edgebank.

> City Challenge has resulted in some improvement but not enough to turn things around. Through them, though, I found out about where to go – who to complain to. (Chair of residents association, owner-occupier, Edgebank)

> LH: (Regarding current and past regeneration initiatives): *Are/were the needs of your community being addressed, in your opinion?*

> A little bit! But not made a huge difference. Marginal improvements . . . such as the 'safe and warm' project. (Residents association member, owner-occupier, Edgebank)

> City Challenge was good once we got to know about it. The [named] tenants association got funding for environmental improvements and the good food project. It's a pity it was only for five years. I was and still am involved in the Community Progress

Group,[3] which is staying in place for another three years. The funding is going to come from the rental income of the [business] units built by City Challenge. A proportion of the income from the units is to be used for economic regeneration. (Tenants association member, local authority, Edgebank)

City Challenge has been very good on the whole. (Tenants association member, local authority, Edgebank)

When interviewees in Edgebank were asked about the regeneration initiatives that they were aware of in their vicinity, whether they were community activists or not, almost all said they knew about City Challenge. Many could point out one or more benefits the initiative had brought with it. These included accessible education through 'neighbourhood colleges', funding for improvements to play areas and a 'safe and warm' initiative (see Chapter 4), which seems to have benefited a number of older people especially. Similarly, the enduring Community Progress Group established by City Challenge was for the most part considered an important mechanism for promoting community involvement in local decision-making structures.

Nevertheless, most community-group members, in both areas, reported that on balance the needs of their community were not being addressed by local regeneration initiatives. The following comments from Earleschurch were commonplace.

People feel disaffected, hopeless. They feel no sense of stake. (Private renter, Chair of a mixed-tenure community association, Earleschurch)

There are lots of good things happening now but there's a need to make sure that things are approached democratically. There has been a great deal of nepotism going on . . . the large number of con-sultancies and the public money spent on consultancies and the lack of money that is used for visible projects in the area is a scandal. There have also been problems of openness and of democ-racy. It's a 'money go round'. (Representative of the mixed-tenure, community-wide association in Earleschurch)

City Challenge was located in this area. It was a complete rip-off! Public money was used to do up [a bar] on [Named] Street. Private money had been used to do it up only one or two years before that. They promised to create short-term jobs as part of the refurbishment and permanent jobs as a result of the investment, but it has closed down now. It doesn't seem viable. The regeneration projects seem to bend over backwards to accommodate projects where external funding can be obtained, at the expense of the residents' views or any proper consideration about viability. They're the pits! There are jobs for professionals . . . some people in this street are self-employed. For working-class people most of the jobs available are low paid, temporary, with little notice of being made redundant or laid off. They often involve anti-social hours. Poor quality jobs, if any. It's the pits! (Owner-occupier, residents association in Earleschurch)

Community representatives often regarded non-local people, or those not in greatest need, as being the main beneficiaries of regeneration activity. In other cases, particularly in Earleschurch, dissatisfaction was expressed with the structures ostensibly there to facilitate their involvement. In Earleschurch only two community-group representatives were, on the whole, positive about regeneration activity. In one case their approval was closely connected with environmental improvements that had been undertaken. In the other it was felt that the regeneration projects represented an important step toward the renewal of their area. In this case the community group was largely made up of professional people. That said, local people did not simply reject regeneration. In most cases residents recognized *some* benefits that regeneration had brought to their locality Bringing disused buildings back into public use was the most mentioned benefit.

In the main, representatives of community groups involved in participatory relationships with regeneration bodies tended to be less cynical than those not involved in local groups about the *potential* for improvement in their locality.

Our needs are not being met at the moment. Although, that is not to say they won't be in the future. People are quite quick to criticize. The residents association goes to the [project's name] meetings. I represent them there as the Chair. We can't make decisions, though; we only act in an advisory role. We are consulted about grants to organizations and businesses, especially about properties. Some are really silly – there are clearly no employment opportunities or possibilities – people just want the grants. My personal opinion is that these projects face a lot of criticism but it is really too early to say that it is not a good thing – things do not happen overnight. They are not doing enough for ordinary people though. (Chair of a local authority tenants group, Edgebank)

Other research in the region has arrived at similar conclusions (Kyprianou 1997), though it is important to recognize that there were differences between the main study areas in the current research. A less cynical disposition was found to be more prevalent in Edgebank than Earleschurch, perhaps in part because neighbourhood regeneration activity is a more recent feature of neighbourhood life in Edgebank. In Earleschurch, billboards advertising a variety of funding sources for local regeneration projects are a more established part of the local landscape. Nevertheless, community groups in Edgebank maintained strong reservations about the extent to which local people would be helped by regeneration activity as it was being pursued. The following extracts reflect views not untypical in Edgebank.

There has been quite a lot of rejuvenation around [the neighbourhood] and elsewhere in [the town]. The [project's name] promised to use local labour, but we will wait and see. Some of the other schemes didn't use local labour. They brought people in from outside – from Rochdale and elsewhere. Lots of local people are angry about it. Unemployment has always been a problem for people – it hasn't really changed while I've been here . . . Some of the projects are quite good, they are improving the image of the area and that was needed. The latest [SRB-funded project] is going too much 'up-market' though – trying to bring in a load of 'arty stuff'. There isn't enough mixed facilities – facilities that can be used by local people as well as bring people in from outside. (Chair of local authority tenants association, Edgebank)

It is getting much worse. A lot of money is being spent on training and education but what for? (Residents group, owner-occupier, Edgebank)

Pathways is more interested in training, but for what – there are only unskilled jobs, if any. (Tenants association member, local authority, Edgebank)

I would describe the situation as getting worse. The only jobs that are available are low-paid part-time, low-status, and short-term contract work. Some jobs 'round here have been advertised as low as

40 pence an hour! And the Job Seekers' Allowance is insulting. It is not worth getting out of bed for some jobs. If you are on the dole and you are offered a low-paid part-time job for a short term it is a risk because when you sign on again you will be worse off under the new system. It is worse if you need childcare or other help. There are no facilities. People cannot afford to come off benefits. People also need better education. There are a number of people, families, on our estate, in our street, who can't read or write. How can people get jobs? No barriers are being broken down. (Tenants association member, local authority, Edgebank)

[Young people] experience impoverishment, complete lack of money, low self-esteem, lack of information, they suffer from discrimination – everyone thinks that they are trouble-makers, 'yobbos'. There's little for them. (Youth worker, Edgebank)

In general, it would be fair to say that few people (residents and, indeed, some regeneration partner representatives) expect those initiatives that were operating at the time of the research to deliver large numbers of jobs for local people in the inner areas. In Kyprianou's recent survey in the 'Pathways' areas in Liverpool, 478 people were interviewed of whom 22 per cent felt that no new jobs would be created, 24 per cent felt there would be some, 17 per cent said some but not many. Community activists, as in the current research, were generally more positive: 38 per cent responded that the partnership in their area would create some jobs in their area, though 25.5 per cent said that there would not be many. The general lack of optimism is not surprising, given that 'key people' in the 'Partnerships' were 'not confident' that much employment would be created, since, in part, they doubted that any major employers would come to the area (Kyprianou 1997).

Most residents, in both areas, welcomed the environmental improvements that had been brought about by regeneration initiatives; they approved of derelict and neglected buildings being renovated. But few respondents felt that local people, and especially the most needy, would benefit from regeneration activity as it was being pursed (see also Kyprianou 1997). As the extracts have indicated, developing arts and cultural industries has been a key plank of renewal policy in these localities. Because of this focus many local people feel that the end-product of regeneration is not geared toward local, less-affluent people. The nature of projects (museums, private housing or housing provided on a shared ownership basis, for example) or the costs of using facilities (expensive cafes, for example) are referred to by local activists when making these points.[4] Managers of regeneration initiatives acknowledge that the kind of provisions being promoted are not really aimed at local residents. Rather, they wish to attract people from beyond the town to the cultural amenities and tourist facilities that were being developed. They expected local people to benefit from employment opportunities that would be afforded as part of a 'trickle-down' multiplier effect. Many respondents voiced the view that these jobs are second-rate or 'not proper jobs'.

> There is a lot of unemployment. Huge. There are some jobs in the arts, in music and in cafes but the jobs are often short term, with high rates of turnover. The arts stuff tends to grow and shrink – subject to fashion and funding. It is very insecure and low paid. There are a core of okay jobs and a lot of insecure short-term stuff revolving around these jobs. (Private renter, Chair of a mixed-tenure community association, Earleschurch)

In response to this kind of view, one SRB-funded project manager commented, 'Many people feel that jobs in the arts and in cultural industries are not as important as jobs in manufacturing; they should be regarded in the same way.' She went on to add that 'People look back with rose-coloured glasses to the days when port-related industries were large-scale employers – those days are gone forever.' Note that this perspective, and the employment output performance indicators by which regeneration projects measure their success, neglect to consider the quality of employment opportunities in the service sector in these localities.

Local authorities have been the lead agencies in trying to attract urban regeneration funds, from central government and elsewhere, to the region – though the kinds of projects that can be developed using funding from such sources is circumscribed. In view of the limitations of urban regeneration under frameworks current at the time of the research, and in recognition of persistent problems of poverty and inequality, some local authorities and voluntary-sector bodies have begun to develop anti-poverty strategies.

In its draft strategy, Liverpool City Council clearly demonstrated the need for action. At least 65 per cent of households in the city live in, or on the margins of, poverty; unemployment in 1996 was more than double the national average; and 73 per cent of jobs advertised in

Liverpool's job-centres in 1995 paid less than £3.55 per hour. Liverpool pledged itself to research and evaluation (of Housing Benefit and Council Tax Benefit take-up), income maximization and economic development. It promised to continue to establish and support Local Exchange and Trading Systems (LETS) and credit unions in areas of poverty. Food co-ops were to be encouraged and welfare rights' advice supported. The council has a good track record of trying to ensure that water services are afford-able, such as by opposing the installation of water meters, for example. And as part of the strategy, the council said it would engage in wider campaigns and play a proactive advocacy role for those in need through a range of forums. Clearly, however, the actions of local authorities are limited; 'anti-poverty is not a statutory function'[5] and widening poverty has resulted from changes in national social policies and in the economic fortunes of the region. Nevertheless, the council recognizes that there is some scope for councils to take action to alleviate the effects of poverty, and to some extent address the causes of poverty.

Other councils, housing associations and voluntary agencies in the region have tried to develop schemes to alleviate poverty and improve access to services. The residents and tenants associations in the study areas have drawn upon some of these resources over recent years. In Earleschurch, LETS schemes are operating and there have been moves to establish a credit union, and in Edgebank's vicinity there are credit unions operating. Nevertheless, community groups had strong reserva-tions about the commitment of local authorities to residents in their area.

Residents' perceptions of the local authorities in the study sites

The Crime and Disorder Act urges local authorities and police forces to undertake 'community consultation' in the establishment of Community Safety Plans, and promotes local peoples' 'involvement' in their implementation. Though the research for this study took place before the introduction of the Act it nevertheless provides important insights. The following extracts suggest that the local authorities, despite their attempts to develop initiatives to ameliorate living conditions for the most marginal residents and communities, are estranged from the communities they ostensibly serve; all community groups were critical of the role of the local authority in their area. In turn, this raises questions about their ability to form durable partnerships with these communities without substantial effort on their part.

There are problems with street maintenance and litter. Oh! About the litter! We have them on 'family and friends'![6] The police and council deal with things as they come up, in crisis. The roads and paths are awful, for people with prams . . . a nightmare. We have to push on everything. (Representative of a mixed-tenure community group, Earleschurch)

Appalling, inept, badly managed, one arm doesn't know what the other is doing . . . (Owner-occupier, community group in Earleschurch representing mostly professional people)

There is plenty of lip-service paid to addressing the needs of residents in mixed commercial and residential areas like ours but when the chips are down there's a feeling that the council will usually back the commercial interests. (Owner-occupier, mixed-tenure group, Earleschurch)

Sometimes more powerful people like the council and the health authority just don't listen to our needs – well not really. (Owner-occupier, mixed-tenure residents group, Edgebank)

Many owner-occupiers in Edgebank held the opinion that the council was only interested in local authority housing and tenants – a view, not surprisingly, rejected by council tenants, who felt that the local authority's environmental health and housing departments did little to address the deterioration of property and problems of social and physical disorder in their neighbourhoods, for example. Members of local authority tenants' associations felt, on the whole, that they could make a small difference by keeping up the pressure for improvement. Some had resorted to legal action to improve their schemes.

Before the residents' group the council quite simply did not respond to our needs. We had awful problems with damp. I mean awful! There were mushrooms growing in the wardrobes and black mould on the walls. The house was condemned. I, later with the residents' association, took the council to court. We won compensation. Since the residents' association was formed we have monthly meetings and we monitor repairs. They pay more attention to us now. (Local authority tenants association, near Edgebank)

In sum, most community activists said that the local authority neglected their area and the needs of their members; the improvements they were able to secure came about only after a prolonged period of pressure-group activity. I turn to some of these matters more fully in the following chapter.

Spatial divisions: employment inequalities

Census data for the period between 1981 and 1991 show considerable divisions emerging between those in work and those without employment in sections of Earleschurch. In the years that have followed, these divisions revealed themselves spatially across the neighbourhood to an even greater extent. Though the picture is not clear-cut in any simple sense, those living on the western side of the neighbourhood have fared better than those in the east in the period from 1981. The south-western part of Earlschurch fared the best. Small area statistics from the Census indicated that unemployment, though remaining high at 28.9 per cent, was the lowest in the neighbourhood; youth unemployment was also the lowest at 32 per cent of 16- to 24-year-olds. The population had increased by over 15 per cent and the economic activity of both men and women had more than doubled during that decade. Between 1981 and 1991 the population in the eastern side suffered from higher levels of unemployment, particularly among men and the unskilled. In 1991 in the north-eastern corner of the neighbourhood 42.3 per cent were unemployed (50 per cent for 16- to 25-year-olds) and, though women's economic activity increased (by 7.3 per cent), economic activity for men declined by 18.2 per cent. The population here has, like the area as a whole, declined. However, population loss has all in all been less dramatic on the western side, and in some streets the number of residents increased. The enumeration districts in the middle of Earleschurch show a more complicated picture; they reflect trends occurring on each side of the neighbourhood. In the three enumeration districts that make up the centre of Earleschurch, unemployment is similar to the neighbourhood average, though unemployment among young people is 58.3 per cent and in one area as much as 65 per cent: 15 per cent higher than the neighbourhood average. That said, economic activity increased among men and women in these areas as a whole, though in one of the districts men's economic activity declined by 7.5 per cent. Again women fared better than men. In one of the districts women's economic activity more than doubled, in another there was a more modest increase of 7.7 per cent.

These data suggest that during the period 1981 to 1991 Earleschurch was becoming polarized, with poorer people in the eastern side and

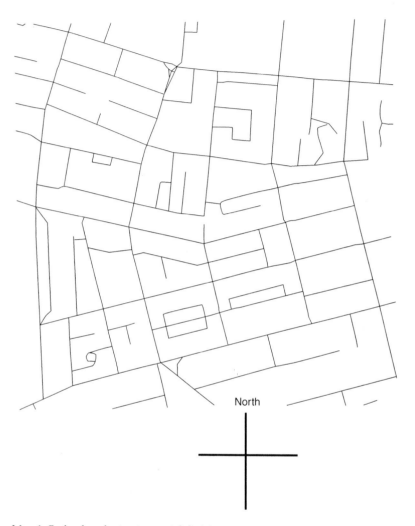

Map 1: Earleschurch streets: spatial divisions

more prosperous residents occupying pockets of the western enumeration districts. Without more recent data from reliable sources it is
difficult to establish changes in economic activity in Earleschurch. The
regeneration initiatives record or 'estimate' the number of jobs they
have created, directly and indirectly. However, at the time of the

research (1996–8) there was no central database (and there was the potential, at least, for employment outputs to be counted more than once, as I indicated in Chapter 2). Employment figures are very much a delicate topic. Not surprisingly, regeneration initiative spokespeople were quite often reticent or unable to provide clear and unambiguous data regarding the number of jobs created as a result of their endeavours, especially for local people. Furthermore, as we have seen, local people are concerned about the *quality* of the jobs that have been created, particularly in the arts, cultural and tourist industries, which are subject to seasonal fluctuations. And job losses, particularly in manufacturing, continued in the region during the 1990s. Nevertheless, despite the lack of quantifiable data, other local data can help to build a picture of the area and its socio-economic make-up in the late 1990s. For instance, the largest housing association in Earleschurch reported in spring 1997 that about 80 per cent of its tenants were claiming housing benefit, a proportion similar if not slightly higher than 10 years earlier. Further evidence regarding the spatial divisions that have emerged over recent years is elaborated below.

Edgebank has seen a decline of about 10 per cent of economically active males across the neighbourhood between 1981 and 1991. But 5 of the 9 Census sub-areas saw a decline of between 11 per cent and 17 per cent, and some saw a fall of more than a quarter of all economically active men. The west side contains a high number of young adults and lone parents. Unemployment in the west side varies between 22.3 per cent and over a third of residents, and for young people between a third and a half of the population between 16 and 24 years. The most prosperous enumeration district is in the east side where just fewer than 13 per cent were unemployed in 1991, and youth unemployment was only 10.5 per cent. This area had also seen an increase in residents and in economic activity among both men (an increase of 16.7 per cent) and women (an increase of 22.2 per cent). Women, more generally, did better than their male counterparts even in less fortunate areas. In the far western side, for example, where unemployment was over a third and youth unemployment nearly half of young people aged 16 to 24, women increased their economic activity by 11.3 per cent against a male decline of 13.8 per cent. Again, the areas in the middle complicate a clear picture. Like Earleschurch, there are a number of contradictory trends occurring, perhaps to an even greater extent.

As in Earleschurch there are problems associated with gathering quantitative data that will illuminate the economic fortunes of local people in Edgebank after 1991. Nevertheless, the qualitative data (above and elsewhere in this volume) suggests that there has been only a limited impact upon joblessness (particularly amongst men and young people), under-employment and poverty. A number of housing associations in Edgebank noted, for example, that on average the percentage of tenants on housing benefit, like Earleschurch, was around 80 per cent. Without exception they said that the people in their property were increasingly poor. Invariably they said that their tenancy had changed over recent years: Some said that there had been a marked increase in the number of lone parents, people with mental health problems and other vulnerable groups. Managers often described properties as being difficult to let in a way that they were not only a few years earlier. Others noted that people used to carry out their own repairs 15 years ago. Nowadays housing associations are called to help with repairs for which they are not responsible.

Housing regeneration

In Merseyside housing associations have traditionally focused their activities in inner areas like Edgebank and Earleschurch, as I indicated in Chapters 1 and 3. The proportion of stock in this sector is well above the regional average and is the majority tenure in one, Earleschurch. The associations' role in regenerating housing in these areas before and after the 1974 Housing Act, which provided grant aid for rehabilitation, should not be underestimated. Nevertheless, more recently this sector has experienced considerable difficulties maintaining the stock, let alone improving it to modern standards, or reconverting it to meet changing needs.

Several small council-controlled schemes in Edgebank and its vicinity have been improved using Estate Action funding (through central government), often in partnership with housing associations. Indeed, housing associations or private interests, or a combination of both, have been key sources of housing regeneration, particularly in Earleschurch, although housing associations are no longer recognizable as local charities taking on portfolios of deteriorating properties, often from the private rented sectors, to secure their rehabilitation as they had in the 1970s.

The number of converted properties is comparatively high in Earleschurch and Edgebank and substantial parts of this stock need upgrading. Most are social or privately rented. Privately rented properties in both areas account for over a fifth of the stock (see Chapter 3). While many are poorly maintained, the houses in multiple occupation are the poorest. Owner-occupiers, particularly in Edgebank where the sector is large compared to Earleschurch, also find improvement difficult and should not be ignored. The following comments are not untypical of the older owner-occupants in Edgebank.

> Everyone's much more interested in the council sector. They get more investment and renovation. I feel that I have been careful with money and scrimped and saved all my life and haven't benefited at all. People like me and my husband have lost out because nobody cares about owner-occupiers, people think that we're rich . . . Until someone from City Challenge came, nobody told us that we were entitled to council-tax benefit, and we really struggled to get by while paying full.

Chapter 3 discussed housing problems and their implications for crime and disorder more fully. What is more important for our present purposes is that during the 1990s housing policy has failed to address the needs of inner-city mixed-tenure areas. Some housing associations, building upon their historic role in the region, have tried to address the problems associated with their stock, and the needs of their tenants. In so doing they have tried to re-establish their place in community regeneration.

Some associations drew upon their reserves to carry out improvements and maintain standards. Others developed plans for areas regarded as being in strategic need, as I discuss below. Staff were trained or mediation schemes were established in an effort to deal with neighbour disputes, for example. There have been attempts to develop community-sensitive lettings; and one association in particular, in Earleschurch, made strenuous attempts to obtain funding to reconvert small dwelling units into family properties, in response to local demand, and to stabilize the population, as I alluded to in the previous chapter. As the housing manager in this association put it:

> Five years ago [Earleschurch], like other neighbouring areas, was going down the pan. We thought it was right that there was a lettings policy based on needs, but it was based on need to the exclusion of everything else – such as the needs of tenants or the community. Because of this, localities become destabilized even

where they weren't before . . . Property was difficult to let. It is important to have a mix of people – [Earleschurch] had always been like that. It is important to improve and spend more money on security. The security package that had been in place in [Earleschurch] for a while was extended. Do you remember the improvements to [named] Street? Improvements are now in their third phase. But there was a shortfall in the funding. In general, we have been investing in the stock in Earleschurch for about four years. There are efforts to upgrade the heating, renew kitchens, bathrooms, and bring them up to modern standards.

He continued:

[Earleschurch] has always been saveable. There are some positive things happening here. Arrears have declined to less than three weeks, on average, and turnaround time between tenancies has reduced to three weeks. There's increasing demand for properties. People are asking for Earleschurch for their first choice now. There's willingness on behalf of other housing associations in the area to cooperate. About two years ago a number of housing associations got together and each presented on an area that had gone down the pan in their area. Each said that they couldn't cope and that they needed to cooperate and do something about it. They recognized that housing policy was a key reason for the decline of the areas – mainly lettings policies.

Improvement in this case was funded through the association's reserves; income saved by reducing letting time; moving money from day to day repairs to planned and cyclical maintenance; and rent increases. Rents increased for two main reasons: declining subsidies (there is no longer a capital repairs grant, for example) and because the Rent Assessment Committee for fair rents took into account market rents for the first time in 1996. This resulted in an increase of up to £17 per week for some flats (a rise of approximately £1 per week for many properties), which created more rental income than the association expected. Though housing benefit covered most of the increase, my respondent was concerned with the way that this creates a poverty trap for tenants trying to get into work.

However, some associations have not been able, or willing, to commit the kind of funding needed to address the problems of deteriorating quality and instability from their reserves. Furthermore, because of cuts from 1988 to the amount of capital funding available to associations, the extent to which improvements can be made remains limited. Some housing associations in Edgebank were questioning the viability of some of their difficult-to-let properties and were considering selling them on the private market.

Housing associations have been keen to develop income-generating projects, some of which have lain outside the traditional framework of providing housing for those in greatest housing need. In Earleschurch, associations had been involved in the provision of accommodation for students and staff working in local hospitals, as a business venture. In some cases the income has helped to support improvements to the socially rented stock. Similarly there had been increasing interest in improving property for sale and shared ownership. In undertaking these new ventures, housing association managers in both localities felt that there was a regrettable move away from the idea of community-based, charitable, social landlords, towards more business-oriented concerns. But in 1997 all felt that the trend was likely to continue. This activity was beginning to have other small knock-on effects: stimulated by physical, housing and economic regeneration, house prices were rising in Earleschurch.

One of the aims of a recent SRB-funded regeneration initiative near Edgebank was to increase the residential population of the town centre threefold over the lifetime of the project. Housing association activity, without keen interest from private developers alone, was one of the ways in which this was to be achieved. Housing Corporation funding, available through the Merseyside Special Allocation, in place because of Objective One, made housing association involvement possible. Their objective was to increase the number of town centre living spaces; ideally they would be provided on a mixed-tenure basis. In turn, housing associations were expected to raise confidence in the area and encourage private developers to invest. This was beginning to take place on a small scale during this research, according to project managers.

In Earleschurch especially, some residents thought aspects of housing association activity, particularly schemes that involved owner-ship rather than social renting, were furthering a process of uneven gentrification and polarization. Some residents felt marginalized in this process, perhaps understandably given that most had not benefited from the small-scale improvements that housing associations were able to bring about under the financial regimes in which they were operating at the time of the research.

Spatial divisions: housing and economic regeneration in Earleschurch

Those areas experiencing the greatest 'gentrification' have been in the western part of Earleschurch. The streets that remained single-family dwellings are, for the most part, to be found in this area. Perhaps because they remained intact and were therefore relatively less expensive to improve or convert, they were attractive propositions for private interests, housing associations seeking to develop housing for sale or shared ownership, or for purchase by more affluent people. A few streets contained (unconverted) houses owned by the local authority. This is significant because of the implications of the 'right to buy' legislation in 1980, though its effects would not be clear until later in the decade, after the urban disorders of 1981. But as investment in the wake of the urban disorders grew, local authority tenants increasingly exercised their right to buy and, later, to sell. Because members of professional groups were willing to come to live in the area, these tenants were then able to move to areas they regarded as being more desirable. Thus we see that the number of council owned properties declined from 11 per cent to just 6 per cent between 1981 and 1991 (see Chapter 3). Though this trend remains patchy, and confined mostly to specific streets in this sector, there is considerable evidence to suggest that this is redefining the social composition in Earleschurch. As one respondent in such a street noted

> Over the past 10 years the area has become much more middle-class. There are now more middle-class people in this street than there are working-class people. The relationships are less comfortable. On the other hand, there are a lot of strong women in the street, and the men are also very comfortable to be with. Unlike most of [Earleschurch], in this street almost all the houses are family houses; they are not subdivided. Incidentally, [street name] is the same. But the houses have increasingly gone from council-rented to owner-occupation. A number of tenants have exercised their right to buy and the number of tenants has declined, some have sold the houses on and moved away. As a result there are more owner-occupiers in the area. I personally regret that we are losing the sense of social mix. I think that society benefits from social mixing.

Other commentators made similar observations. Many of the middle-class people who have moved to Earleschurch are committed to the area and economic regeneration, as the following extract from one of the early newcomers illustrates.

> I used to live in suburbia, in Crosby, but it was a conscious decision [to move here], because we felt that professionals should not flee the inner city, we were interested in regeneration. People should argue for the place. This is a very large family house with a garden and garage; it has five bedrooms and four reception rooms. It allows for a very civilised pattern of living. It was relatively cheap to move here 15 years ago because professionals didn't want to move here. The road was held in leasehold to the council, who was reluctant to sell. This had implications for people who wanted to buy properties because people couldn't get mortgages because of the short terms left on the lease. (Owner-occupier, community group in Earleschurch representing mostly professional groups)

Nevertheless, the redefinition of the social composition of Earleschurch was also redrawing lines of affiliation in the neighbourhood. For example, representatives of the community-wide residents association noted how 'the [street name – western] end of [Earleschurch] had different interests' to the remainder of the area, where residents tended to identify with neighbouring (and poor) areas nearby. There had been some environmental improvement during the course of regeneration initiatives through the 1990s, and small sections of converted properties had been improved (see above), along with the upgrading of a purpose-built housing association scheme in the eastern side. Nevertheless, the bulk of visible improvement and economic investment (public and private) appeared to residents to be concentrated in, or in proximity to, the streets on the western side. The separation of interests became manifest in a debate over which regeneration 'Partnership' to join and whether Earleschurch should be split down the middle to reflect divergent interests. The alternatives were to join a partnership with a clearer remit to address the needs of the town centre, or to join that concerned with the more residential (and impoverished) area lying to the south-east. The outcome of this debate was to hold the area intact and to join the latter partnership. But community members and other commentators remember the conflict that surrounded these negotiations.

The experience of victimization appears to be closely connected to the fortunes of the various subsections in the Earleschurch neighbourhood. In those areas that have witnessed gentrification a variety of crimes are reported at a much lower rate than those that have experienced decline, or a mixture of decline and renewal. I explore these issues in the next section. I focus upon the Earleschurch neighbourhood, in part because its experience of regenerative activity is longer and the divisions that are emerging are more evident.

Socio-spatial divisions and victimization in Earleschurch

Earleschurch as a whole has high rates of property crime, as we saw in Chapter 3. But it is the eastern part of Earleschurch that reported the greatest amount of property crime, burglary, robbery, neighbour disputes, minor and serious disorder, despite under-reporting, for the years 1992–4. The streets in the south-western part of the neighbourhood, the area that has experienced the greatest amount of gentrification, had the lowest rates of reporting as far as property crimes in general, assaults and neighbourhood disputes are concerned. These offence categories are reported at a rate half the Merseyside average or less for 1992–4. The exceptions to this rule concerned calls about robbery and sexual offences. Robbery offences were reported at a rate nearly two and a half times the Merseyside average, and are the most common problem in the neighbourhood as a whole. Nevertheless, robbery in this section remained below the neighbourhood rate for these years. That said, residents in the western sections made an increasing number of property crime calls in the mid to late 1990s, according to command and control and Victim Support data. Residents in the western, gentrified, sections are more likely to report their (lower level of) victimization to the police.

Despite reluctance to report to the police in the enumeration districts to the east, calls regarding property crime in general, burglary, robbery, neighbour disputes, minor and *serious* disorder were, in general, several times higher than the Merseyside average. For example, regarding burglary, residents in the north-eastern corner report burglary at a rate nearly four and a half times the Merseyside average. The neighbourhood average is 2.74 times the Merseyside average. Here property calls accounted for 24.6 per cent of calls to the police in this period, against the neighbourhood average of 13.4 per cent. Towards the south-eastern corner of Earleschurch, burglary is reported at a rate more than 7 times the Merseyside average. Robbery is nearly 10 times this average, assaults more than 4.5 times, and disputes 4.74 times. Property offences in general account for nearly 28 per cent of calls to the police. The enumeration districts in the middle are more complicated. There are no clear patterns but robbery is consistently higher across each of the three areas.

Reports regarding juvenile disturbance are consistently lower than the regional average in Earleschurch. This is a reflection of the age structure of the population, which includes a high number of adults but not children and old people. It flows from the housing units available (many small flats); families find it difficult to remain in the area because of the nature of the properties available. As a consequence, those young people who live in Earleschurch are more often found on the eastern side, among poorer families, living in dwellings that lack sufficient space within them for children to play. Few dwellings have private gardens; there are no play areas for these children in the neighbourhood, and as a consequence they are more likely to be found on the street. Some become involved in petty crime and socially disorderly behaviour, causing annoyance to neighbours, and as a result they come to the attention of the police.

A youth outreach scheme, intended to divert young people in the neighbourhood from 'trouble' and crime was funded on a short-term basis in the 1990s; the project was not renewed. Some commentators suggested that the scheme was not cost-effective because of the low number of children and adolescents. And, while there is one youth centre on the edge of the neighbourhood, the provision is regarded by many local people as being inadequate, old-fashioned and 'boy-oriented'. In contrast to juvenile disturbance, a disproportionately high number of calls are made regarding sexual offences, when compared to the number expected in Merseyside as a whole, which are related to prostitution and associated activities. The issues associated with these phenomena are complex and require separate treatment. I examine them in the following chapter.

What is clear from these data is that patterns of victimization reflect the social divisions that have emerged in Earleschurch since the 1980s, though it is likely that the full implications of this are hidden because of under-reporting in the eastern sections. Victim Support, for example, registers the wide variety of crimes that are reported to them through 'self-referral' in the eastern sections. Reports of racially motivated incidents and complaints about policing (harassment and failure to respond) to Victim Support come, for the most part, from this part of Earleschurch. The ethnographic work, data from the police and Victim Support indicate the following reasons for the geographical disparities in reporting in Earleschurch.

First, people living in the eastern sections are more likely to mistrust the police and are less likely to report directly to them. A range of people are concerned about police reactions to their 'backgrounds': black and minority ethnic groups, and poorer people more generally, prostitute women and those who have been involved in criminal activity, for example. These groups are more likely to be found in streets to the east. Second, residents from these social groups often feel that there is little to be gained from making reports to the police. Insurance levels (according to a Victim Support survey of residents reporting a problem), for example, show that only 4 per cent of people in that part of the locality have home contents insurance because of the prohibitive level of premiums. Those living in the east are more likely to 'fear reprisals'. People are afraid of being called 'a grass'. And, residents talked about the 'stigma' associated with having a police-car outside their homes. Third, middle-class professional people in the west are more likely to call the police and 'argue their case', and are more likely to be able to afford the relatively high cost of home contents insurance cover, and the 'excess' costs of making a claim.

> I know for a fact that people don't report to the police. They think 'what is the point'. Most of the theft is for smallish items – it is not worth claiming because often you have to pay large amounts in excess. If it's not worth making a claim there is not much point calling the police. You have to call the police if you are going to make a claim. (Private renter, Chair of a mixed-tenure community association, Earleschurch)

Interestingly, 'cleared up' dwelling burglary data showed no discernible difference between the eastern and western sections of Earleschurch in 1994–5.

Residents' responses to policing

In Earleschurch and Edgebank there are clear divisions between people who report getting appropriate service from the police and those who do not. Those who report receiving a poor service tend to be the more economically marginalized groups. In Earleschurch in particular, this is recognized even by those who say they obtain a decent service. The following extract taken from an interview with an owner-occupier in one of the gentrifying streets is illustrative.

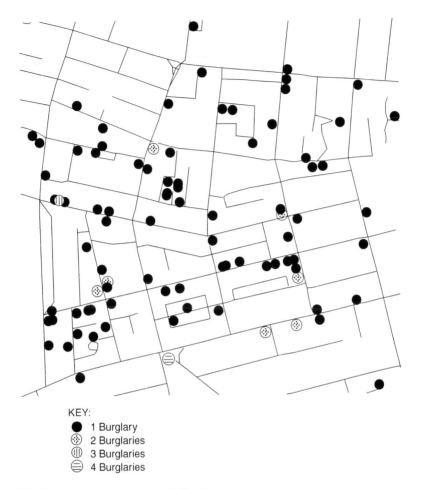

KEY:
- ● 1 Burglary
- ⊛ 2 Burglaries
- ⑪ 3 Burglaries
- ⊜ 4 Burglaries

Map 2: Earleschurch burglaries, 1994–5

We reported a sneak thief recently [someone who had come into the property while the front door was open and the resident occupied]. A uniformed officer arrived within minutes, followed later by a CID pair . . . and then eventually by another CID pair. But we fear that other people have had difficulty in getting a quick response to really serious crimes. (Mixed-tenure group representative, Earleschurch)

Residents in the study areas felt that more foot-patrols would increase confidence in the police and the locality, a finding reflected in many studies in the UK (McConville and Shepherd 1992). Invariably residents in Merseyside wanted Community Beat Officers (CBOs) that are sensitive and respond, fairly, to the needs of residents and their communities. In the Edgebank area respondents were more likely to suggest that their CBOs behaved in this manner. One of the local beat officers referred to in this way suggested that this was because of the personalities of those involved and a management structure that was relatively supportive of community beat policing, though the reasons were not simply a response to community wants and needs. Rather, public relations, less opportunity for promotion and the need for intelligence shaped management responses. Nevertheless, as a consequence, managers try to avoid moving community beat officers from duties, though sometimes this is unavoidable.

According to this respondent, some of the other CBOs working in beats near Edgebank, prefer not to be involved in arrest-making. This particular officer did not concur with this point of view. What was more important for this officer was that people are treated fairly: 'You should treat every-one the same way, with respect, even if sometimes you think that they've not earned it. I don't make arrests for the sake of it.'

Two key factors were said to inhibit his ability to carry out his role and disrupt his relationship with the community. The first referred to the way that harsher policing styles (the work of the Operational Support Division, for example) were sometimes detrimental to his work. 'It's not right to be the community's friend and then have the "heavies" come in and arrest people – this doesn't make my job easier.' The second con-cerned the way his decisions, advice or information were sometimes either ignored, overruled or overridden. As a consequence, his credibility with the community was threatened. 'Some other officers wanted to go against decisions made on the ground – not to arrest on a particular occasion, for example – because they wanted the credibility of arrests and didn't worry about the impact on others.'

All community-group respondents in and around Edgebank approved of their beat officers and most knew their names and contact numbers. That said, a number of community activists reported that fear of being labelled a 'grass' resulted in their neighbours being reluctant to report. However, there were strong feelings in some areas, in and around Edgebank, that some policing styles were a problem in themselves. As one local authority tenants association Chair commented:

People here are often upset at OSD vans coming into the area at night. People look out their windows and some come out. I've gone out in the past, and tried to help people who were being dealt with unfairly.

Similar views are found in Earleschurch. However, interview data revealed that it is not simply the policing style that is important, but the disposition of the officer (as my respondent above suggested). Two officers hold responsibility for community liaison work in Earleschurch. One is very highly regarded; the other has been unable to secure the confidence of the community. The following extract reflects widely-held views in Earleschuch, not only on behalf of residents but other voluntary agencies too.

We have two community beat officers [name] and [name]. I can give you their phone numbers if you want. [Name] is really good, he believes the community can build itself, he believes that people have a stake in the community and want to be safe. He also understands that people are tolerant. [Name] on the other hand is a nightmare. He was the one that, at a public meeting, said that the trouble was black youths in the area. The audience challenged him as they would. (Woman, community-wide residents association)

The experience of working in Earleschurch for the officer who held the confidence of the community reflected the experiences of the CBO in Edgebank in some ways, though he was more worried about cuts in the budget for community beat policing, and felt his role undermined by the risk, or reality, of being removed from his jobs to other policing tasks. In this way he appeared to have less organizational support than his Edgebank counterpart. This officer felt that he would be assisted by more trust from the community. Building a relationship with the community was a slow process because, as he put it, of 'distrust of the police in the area'. And indeed, though he acknowledged the necessity of the OSD, he was critical of these units; they undermined his role.

Many community commentators in Earleschurch resented harsh policing styles, as they had in Edgebank. Furthermore, during the Spring and Summer of 1997 armed police, in part associated with the special policing operation discussed in the previous chapter, became more visible in the town centres adjacent to both of the study sites. There was considerable evidence of mixed feelings amongst the various residents of Edgebank regarding this operation, but feelings were transparent in Earleschurch.

> I am worried, horrified, at the armed police in the area. I challenged this at a public meeting and was not satisfied with the kind of response that they gave – that it was in the interest of public safety! I have to say that to some extent the community is self-policing – people sort things out between themselves to some extent. (Woman, community wide residents association)

In 1997, residents, and other agencies reported a toughening of policing activity in both study areas. In Earleschurch, some residents said that there has been an increase in stop- and-search in so far as many believed the 'sus law' to have been rekindled. Some interviewees said that they thought that the police were reacting to a belief that they had been 'too soft' since the urban disorders of the 1980s; or that the police have been influenced by zero-tolerance debates and styles (the zero-tolerance initiative in Edgebank, discussed in Chapter 4, had been reported widely in the media). Young people and lower-order offences were said to be receiving increasing levels of police attention. But, by far, the most draconian action was taken in relation to prostitution, in both Edgebank and Earleschurch (as discussed in Chapter 4).

In Earleschuch, widening social divisions and polarization resulted from selective housing improvements and improvements in the economic well-being of some. Regeneration, the appeal to 'public opinion' and the need for measurable results blended to generate a zero-tolerance initiative in Edgebank, which had ramifications for other communities, notably Earleschurch. In a number of ways this compounded the marginalization of the most powerless groups. Furthermore, it could be argued that these processes could, ultimately, hinder the policing task since their (perhaps most useful) information comes from these groups; not the incoming gentrifiers.

This is not to argue that economic regeneration, housing and environmental improvement are inevitably bound to produce these kinds of effects. There are a number of reasons why they took the form that they did in Earleschurch. The availability of unconverted houses in specific streets, in the western sections, is important for understanding the gentrification of specific parts of the neighbourhood, for example. Unemployment and disaffection are deeper and more entrenched in Earleschurch, its surrounding area is poorer, and experience of regeneration longer. Nevertheless, policy-makers in areas like Edgebank need to be aware of the effects of neglecting the variety of needs of their poorer occupants.

There is some evidence of good practice in this regard. For in some neighbourhoods new partnership arrangements have aided the ability of local groups to address not only crime and disorder but other problems, such as training, jobs and youth provision, albeit in a fairly limited way. One such example was found in north Liverpool (in an area that was not the focus of this research), where housing associations are developing an area-based strategy for a locality identified as being in need of 'strategic regeneration': impoverished, experiencing high levels of crime and disorder, difficult to let and unstable. Addressing the housing problems is obviously a key focus, but like a number of other associations pursuing 'housing plus' policies elsewhere, social and economic issues are also important. Because the associations were not constrained in the same way that local authorities were, they could respond to local people's demands to employ local labour. However, the availability of funding through the North Liverpool Partnership (SRB) and, because of this, from the Housing Corporation, was instrumental to the development of the strategy in that locality.

Project managers hold that commitment to, and of, the community and residents associations are fundamental to the success of this project. But most community groups in the areas where this research was carried out have, as I have shown, not yet benefited from such a comprehensive community-focused strategy. In this context they have tried to address community problems, including crime and disorder, in other ways. I explore these in the following chapter.

6
Community Responses to Crime, Decline and Disorder

This chapter examines community-group responses to crime and disorder. It begins by looking at the value and place of community involvement in community safety strategies. It examines how collective initiatives revealed themselves in the study areas and addresses the question of how best to understand the community-based actions in Merseyside. Some observations will be relevant to other neighbourhoods elsewhere in the UK and beyond. The chapter suggests that police and other policy-makers, and indeed criminologists, often make unwarranted assumptions about community responses to crime and disorder. In the course of so doing, the chapter draws attention to some of the methodological issues associated with making sense of community responses (see also Chapter 2).

We have some understanding of the ways *individuals* perceive and respond to crime and disorder, through research carried out by academic researchers and policy-making and service-delivering institutions. However, there is relatively little literature that examines collective, grass-roots responses, particularly in the UK. As Dubow et al. noted in the US context: 'What at first appears to be a fair amount of literature and research on community crime prevention turns out to be primarily studies of programs run by the police or other governmental agencies attempting to involve citizens in their programs' (Dubow et al. 1979, in Podolefsky and Dubow 1981: 4). In the UK we can also include the initiatives of voluntary-sector bodies: NACRO, for example. However, the point remains valid in this setting and several years later: there have been few examinations of actions around crime and disorder arising from communities themselves.

The importance of local community groups in community safety?

Despite the lack of attention to 'what communities do' (Podolefsky and Dubow 1981) in response to crime and disorder, their role in community safety has been promoted by commentators across the political spectrum. Those on the right have been motivated by concerns about the diminution of morality and community, while 'left' commentators have been informed by a critique of local and central state interventions (see Hughes 1998). Most recently, the role of the community in implementing provisions of the Crime and Disorder Act was promoted by government. And community groups, voluntary organizations and citizens' panels are or have been consulted and, in some cases, involved in the development of community safety strategies and policies in local authorities across the country. In some cases (though the number is unknown) building 'community' is at least part of the community safety strategy itself.

Some writers have argued that the central state's capacity to impose its will on local people and groups has been enhanced by these developments. Others say that *some* scope to resist dominant authoritarian populist discourses around crime and disorder, social policy and criminal justice can be wrested from these arrangements (see Hughes 1998). This chapter does not specifically engage with these particular debates. Nevertheless, for those who wish to do so, it may be of value to note that, for the most part, community groups in this research responded to the problems faced by their communities in ways that cannot be described as authoritarian and populist.

Still, urban communities have often been portrayed as sites of tyrannical responses to crime and disorder over recent years. This is not surprising given print and broadcast media attention to the actions of some community groups against, for example, sex offenders, and a lack of interest on behalf of the media and academic criminologists regarding the daily business of responding to crime and disorder in inner-city neighbourhoods. In part, this lack of attention to community activities can contribute towards another (contradictory) view: that of the 'victim community', a powerless community where members live under siege conditions. Let us be clear: communities are not necessarily enduring crime- or disorder-ridden conditions until a local or central government funded project arrives to rescue them. As I show below, and as Podolefsky and Dubow (1981) demonstrated in their study of 10 neighbourhoods, in 3 cities in the United States, collective grass-roots activities are not rare events.

Nevertheless, the effectiveness of 'community organizing' programmes on crime remains unclear. Writers (e.g. Hope 1995; Skogan 1988b) have noted an absence of evidence to show the success of community programmes, which may be related to one or more of the following: the problems associated with the theories, and/or assumptions underpinning them; implementation failure; inadequate evaluation data. It has often been assumed that if lack of cohesion and disorganization is the problem 'organization is the solution' (Skogan 1988b: 40). Such a view is simplistic, as a number of writers have argued (see also Hope 1995; Bursik and Grasmick 1993; Chapters 1 and 3 in this volume), though the potential contribution of community programmes to crime prevention may have been underestimated (see Bennett 1995).

Recent writers on 'social disorganization' or 'collective efficacy' have argued that community cohesion may influence crime rates if coupled with a willingness to intervene 'on behalf of the common good' (see Sampson et al. 1997: 918). These new developments in 'social dis-organization theory' are important, as we saw in Chapter 3, because they recognize the importance of the vertical dimensions of social relations: they properly locate neighbourhoods within the wider social structure (see Bursik and Grasmick 1993). Nevertheless, problems with the model remain. For, although the revised model, as Bottoms and Wiles (1997) noted, recognizes the wider contexts in which neighbour-hoods exist, proponents rarely examine whether those institutions who can or do direct resources, particularly policing, into a community are considered legitimate or not. This is significant not only for com-munity safety or crime reduction policy in the current context, as I suggested in Chapter 5, but because, as we shall see, the ways in which these institutions are regarded by community groups can have important implications for the manner and means of community mobilization.

Community organizations and crime: some preliminary observations

The present research focused on community *groups* and as such it has its limitations: *all* views within a locality were not necessarily collected (though efforts were made to reach non-members and non-activists). That said, communities that are mobilizing to address crime and/or disorder are likely to add their concerns to the agendas of existing organizations. Communities are less likely to establish new groups around these matters alone (Podolefsky and Dubow 1981; Skogan 1988b). Where problems of crime and disorder are evident but mobilization does not occur, we *may* gain insights into the nature of urban communities, and the constraints associated with organizing around crime and disorder. Still, perceptions of crime and disorder alone do not influence community-group responses to crime (Podolefsky and Dubow 1981). Rather they, and indeed anti-crime pro- grammes, are interpreted through the 'local cultural context', which may in turn influence both local crime conditions and collective responses in an interactive fashion (Podolefsky and Dubow 1981: 12). This in part explains variations in collective responses in Podolefsky and Dubow's study areas, and those discussed in this chapter. Figure 1 expresses the dynamic nature of these relationships.

Podolefsky and Dubow (1981) discuss a wide range of activities pursued collectively in neighbourhoods in Chicago, San Francisco and Philadelphia. In total they distinguished 47 different anti-crime activities. Many would have been missed had *a priori* categories been used by the researchers, and this alone signifies the importance of the kinds of methodologies that researchers employ to discover 'what com- munities do'. In their study the researchers used a 'discovery-based

Figure 1: Podolefsky and Dubow's preliminary conceptual framework

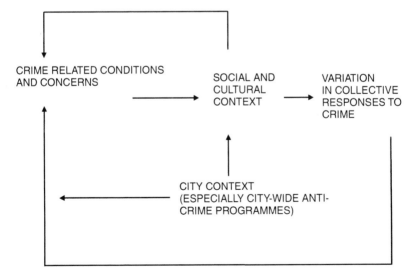

Source: Podolefsky and Dubow 1981: 13.

approach', as I did here. Variations in responses to crime and disorder across different neighbourhoods were explained by differing urban contexts and divergent local, social-cultural contexts, which in turn reflected and created different opportunity structures. I return more fully to these matters below. For now, we may note that in the Merseyside context, though there were some activities which groups engaged in directly, community groups for the most part played a lobbying or pressure-group role. While it is difficult to be conclusive, because some literature fails to distinguish between provisions secured through lobbying and those directly provided by groups themselves, for example, community groups in American cities appear to be more directly involved in anti-crime activities. Furthermore, while groups in Merseyside occasionally approached private businesses to support some of their activities, this also appears to be more common in the USA (see Podolefsky and Dubow 1981). This may arise because of differing opportunity structures and different perceptions of the role of the local state (and other city authorities) in the 'causes of crime', and community groups' perceptions regarding the degree of obligation placed upon these authorities to resolve neighbourhood problems. Without more research (of a comparative nature) we can only speculate, but what is significant here is that this observation foregrounded the importance of community groups' lobbying activities and their relationships with dominant city authorities.

Seen in this way, collective responses are not simply reactions to crime, but they are part of the urban context (Podolefsky and Dubow 1981). Moreover, they are an integral part of urban politics, albeit a neglected one. The idea of urban politics invokes thoughts about local government, elections and council meetings, rather than the activities and struggles of tenants, community and residents groups. Consequently, *local* pressure-group activity has often been a neglected area of study, even for political scientists (Stoker and Wilson 1991). Furthermore, the subject-matter itself, crime and disorder, complicates efforts to apply political science or urban sociological frameworks in any simple sense to explain and understand these phenomena.

Some empirical evidence on the relationship between neighbourhood organizations and crime suggests that they are most successful in the areas that need them least (Shapland 1988; Skogan 1988b; Skogan and Maxfield 1981). As a consequence it is possible that resources are deflected away from those who need them most (Skogan 1988b). Low-income, heterogeneous, deteriorating, rental, high-turnover, high-crime areas, for example (Skogan 1988b).

Skogan also found:

- Community organizations are less frequently found in stable, cohesive, working-class areas, where informal networks are likely to substitute for more formalized channels.
- Successful organizations are more common in homogenous areas where common problems are easier to discern.
- In gentrifying areas there may be divisions that preclude community-wide support as new residents' and property developers' interests (exchange values) may not coincide with long-term residents. Their influence may result in actions against undesirable people and land uses.
- Participants lose interest and enthusiasm over time, or their function(s) change.
- Community groups rarely form in response to crime problems alone; rather, it is more likely that existing groups add crime prevention to their agendas, and later drop it.

For some writers, crime is an inhibitor of collective activity. Crime affects individuals, not groups, and tends to have an atomizing effect (see Skogan 1988b; Skogan and Maxfield 1981). This may help to explain why it is difficult for community organizations to win visible victories over crime; though success is necessary if sustained action is to be achieved (Skogan, 1988b). And, these observations may go some way to illuminating why crime is often dropped from community organizations' agendas. That said, as I indicated above, the relationship between crime and collective action is not straightforward. Podolefsky and Dubow put it thus:

> Not only do we question the impact of fear of crime on involvement in community groups, but more importantly we question the salience of crime perceptions for an understanding of why people participate in collective responses to crime when a full range of anti-crime activities is examined. We suggest, alternatively, that participation in collective responses to crime develops out of more general involvement in community groups. (1981: 104)

In these authors' view, participation in collective anti-crime activities is related to group involvement, which in turn is related to social integration. Moreover, the evidence provided by Podolefsky and Dubow suggests that it is not crime *per se* that impacts upon collective action, but other contextual factors such as 'social solidarity', the definition of 'out-groups' and 'local theories about the causes of crime' (1981: 15).

Podolefsky and Dubow were concerned with evaluating the idea that fear of crime or victimization may *promote* involvement in collective activities. Nevertheless, given the importance of these conditions, the contention that fear of crime, deterioration and disorder inhibit collective activity should be tested empirically. For, more recently, Taylor's (1996) study of 66 neighbourhoods in Baltimore, Maryland, found evidence that attachment to, involvement in, stability of, and the social climate found in neighbourhoods are not only important for collective responses to disorder, 'but also to cognitive, behavioral, and emotional responses to disorder' (Taylor 1996: 69). Thus, he argued, 'we need to know more about the community and perhaps historical conditions shaping these responses' (p. 70; see also Donnelly and Majka 1998).

In Skogan's work, 'preservationist' and 'insurgent' groups are distinguished (Lewis, Grant and Rosenbaum 1985 in Skogan 1988b: 42). The former are concerned with the maintenance of local interests, customs and values, and are likely to be found in the better-off areas. The latter aim to challenge the status quo (the distribution of status and property) and the institutions that maintain it (Skogan 1988b). In the Merseyside data, however, groups did not fall easily into these categories. I return to these issues below. Nevertheless, Skogan's work is useful and a number of his observations were germane in the Merseyside context. For example, the ability to secure resources, particularly staff or others who could devote time to their cause, was regarded as being essential for sustained involvement. In Podolefsky and Dubow's terms, resources influence community groups' capacity to respond to crime and disorder. Capacity to respond intervenes between the inclination to respond and the types of action undertaken in their model. But, as Skogan (1988b) noted, an organization's goals can be transformed as a consequence of securing resources; the preferred strategies for dealing with neighbourhood problems promoted by bodies funding crime prevention often do not match those at the grass-roots. In some cases funders' views about the causes of crime are in opposition to those of local people (see also Podolefsky and Dubow's discussion of the SAFE project in the Mission, 1981: 192–5). Discord between local groups' assessments of the causes of crime, and those manifested in the programmes of local agencies, was apparent in the study areas in Merseyside. I consider these observations below; they raise important questions for current crime reduction strategies as they are being pursued under the Crime and Disorder Act (1998).

Let us now turn to the kinds of activities that communities engage in when they respond to crime (and disorder). Skogan (1988b) suggests that groups try to:

- *Get others to help* – often the police – though for insurgent groups policing may constitute part of the problem and they may call for greater accountability, for example.
- *Identify institutions and processes* that originate outside of the community – for insurgent groups this often means addressing the 'root causes of crime' and addressing social, economic and political issues.
- *Push crime prevention* – here insurgent groups may develop drug prevention, treatment, job programmes and a myriad of social programmes. However, trained staff and funding are required to pursue them, and with this comes the danger of co-optation.

Podolefsky and Dubow's work provides some useful insights regarding variations in community responses, as Figure 2 illustrates. Thus crimes, and what is perceived to be the criminogenic environment, are interpreted through the local, social-cultural context of the community. The socio-cultural context influences the structure of opportunity and thus the capacity to respond. It also also influences the inclination to respond through conditioning perceptions of the causes of crime (and in-groups and out-groups who may perpetrate crimes). This context influences beliefs about appropriate types of response. Podolefsky and Dubow (1981) note, for example, that in areas where people refer to local youth as 'our youth' and the community as 'our community' and so on, the outcome is likely to be activities that focus on positive youth activities. As such, family composition and social integration are key to understanding inclination and strategy. Socio-economic status is related to the capacity of a community to respond. And 'race' and 'ethnicity' are linked not only to perceptions of 'in-groups' and 'out-groups' (which in turn are related to the inclination to undertake action against perceived perpetrators), but social divisions such as these are likely to influence action in other ways. These authors note that involvement with police programmes is likely to be viewed more antagonistically in areas where minority ethnic groups are active, for example. In these areas there is likely to be more inclination towards a social problem approach, since local groups are often sensitive to the lack of opportunity facing minority ethnic groups, and the link between young people's delinquency and lack of opportunity is more likely to be made.

Community organizing, crime and disorder in Merseyside

In common with the findings discussed by Podolefsky and Dubow, the groups encountered throughout this research had all engaged in some kind of action around crime and disorder. And, like these authors' findings and those of Skogan (1988b), few had mobilized simply around crime. The kinds of actions varied, some were perceived to be more successful than others, but similar strategies were discernible. What is notable is that actions took place precisely in areas thought to be difficult to organize (see also Donnelly and Majka 1998). I therefore faced a task similar to that of Donnelly and Majka (1998) when they tried to explain their 'negative case', residents' actions in Five Oaks,

Figure 2: Podolefsky and Dubow's model for thinking about variation

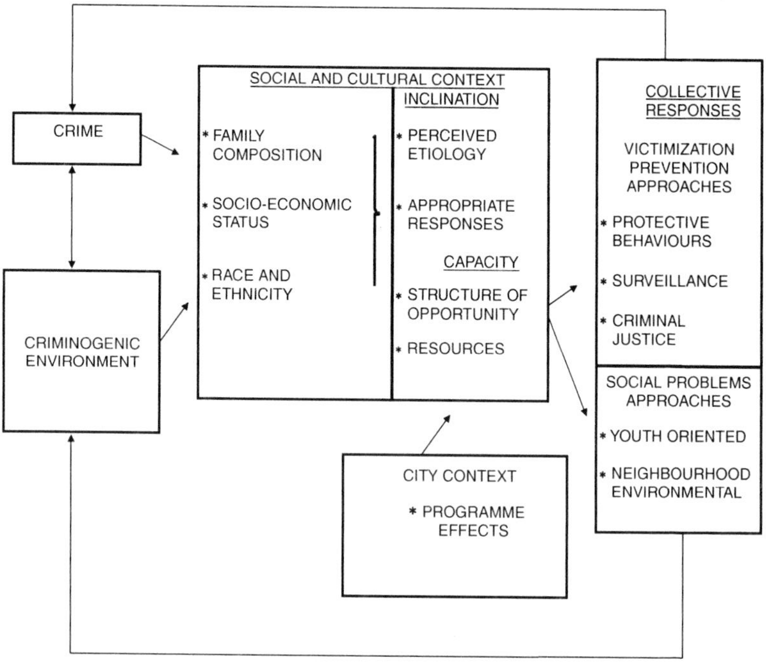

Source: Podolefsky and Dubow 1981: 138.

Dayton (Ohio). Five Oaks, an inner-city, racially and economically diverse neighbourhood experiencing increasing levels of crime and disorder, did not fit into previous models; while it experienced considerable instability and increasing heterogeneity, for example, it remained relatively cohesive and its residents retained the capacity to engage in collective action. Donnelly and Majka argued the importance of a historical experience of local organization in their explanation, a factor clearly reflected in the present study. Indeed, Merseyside's well-established community-group infrastructure has been noted by many writers (Middleton 1991, for example), even in the most impoverished localities (Anderson et al. 1998). And, as we have seen, collective responses to crime develop out of more general involvement in community groups (Podolefsky and Dubow 1981).

Part of the reason for the existence of community groups (whether formally constituted or not) can be found in the way that economic, social and physical regeneration initiatives have been active in the region for many years. In some neighbourhoods they have been present almost continually for the past 30 or so years. Many have tried to involve or develop community organizations as part of their remits. More recently, residents' 'participation' and 'involvement' have become essential if a local authority's bid is to receive funding under urban regeneration programmes. However, even before such developments, community groups were involved in participatory arrangements because lead agencies felt it important to involve local residents in their activities. We may understand the desire to consult communities by referring to local authority officers' progressive professionalism, to past mistakes and to experience of other statutory requirements (especially those associated with urban planning). This is not the place to discuss the adequacy of these arrangements. In any case, the 'past mistakes' element is useful to our understanding of the history of community organizing and politics in Merseyside. Many tenants and residents groups can trace their origins to struggles over slum clearance and other housing policies, in which failure to consult and respond adequately to the needs and demands of residents resulted in conflict with local authorities in the 1960s and early 1970s.

Indeed, the 'neighbourhood' as a political entity has a longer history in some parts of Merseyside. For, despite a reputation of militant trades unionism and working-class politics, the history of Liverpool has been for a long time one of conservatism in 'formal' politics (Smith 1984). It was only in the 1950s that the city managed to elect a Labour council (Smith 1984), for example. According to Smith, historically, political action in Liverpool, when it occurred, took the form of 'riots', usually along neighbourhood lines, which were often defined on sectarian grounds. Lacking strong working-class organizations, partly as a result of the predominance of casual, unskilled labour and partly because of the importance of other lines of affiliation, the politics of neighbourhood and of 'riot' became a distinctive feature before and after the First World War (Smith 1984). The important point is that the historical experience of organizing is relevant to our understanding of community action and crime in those areas that are seen, ostensibly at least, to have the least capacity to organize. Moreover, some of these experiences facilitate their ability to conduct actions (though of course failed actions can undermine future ones), and those involved in earlier actions can facilitate those of neighbouring groups.

Doreen Massey's discussion of the 'uniqueness of place' provides urban criminologists with useful insights when considering these matters, as I indicated in Chapter 1; it illuminates our understanding of community responses to crime, disorder, decline and regeneration. In particular, variations in local organizations' responses to the agencies associated with the management of these phenomena are also informed by Massey's account. It also helps us to understand how some urban regeneration or crime prevention policies produce unintended consequences in certain settings. For our present purposes, Massey's framework helps us to understand why we find evidence of community organizing around crime- and disorder-related issues in Merseyside (and elsewhere) that is at odds with some studies.

Crime and disorder: local authority controlled areas

a) The role of dominant city authorities

Urban sociologists have noted that, historically, direct action undertaken by tenants is much more likely in areas where local authorities have failed to respond to the needs of their residents. If, for example, a local authority's stance has been to oppose national legislation to increase rents, tenants have failed to organize. If they have been compliant with legislation of this sort, residents are much more likely to mobilize (Lowe 1986; Sklair 1975). The action is directed first towards the local authority. Similarly, residents are more likely to mobilize around crime and disorder when the very structures and procedures that exist, ostensibly, to deal with or manage neighbourhood problems fail to do so. The following case study (Case Study A) is illustrative.

A group in a late 1960s or early 1970s council estate, near Edgebank, formed primarily as a result of concerns about crime and disorder, mostly the latter. It was the only one to do so in this research, though two points should be noted in this regard. First, it soon developed beyond being a single-issue presure group. Second, physical and social disorder, and some types of crime, impact upon communities (or sections of them) and not just individuals. Thus, the atomizing effect may be less powerful; there may be more of a basis for collective action. In this particular case, the physical fabric of the dwellings (maisonettes) had deteriorated from the beginning of the 1990s. The estate's desirability had fallen as other housing estates had been redeveloped (a pattern familiar in many studies of neighbourhood decline and crime; see Chapter 3). Vandalism (graffiti, broken lights, for example) and public drinking (amongst young people) became more prominent. Stolen cars were dumped on the (relatively small) estate, 'chaotic' drug-users were more visible and young people congregated on the open landings and stairwells. The turning point, which led to the formation of the group, came when one tenant, later to become the chair of the residents association, felt terrified during a weekend of 'trouble' on the landing above. All the windows on it were smashed in an incident that was described to the author as being 'drugs related'. She called the police. Later, the residents' group was formed, which was to reflect a broad section of the population of the estate.

Before calling the police on this occasion, individual residents had taken their problems to the council, its housing and environmental health departments; offices whose remit included dealing with housing management and nuisance issues. The problems residents faced were twofold. First, insufficient numbers of employees of these agencies worked at weekends, when most problems were occurring. Second, they felt that the local authority departments were not listening to them. In part, this related to the difficulties the housing department faced. The tenants were often seeking 'exit'; but the housing department either would not, or could not, rehouse them. Advised of the long waiting list to transfer, tenants could either accept their situation or mobilize (and exercise 'voice', in Hirschman's terms). The incident described above triggered the latter strategy.[1] This example illustrates a number of issues to which I shall return. For our present purposes it demonstrates the importance of how powerful agencies (in this case the local authority) behave for residents' anti-crime and disorder activities. Furthermore, an examination of the interaction between these groups and the relevant authorities reveals that the institutions themselves often become *the* focus of action. Here is the source of many groups' difficulties, because these structures can debilitate local efforts to deal with problems.

This is reflected in another example of community organizing over problems of crime and disorder on a local authority estate approximately a mile and a half away from that referred to in Case Study A. Here a residents association existed before the adoption of crime prevention as an organizational goal. Housing repairs had traditionally been their main concern. As in Case Study A, the area was relatively economically impoverished. Two-thirds of the population over 16 years old were unemployed. In this case, the neighbourhood was more stable and cohesive. It was one of the few cases where residents exhibited no hesitation when describing their area as having 'a strong sense of community'. Many people had local connections and wished to remain in the locality. However, should people want to leave they often could not do so because 'the housing department won't let them', as one local authority officer commented. The area has a poor reputation relative to other housing estates and it was in the interests of the department to maintain reasonable levels of occupancy. The important point, as Hirschman (1970) noted, is that where opportunities for 'exit' are unavailable, exercising voice, when conditions are unsatisfactory, is more likely.

This group (we will call it Case Study B) employed a number of strategies to improve their area both directly and through lobbying. They removed graffiti from a high wall that overlooked the estate. They felt that they had successfully addressed the problem of young people 'joy-riding' through the neighbourhood. Furthermore, they had managed to secure funding to improve a local cemetery that was frequently vandalized, and several thousand pounds to develop a new play area for children. Open drug dealing had declined, the physical appearance of the area improved, central heating had been installed, and demand for housing in the area had increased somewhat (new tenants tended to be younger), though considerable problems remained. These successes were important for the collective confidence of the community and, as such, they were important for the group's subsequent actions. In Podolefsky and Dubow's (1981) terms, they added to the capacity and the inclination to undertake action to improve their neighbourhood. Against this, some attempts to secure funding to improve neighbourhood facilities failed.

b) Socio-cultural context, history and the reactions of dominant authorities

Case Study B illustrates a number of themes outlined in our earlier discussion. It highlights the importance of recognizing the socio-cultural and historical context of neighbourhoods and the reactions of dominant authorities to their members and groups. For example, in this case, though the residents' association identified 'youths causing annoyance' as one of the main problems facing the area (70 per cent of calls to the police), this is certainly not to say that the residents association was unsympathetic to their plight. In describing the disaffection faced by young people in the area, the Chair of the association noted how there were 'no jobs – only pot', that the nearest cinema was several miles away, and the nearest leisure facility was a tennis centre charging £11 for each half-hour on court. And, indeed, the Chair had made an international telephone call to the New York Police Department, after watching a television programme about a sports initiative developed by community officers, to obtain further information in the hope of setting up a similar venture. No help was forthcoming from local agencies. On another occasion, he had developed a proposal, with local young people, to procure an innovative youth facility where young people would be able to develop activities and where they would play a part in its management. Again, the local authorities and regeneration initiatives lacked interest.

This activist recognized the need for young people to be involved and have a stake in the development of facilities that were seemingly 'provided for' them. In Podolefsky and Dubow's terms this group clearly regarded those 'youths causing annoyance' to be 'our children' – not an 'out-group'. Moreover, it was common knowledge, amongst local people in the town, that a youth centre in another neighbourhood had suffered thousands of pounds of damage at the hands of local kids only a few months after its opening. It had been funded by one of the regeneration initiatives – and many felt that there had been insufficient input from local people, especially young people, in its development. Moreover, the decision-makers were regarded as being ignorant of local sensibilities; in this case of historically rooted conflict between local groups of young people, some of whom were self- or otherwise excluded (by others or the management team) from using it. It is not too dubious to suggest that, for many decision-makers, who funded the centre and who lacked sufficient knowledge of local sensitivities, the episode was likely to have created or reinforced notions of undeserving groups of young people.

That said, however, the residents association Chair said, without being too censorious, that his area 'always had the potential for disorder – serious disorder'. Twenty-five years ago there had been a series of 'riots' in the neighbourhood, involving clashes between groups of young people from inside and outside the locality. They had become part of the collective biography of the neighbourhood; they were remembered by locals, housing officers and the police; they formed part of the backdrop to the local, socio-cultural context. Also part of the local context was the historical antagonism between members of the community and the police; though people talked favourably about the local community beat officers who were regarded as being able to identify with the area and its problems. The Operational Support Division, a special unit, in particular, was regarded with resentment. Significant numbers of residents would come out onto the street, to protest, if they thought that local people were being dealt with unfairly (as I discussed in Chapter 5). Experiences such as these clearly helped to shape community views about the causes of crime, appropriate responses and preferred strategies to deal with crime and disorder. This is not to say, however, that offending behaviour was sanctioned by local people or the residents association. Rather, the association wanted the police and local authority to respond sensitively to their needs. When they failed to do so, sometimes they took matters into their own hands. This was reflected in one story related by a member of the association, in which a family deemed responsible for a 'mini-crime wave' of dwelling burglaries was 'persuaded [he did not elaborate] to move from the area'. I should add that the residents association had, for some time, been given some power over local lettings, but the property had been let without their knowledge or consent some time before.[2]

c) Resources

The efforts to improve the neighbourhood in Case Study B had been assisted by a community development worker who had been seconded from the local authority to work for the local regeneration initiative. He had helped the community association to secure resources to lay 'sleeping policemen' in an effort to deter 'joy-riders', and to clean up graffiti, for example. The same worker had been important for other groups in this research. Moreover, the 'alliances' that his liaison role afforded were instrumental for other groups' actions. The loss of this worker, after the regeneration project's funding ended, was a blow to some associations (see also Chapter 4). *Direct support* was regarded as important to many groups' ongoing activities. Against this, the funders argued that residents associations should be self-sustaining by the end of the funded period.

An activist in another local authority controlled neighbourhood near Edgebank, facilitated the action of the group in Case Study A. Indeed, the community development worker (above) also played a part in its mobilization (as a favour, because it lay outside the geographical area to which he was assigned). Together, they sought the support of significant others, for example, councillors, the police and so on. Following their failure to obtain transfers, they took action to improve their neighbourhood. First, they demanded that the maisonettes were 'down-topped', the landings removed and the dwellings converted to houses. Later they argued for a complete redevelopment, probably after seeing the transformation of the estate nearby, where the visiting activist lived. There the group had achieved considerable physical and social change, following a campaign. And the chair of the group had gained considerable experience of local authority structures and policies, the law, and 'how to get things done' following her earlier conflict (which went to court) over structural problems and repairs (see Chapter 5). This knowledge not only helped her action but was now benefiting that of others. However, in this later case (Case Study A) the outcome was not as favourable.

In November 1996, the council agreed that the scheme should be demolished and decided that the area would be redeveloped by a housing association. The contract for the redevelopment would be put out to tender under the council's supervision; tenants understood that they were to be given the right to be involved in the negotiations and would have the right to return if they chose to do so. Later, one of the regeneration initiatives informed the author that it would be funding half of the redevelopment and the project was *not* going to be put out to tender. Instead, a [named] housing association would redevelop the site; it had a grant from the Housing Corporation, which needed to be 'spent'. A decision had been made that the area would be redeveloped on a mixed-tenure basis, which would include some rented accommodation and some units provided on a co-ownership basis. Many tenants would not be able to gain access to these types of tenures. It was apparent that tenants (who had campaigned for redevelopment) were now becoming increasingly marginal in the policy process, as discussed in Chapter 2.

Community action, crime and disorder, and the new urban governance

I have devoted some time to describing what happened in these examples of community organizing because, in addition to the themes already outlined, they illustrate the need to place an analysis of community responses to crime and disorder, and community organizing more generally, in a framework that recognizes contemporary forms of governance. In so doing, we can appreciate why community groups may demobilize in the face of problems. In making sense of these findings, the idea of 'policy arena', discussed in Chapter 4, is of particular value: it allows the analyst to envisage a situation where actors emerge and disappear, relationships and outcomes stem from antagonism and negotiation, and are shaped by pressures external to, but impinging upon, the actions of those concerned (Wilks 1995). The idea is valuable for understanding how some communities, and sometimes sectional interests within them, have achieved access to the policy arena, and have subsequently found themselves excluded.

Some of the mechanisms that have resulted in the exclusion of community groups from the policy arena can be found in the context of urban policy-making in the late 1980s and early 1990s, discussed in Chapter 1 – though in some cases these developments have also promoted consultation and involvement as the legislation underpinning them in some areas of social policy (housing policy, for example) made community consultation mandatory; and they were often ushered in with rhetoric that suggested that governments were promoting 'consumer sovereignty', for example. Be that as it may. Suffice it to note here that central government's control of local government expenditure and the range of agencies responsible for urban policies and service delivery grew considerably over the 1980s and 1990s. These changes had implications for the ways community groups mobilize. Most obviously they had implications for their considerations about which bodies they needed to gain access to, so they could influence urban policies and services.

In some neighbourhoods the new arrangements have aided the ability of local groups and organizations to address not only crime and disorder but other problems, such as lack of training, jobs and youth provisions, albeit in a fairly limited way, as discussed in the previous chapter. (In others they clearly have not.) This is important because community groups do not regard problems of crime as ones simply of law enforcement and 'crime prevention'. As Podolefsky and Dubow (1981: 223) noted, 'Community groups do not wish to isolate crime

from the myriad of social problems.' This is also reflected in the preferred strategies for addressing neighbourhood problems in Case
Studies A and B and in those discussed below.

Community organizing, crime and disorder: the mixed housing areas

In Earleschurch there have been approximately 10 residents and
tenants associations operating for a number of years. Some are street
organizations; others are defined by their relationship to particular
landlords (council tenants and housing association tenants, for
example). Others reflect particular interest groups (regeneration and
environmental issue-based groups are notable in this category). In the
regeneration and environmentally oriented groups, middle-class
people (often owner-occupiers) are over-represented. There is, however,
a community-wide residents' association that aims to represent the
interests of the area as a whole. As I will show in this section, the heterogeneity of the area can sometimes make effective action difficult
(see also Podolefsky and Dubow 1981), when compared to the actions
of tenants in local authority controlled areas where everyone shared
tenurial relationships with the local authority, but the process is not as
straightforward as this statement might suggest. The following section
seeks to delineate some of the complex processes that are at play in the
mixed housing areas in this study.

A number of the housing association-based tenants associations in
Earleschurch had been pressing for improvements to the security of
their homes for some time when this research was carried out. For
many, their greatest concern has been to stabilize the population of
the neighbourhood. Instability was identified as a 'root cause' of the
area's problems (see Chapter 3). For tenants in one housing association
their actions resulted in a package being made available to them during
the early 1990s, which was later extended (see also Chapter 5). Other
problems were associated with the hopelessness and disaffection that
results from poor employment prospects – particularly on the eastern
side of the neighbourhood.

Because the majority of properties in Earleschurch produce instability, there has been pressure to reconvert properties for family occupation. There have been some small sections where this has been
achieved by one association in particular, that referred to above, which
has been willing to invest some of its reserves in stock improvement
(see Chapter 5). However, because of cuts to housing association
capital spending, addressing housing problems on a large scale was not

possible during the period of this research. Other associations in the area either lacked the resources, or were unwilling to commit them to improve their properties. Indeed, some commentators reported that some *lowered* their standards because of the need to reduce costs. Derelict properties have also been identified as a problem; and efforts to reduce their numbers have had an impact over recent years (1990s). But general improvements to housing association properties were not a priority for regeneration initiatives in the locality, or national housing policy, during the 1980s and 1990s. In short, housing associations were limited in their ability to address tenants' (and indeed their own) concerns in the 10 years to 1998.

The situation was, perhaps, worse still in the private rented sector, where tenants' capacity to mobilize was difficult, not least because of the diversity of properties and the number of landlords. Few landlords were willing to commit funds to improve the physical security of their dwellings; though tenants in the social and private rented sectors faced, by far, the greatest level of property crime (criminal damage and burglary). Surveillance measures, employed to address racial harassment (under the auspices of Safer Cities), were available (subject to conditions) to tenants in the housing association and council sectors, but not to private-sector tenants and owner-occupiers. Indeed, there is evidence to suggest that some private tenants have been asked to leave when they made complaints about racial harassment to their landlords; and some private landlords have been reluctant to fit 'antiburglar bars' because 'it detracts from the aesthetic quality of the houses' (see Chapter 3).

Though few respondents would go as far as this, some would go some way to agree with *sentiment* expressed here. Certainly one group in the gentrifying section sees its main aim as the preservation of the appearance of local buildings, and has often made representations to the planning department in pursuit of its interests. Sometimes interests such as these collide with those of others. For example, there is evidence to suggest there is a conflict of interest between those (including this group) who campaign for Victorian-style street-lighting and others who regard it as inadequate. But to describe such groups as being strictly 'preservationist' would be misleading.

It is clear from other views put forward by this group (and others) that they are influenced by a number of complex and contingent factors, and by urban ideologies, which emanate from spatially and temporally variable sources (see also Donnelly and Majka 1998). Indeed, there is some evidence to suggest that members of residents groups in this sector are socialized, to some degree, into the norms and values of the neighbourhood. This manifests itself in the celebration of the diversity of lifestyles that characterize the area (a finding reflected in Donnelly and Majka's study of Five Oaks), and in the relatively tolerant attitude that *all* groups in Earleschurch display towards street prostitution. The groups in the gentrifying section, that are largely made up of professional people and owner-occupiers, are no exception.

Local sensibilities and toleration

Though covering an area slightly larger than the present author's research site, recent research found 95 per cent of residents were aware of street prostitution; 39 per cent said that they felt 'indifferent'; 24.5 per cent said that they felt 'concern for the women' or 'uncomfortable'; 20.7 per cent reported that they felt 'mild' or 'serious annoyance'. Thus, no consensus exists; but only 8.3 per cent said that they wished to have the women removed from the area. Most (92.8 per cent) agreed that the welfare of the women should be a key consideration. Furthermore, residents were asked whether women working as prostitutes were percieved as part of, or seperate from, the community. The responses indicated that 40 per cent felt they were part of it.[3]

Clearly, there are people reporting sexual offences (soliciting and kerb-crawling for the most part). Between 1992 and 1994, calls to the police regarding sexual offences were 21 times higher than the Merseyside average in this research site. Some sections of the area have even higher rates. In the previous chapter it was noted that incoming, more affluent groups were more likely to report crimes, like burglary, since they are more likely to be able to afford the high insurance premiums, and are more likely to have confidence in the police. The geographical spread of the calls, and anecdotal evidence,[4] suggest that it is these groups who are most concerned with activities associated with prostitution. However, it is likely that residents report prostitution-related activities to the police not because they want prostitute women to receive the full force of the law, but because there were no alternative strategies in place for dealing with neighbourhood disorder, including prostitution. These groups were also more likely to anticipate that the police will respond fairly to perpetrators of incivilities, such as women involved in sex-work. It should also be noted that rates of calling, compared with the regional average, while informative in some respects, can be misleading in others. For in the most gentrified sub-area calls regarding sexual offences made up less than 10 per cent of calls (9.5 per cent: 116 calls) to the police in the period

1992–4. Furthermore, across the neighbourhood as a whole, and in the gentrifying area too – despite their low level of victimization (see Chapter 5) – calls regarding property crimes were reported more frequently. Moreover, the qualitative work suggested that those community groups, largely or in part, made up of middle-class people, or 'gentrifiers', displayed a remarkable degree of tolerance towards women involved in prostitution during this research. The following extract illustrates something of the debates around these issues.

> Prostitution, people get het up about prostitution from time to time. Personally I don't mind offering a venue for this activity to our suburban brothers and sisters – provided that they don't leave their used contraceptive equipment behind our back alleys, which unfortunately they sometimes do . . . There is a strong feminist presence in our ABO[5] meetings, much to the confusion of the ABO, which as well as holding the usual view that it's the men, not the prostitutes, who should be arrested also believe that our houses are safer for there being prostitutes in the street. I think this is a very romantic view – but it makes for an interesting debate. (Retired professional male representing a mixed community group of renters and owner-occupiers)

The leader of another community group operating in the gentrifying section, but representing people from a range of backgrounds, outlined a number of problems associated with disorder in the locality but did not refer to prostitution when asked about problems associated with disorder in her locality. Only a passing reference was made in relation to a question about the area's reputation (see also the extacts in Chapter 2).

More research is needed to establish the precise mechanisms that have resulted in residents' toleration of prostitute women and, to some degree, prostitution in Earleschurch. Indeed, the question of 'toleration' more generally deserves more research. What is clear is that toleration is bound up with the socio-cultural context of the area (Campbell and Hancock 1998). Its demography may be influential as part of this context or independently. The nature of the population, which includes a high number of adults but not of old people or children, means that those more likely to be upset by the sex industry are less likely to come into contact with street-walking women. When parents come into contact with street prostitution it is evident that they are concerned about its effect upon their children, as the following quotation shows.

As far as prostitution is concerned people are tolerant . . . because they know the women. People interrelate. But some people have a nostalgic view of prostitutes. Many women are desperate for the next fix – desperate. It is awful to see, for our kids to see women like that. But we don't want to see the women more marginalized. There are more women than ever out at the moment. Some women are dealing. There are, it should be said, different levels of tolerance. People, in general, want the worst effects 'packaged' so that they feel safe. . . . Also, [prostitute] women tell people in the community about what they have seen, they tell people about neighbourhood or people problems. (Woman representing the community-wide residents group)[6]

It is interesting that the resident quoted highlighted other features which explain why even parents in this locality are reluctant to support 'police clampdowns' on prostitution: they do not want to see women disadvantaged further. Indeed, this respondent, like others, suggested that prostitution brings some benefits to the community (see also Chapter 2). When the issue of 'toleration' was explored further, the 'cosmopolitan' population (with the architecture) was amongst the most often-cited attractions of the area. The following quotation from the respondent noted above illustrates the point.

There are so many different levels to it – there are so many different types of people – it is more than a bohemian community, there are people with different histories and experience. The architecture is beautiful. In our street there is a mix of people, there are political activists, heroin users, prostitutes, a fringe award winner, people with important jobs, students – a mix of people with different lifestyles and levels. It is not one community but a number of different communities and networks, we know lots of people. People are not judgemental. It's great! (Woman representing the community-wide residents group)

Numbers and visibility are also important when explaining toleration in this community. The field data show that many, though not all, residents regarded the number of street-walking women to have diminished over recent years, as the geography of prostitution has changed in the locality (see Chapter 2). Other factors may also explain the level of tolerance. For, as Matthews (1992) argued in his critique of the

'Broken Windows thesis', there is a need to recognize that some neigh-bourhoods may have the economic or political resources to withstand or endure 'signs of decline', of which prostitution may be a part. Furthermore, many long-term residents have witnessed periodic police clampdowns on prostitution over many years and have concluded that these simply displace prostitute women, without addressing any of the underlying issues. This, in part, explains why residents are reluctant to support zero-tolerance policing styles. Our understanding is aided further by a discussion of how residents view policing more generally (see Chapter 5).

Other factors may also play a part in forging these responses amongst groups in the gentrifying sections (or may contribute to their members' socialization). For one of the most influential of these groups makes up part of another association that campaigns to attract inward investment. In this context, campaigns to remove socially disorderly behaviour and crime (which contribute to the area's reputation) can have adverse public-relations implications, as Skogan (1988b) observes; though at the same time such actions may be in their economic inter-ests. The more affluent groups also have the option of 'exit'. Yet, for the most part there was considerable 'loyalty' (Hirschman 1970) to Earleschurch – as a whole (see also Donnelly and Majka 1998). The use-value of the neighbourhood, particularly to these groups, and their commitment to it (see Chapter 5) is arguably important for influencing their response to crime and disorder (Taylor 1996) and their willing-ness to campaign to improve the neighbourhood (Donnelly and Majka 1998). The high price of entering Earleschurch (the economic risk for home owners), and the cost of exiting should the neighbourhood enter further cycles of decline, may be important for (1) influencing their adaptations to and acceptance of local beliefs and attitudes, and (2) the promotion of voice to secure improvement (see Hirschman 1970, ch. 7). Furthermore, given the importance of *alliances* to local pressure-group activity, some accommodation of the views of other local inter-est groups would be expedient.

Intra-neighbourhood conflict and lobbying external agencies

Nevertheless, other groups in this section find themselves disagreeing with the regeneration focus of interest groups such as these. Their well-being is not felt to be enhanced by the type of economic regeneration efforts that have been promoted in their area. The noise, litter and some socially disorderly behaviour which are associated with pub and club developments nearby that have been advanced by these initiatives, have been the subject of action on behalf of residents in the streets nearby. (Again, residents were frustrated by the working practices of the environmental health officers, the attitudes of licensing authorities and the policy of promoting 'leisure industries' as a key plank of local regeneration strategy.) Few concede that these problems are offset by job creation.

Faced with problems of crime and disorder, and the difficulties associated with housing-based strategies referred to above, residents' groups in Earleschurch have approached and lobbied a number of agencies to help to resolve local problems. Because the police are regarded with suspicion and hostility in some (the most disadvantaged and ethnically diverse) sections of Earleschurch, there is considerable under-reporting of crime; though, as I indicated in the previous chapter, one beat officer is well regarded (the other has yet to gain the community's confidence). In this context, some community organization members have made reports on behalf of their reluctant neighbours. It should be noted that in so doing residents are often acting in a 'ritualistic' fashion; they do not expect a quick response (if any) but 'don't want there to be an excuse for the police doing nothing'. Occasionally these groups have taken collective action around a particular problem. Two instances stand out in the actions of one group: one when hard drugs were being sold openly on a street close to an area used by children to play, and another in response to a series of confrontational burglaries. On these occasions the police were invited to meetings to hear residents' concerns – they were asked not to speak until the residents had made their points. The co-chair explained that they were displeased with the way that the police had come to meetings in the past and had dominated them.

Creating leverage

Decision-making authorities often argued that they would only respond to a community group that is representative of the whole community. Where a group appears unrepresentative, this can provide grounds for refusing their appeal, though there is evidence to suggest that they sometimes respond to sectional interests. Perhaps ironically, the importance of a democratically elected group seemed to be more important for the 'quangocracy' than for the elected councils covered in this study. In Earleschurch the effects of this have been twofold:

first, issues pursued by the community-wide association were not perceived (by the various subgroups) to be controversial, because broad
agreement between them is necessary. Such issues included efforts to
obtain improvements to the lighting in the area (though there were
disagreements over style – see above), refuse collection and waste disposal. They helped to attract a youth outreach (diversion) scheme into
the area (the youth population is relatively low, but disadvantaged).
And, they have advocated the development of policies relating to prostitution in which the welfare of prostitute women is a key consideration and in which residents' needs can be encompassed. The
community-wide association in Earleschurch was involved in a group
that pressed the council to commission a research project on prostitution to examine the issue of street-walking prostitution and to recom-
mend policy options. Following the reporting of its findings, it helped
to secure funding for a local conference on the issue. Second, many
groups have argued for the democratization of these bodies.

Some urban authorities may need community groups to provide
them with information so that policies and services are developed in
line with users' needs or in ways that avoid waste. This has been the
case where service-delivering organizations (such as local authority
housing departments and housing associations) have expanded, creating a gap between policy-makers and users that would need to be
bridged in some way (see Richardson 1979, 1983 regarding the council
sector). Furthermore, some of the new urban authorities lack the legitimacy of accountability through the ballot box, afforded to local
councils (despite some notable deficiencies), and so these organizations
also need a degree of consent to operate effectively. This may be
secured through the involvement of local communities. These features,
together with the requirement, in some instances, that community
consultation and/or involvement takes place opens up possibilities for
such groups to make their voices heard. Indeed, some groups used the
threat of exit from participation arrangements and the tactic of boycott
in the pursuit of desired goals.

The composition of groups in Earleschurch has changed as the population has changed; and they go through periods of activity and inac-
tivity. Sklair (1974), like other writers, has made the analytical
distinction between the more socially orientated tenants associations
and issue-based associations that arise over particular grievances and
which disintegrate after the campaign into either socially orientated
groups (see Lowe 1986) or virtual oblivion. Sklair noted that there may
be enough trace of an organization to draw upon as a resource in

future campaigns. Certainly in the Merseyside study areas, these groups are *pressure groups* rather than the more established voluntary-sector bodies who provide services in the manner found more frequently in the American literature on this topic. This is not to say that they do not provide some services, or that they do not wish to do so (see above). Organized self-help is widespread in some areas (Local Exchange and Trading Schemes have been established, Credit Unions and food and furniture co operatives are developing, for example), but as usual the problem comes back to resources. Indeed, these community-based services arise at least in part because of lack of mainstream provision. There are no banks in some of the areas covered by this study (and many people do not have accounts), while social security grants are no longer available for furniture – only loans. The important point is that because they are mainly pressure groups they are likely to be relatively ephemeral, especially if they are successful. Where they are unsuccessful in their campaigns, and some reasons for this have been given, it is not surprising that they demobilize.

In Edgebank there is a less-developed community group infrastructure. There are some groups, usually organized along tenurial lines. However, because the history of organization has been more recent, the political education that accompanies campaigning is less evident compared to Earleschurch. The most organized group here are owner-occupiers and tenants of the council estates dotted around the locality. Tenants in the housing association sector are poorer, more mobile and more often preoccupied with day-to-day survival.

In Edgebank, the organized owner-occupiers are mostly elderly, long-term residents who inhabited the area before its (most visible) decline from the mid-1970s. Some blame the new council estates nearby for the decline, but its origins clearly predate these developments. This group provides services (a luncheon club, for example), but they have also campaigned around local problems including some associated with crime and disorder. However, their main concern has been housing improvements. In this respect, their efforts have been frustrated – in part because improvement grants are means-tested, and often a 'value gap' remains. Discretionary grants are available but these depend upon the availability of funding that the local authority can commit for this purpose. It is felt that the local authority does not regard the area to be as much of a priority as some housing areas it controls. These groups believe that the council is not bothered about them; only concerned with council housing and tenants. Many seek exit strategies.

Factors limiting local action around crime and disorder

Individual responses to crime and disorder through the conventional channels are more evident in the Edgebank area. Here residents are more likely to report to the police, though there is also a local authority 'community patrol' that deals with problems of disorder (see Chapter 4). In part, because some of their difficulties could be resolved through these channels (albeit considerable problems remain), the most organized section of this community pursued only infrequent campaigns. Other reasons for this are found in the way other issues (housing, for example) take priority (see Skogan 1988b; Shapland 1988). Nevertheless, there have been a number of campaigns around disorder (notably public drinking, graffiti and litter) when it has been felt that their needs have not been met.

We should also remember that, in all cases, groups identified a number of benefits associated with living in their locality (see Chapter 3). For residents of Edgebank the proximity of their neighbourhood to the centre and its amenities was the most often cited benefit. In Earleschurch, architectural character and the cosmopolitan atmosphere, the mix of population and lifestyles, was valued by its residents, as I have shown. There were no discernible differences between groups regarding this matter. The significance of this is that, as Taub, Taylor and Dunham (1984) have noted, people make 'trade-offs' and weigh the risks and benefits when making decisions about whether or not to move out of disorderly and/or high-crime areas (see Chapter 3). For our present purposes we may note that they also seem to take these into consideration when considering their other option: 'voice' (Hirschman 1970 in Skogan 1988b: 52). It is also important to note that these are not once-and-for-all decisions. They take place in neighbourhood contexts that are changing, where circumstances for individuals within them are shifting, and against a backdrop where the institutions that may provide them with support (community development workers or funding, for example) are also in a state of flux. In some circumstances (such as immediately after environmental improvements were made to an under-used open space in Earleschurch) acquiescence can result from satisfaction – at least for a while. But in a neighbourhood such as Earleschurch, where regeneration has been characterized as a series of small, slow, precarious steps, the need to, almost constantly, defend the neighbourhood is present. Such demands bring with them considerable costs (see Rich 1980) and can be exhausting over a prolonged period. The issue of temporal specificity is therefore important in studies concerned with community responses to crime and disorder, as it is with community politics more generally. Even within narrow time periods social change takes place. And, as Bell and Newby remarked, studies of this nature can often suffer (as well as benefit) from using 'the tools of classical social anthropology' in that they sometimes lack historical perspective (1971: 63).

Other factors that facilitate or inhibit action are highlighted later. Here we may note some of the other conditions that inhibit the formulation of a 'social base' (see Lowe 1986) necessary for mobilization to take place. First, while there may be disapproving 'dominant' values, some residents feel that they benefit from some criminal activity – notably the availability of desired goods at low prices. This is not surprising considering the economic impoverishment of these neighbourhoods. Second, 'disorder' occupied an ambiguous place in the actions of some individuals and groups in one study area. In a couple of instances respondents reported that they highlighted the area's reputation and its disorderly state, drawing attention to litter and used needles, for example, in their arguments to keep rents low. The importance of this point should not be overstated, however, since the practice did not appear to be widespread. Much more commonly, on a collective level, community organizations challenged the reputation of the area, but they also said they were 'unconcerned' about it. And, they also used the reputation, and the presence of social and physical disorder that helps to sustain it, when they campaigned for more resources of one kind or another. In this sense, although disorder and crime may not be 'functional' in the Durkheimian sense (Skogan 1988b), when there are limited tools in an organization's armoury they can serve a purpose.

Local sensibilities, urban ideologies and other contingent factors

The discussion above indicates the importance of local sensibilities, the meanings people attach to their locality and to crime and disorder, when an analyst considers how and why collective action takes place. We can gain further insights from the work of urban sociologists, though their frameworks require some modification in the current context and considering the subject-matter. For example, drawing upon urban social movement theory,[7] Lowe argued that the following factors are significant for conditioning tenants' mobilization in Britain: the political structure and process of local political systems, the identification of social bases and their potential to generate urban movements, and the influence of key urban ideologies (Lowe 1986: 55). I have made some comments above regarding the conditions that hinder the development of 'social bases'. The following section examines other factors identified by Lowe as being consequential.

Lowe's analysis pointed towards the local authority's influence on the activities of local action groups as being fundamental because of its dominant position in determining and executing policy at the local level. The problem with this is that the local authority is *no longer* 'inevitably regarded as the major store of political power' in the current period (Lowe 1986: 60; see also Chapter 1 in this volume). Given this lack of inevitability it is not the case that the 'tactics and strategy of non-party movements are invariably directed towards establishing some form of negotiating position with the relevant service departments' (1986: 60). While this may be the case in the first instance for many groups (see above), others need to reach institutions who are less open to, or in some cases able to respond to, local lobbying: the police, housing associations and the myriad of regeneration initiatives, quangos and 'partnerships'. Moreover, the centralization of power over recent years has meant that decisions are often made away from the locality, in Whitehall. The problems associated with local pressure groups taking action to influence central government have been noted by many commentators (see Lowe 1986).

Lowe's discussion of 'urban ideologies' is useful for understanding the mobilization process around crime and disorder in Merseyside, though he is specifically concerned with tenants' actions (in Sheffield) and urban ideologies associated with local democratic processes. If we adapt his insights to the present discussion, we may suggest that many urban authorities were sending 'messages' to residents in the study areas which promoted their mobilization. The rhetoric of 'participation', 'involvement' at local level, and the notions of 'consumer sovereignty' employed at national level over recent years have been drawn upon by local people during their actions, even those sceptical about these authorities' commitments. The effect has been the creation of 'levers' that community groups can use to further their interests. The need for information and consent (see above) can add to their capacity to negotiate.

Sometimes highly vocal groups of a retrogressive (or progressive) nature are able to negotiate access to the local 'policy arena'. For a variety of reasons, on other occasions they may be unable to do so. Writers have noted that in these instances vigilante activities can occur (Shapland 1988). There were some examples encountered in interviews in this research (most referred to localities beyond these research sites), but it was also clear that such actions were not simply the product of authorities not responding to their demands. Rather, there were a number of different 'messages' that residents drew upon. In short, contemporary social authoritarian rhetoric (national and local) provided a context in which intolerant responses on behalf of some sections of the community were left unchallenged (see Chapter 4).

The ability of groups to mobilize and gain access to the policy arena may be assisted by the kinds of alliances that they can make (Lowe 1986). I have already indicated some of the sources of support for groups in this research. How groups envisaged the solution to their problems was important for decisions about who should be solicited for support. It is imperative, however, that alliances are not simply seen as being based on 'objective interests'; instead we need to be alive to the shifting alliances that are made in practice. Often alliances remain instrumental for a while only.

Leaders are of great importance to the ability to secure resources and are important to mobilization of groups and the success of their actions. While some movement analyses regard non-hierarchical structures as a feature of social movements, having a sufficiently plentiful supply of leaders and officers was clearly important to neighbourhood actions in this research. While this aspect deserves further research, a number of observations can be made. First, many community leaders were women. Second, many neighbourhood group leaders were involved in the activities of other kinds of organizations. This was the case in Edgebank and Earleschurch, though Earleschurch had more organizations and the networks had a greater degree of density as a consequence. Third, a few had experience of workplace-based activities (union activities) or formal party structures, which provided political education and experience. Against these factors, lack of experience, inadequate information exchanges between (and within) agencies and groups (and those who make them up), and lack of material resources (which may hinder information exchange) inhibit mobilization.

Figure 3 shows the conditions that require special consideration when thinking about grass-roots actions around crime and disorder in the Merseyside context. This adaptation of Podolefsky and Dubow's model shows a number of conditions underpinning those factors identified in their work. The pivotal importance of the historical experience of social and political organization to actions, particularly where economic exclusion is marked, is depicted there. This experience forms the backcloth to activities which interact with and influence the social and cultural con-

Figure 3: A model for thinking about variation, revisted

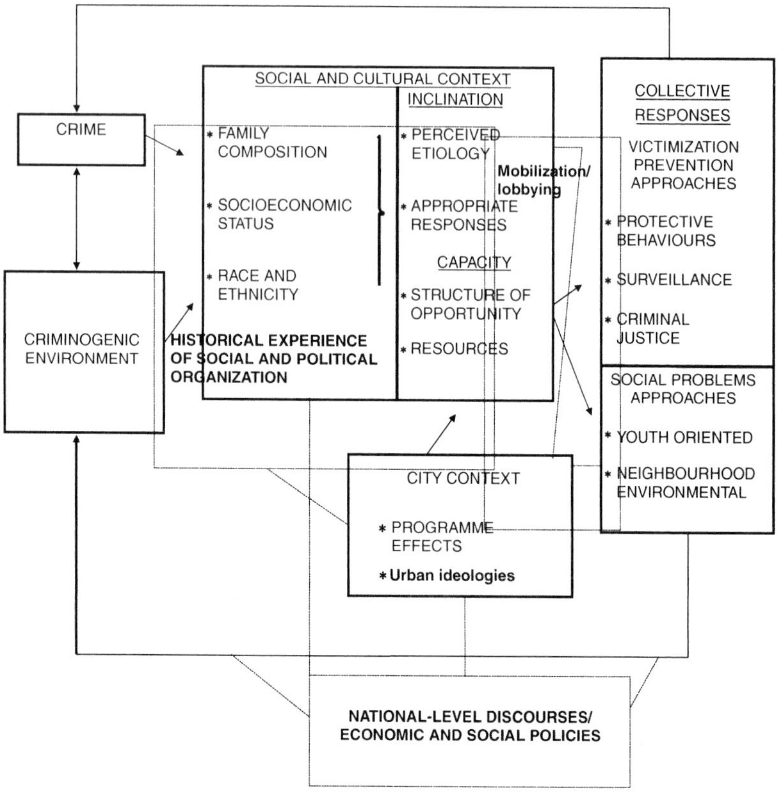

Source: Adapted from Podolefsky and Dubow 1981: 138.

texts of areas; and has been represented as such on the figure. It will also be observed that these experiences play a role in conditioning those factors associated with the inclination and capacity of groups to engage in collective action, included in Podolefsky and Dubow's model. The importance of pressure-group activity is also represented. These additions to the model constitute, interact and relate (sometimes antagonistically) with the city context. 'Urban ideologies', because of their importance, are included as part of the city context in the model. Furthermore, the influence of national-level discourses and economic and social policies have been added, for they condition the city context (including the criminogenic environment) and the socio-cultural context of neighbour-

hoods. Indeed, they have also been shown, above, to influence collective responses.

National-level housing policies during the 1980s and early 1990s, the 1988 Housing Act in particular, produced a context in which reconversion of properties, to family accommodation, and rehabilitation more generally, for example, were disfavoured. New-build became a key plank of housing association activity. In this environment the structure of opportunity to address what tenants groups in Earleschurch saw as the perceived cause of crime, instability, was for the most part blocked. As we have noted, a key housing association in the area, in response to tenants' concerns, made a security package available which largely consisted of physical victimization measures (anti-burglar bars, etc). Though welcomed, it did not address what many regarded as the underlying problem. In this way, and through this example, we can see how external influences modify the capacity of community groups to achieve their desired ends.

The confounding effect of crime prevention policies

The physical crime prevention measures were appreciated in part because of other local factors, notably the view that property crimes are committed by local people and non-residents of the neighbourhood, who, because of instability and transience, are difficult to identify. Nevertheless, this and other evidence from this research show how community activists modify their goals and revise their expectations to reflect what is felt to be achievable (their prior experience plays a role in this process). As Podolefsky and Dubow noted:

> Behaviors are also affected by the existence of institutionalized and legitimized city-wide anti-crime programs which serve to confound the effects of community composition and concerns. Moreover, by following particular approaches, generally victimization-prevention oriented, because the opportunity is made available through these programs, community groups undertake activities geared neither to the local social and cultural context nor to the particular local crime concerns. (1981: 230)

Podolefsky and Dubow (1981) suggest that anti-crime and disorder programmes *can* act as structures of opportunity for community groups when aligned with local definitions of problems and preferred strategies for dealing with them. However, they argue that the local community or *neighbourhood* and its social and cultural context are the important starting points for community safety policies (see also Walklate 1998). This research supports such a view. Moreover, crime reduction partnerships *could* impair the work of locally based collective activities in the event that they are co-opted into current 'partnership' arrangements.

Some writers have suggested that community involvement in policing has meant, in effect, residents are treated as 'clients' rather than partners (Bennett 1995: 76). Moreover, residents can feel intimidated or overwhelmed in meetings with police representatives, unless they have the confidence to exercise some control over meetings, as they had in Earleschurch. Local authority-led partnerships are also likely to be met without enthusiasm in some localities (see Chapter 5). Community organizations participating in police and local authority-led partnerships face several risks in this environment. They may lose support from their more sceptical members, for example. Loss of community support is likely to undermine their internal and external legitimacy (Bennett 1995). Other features of participation arrangements may have similar consequences. Internally, failure to allow sufficient time to consult members and/or the wider community can undermine organizations' legitimacy. Perspectives that are some distance away from officially sanctioned views and policies may come to be seen as unreasonable and extreme, and thus may promote their exclusion from that arena. Relatively short time-scales, the need for clearly defined measurable results, and cost effectiveness, not only militate against effective community involvement but also may result in partnerships 'underestimat[ing] the effects of community organizations' efforts at crime reduction' (Bennett 1995: 84). This is because community organizations are concerned as much with 'process' (community participation, leadership, political education) as 'product' (tangible outcomes), and indeed there may be some trade-off between these necessary goals (Bennett 1995). Each depends on a 'social learning process' (1995: 80) and, if partnership arrangements are to be successful, *all* those involved would need to undergo such a process. Strict time constraints would undermine these processes, even if the political will on behalf of lead agencies was present. Finally, failure to achieve tangible benefits for their members may undermine future actions and involvement. Partnership authorities need to be alive to the political dimensions of communities, as well as the variety of ways in which they aim to achieve safe communities, if they are to be successful (Bennett 1995).

Summary

This chapter, by focusing upon neighbourhoods that are often regarded as the most difficult areas in which to mobilize collective action, has shown that even here community groups can, and do, take action around neighbourhood crime and disorder problems. Key influences on mobilization and conditions which obstruct collective action have been discussed. Importantly, the data drawn upon in this chapter have testified to the importance of understanding the sensibilities that exist in communities, and the conditions that underpin these. The task of discovering them brings with it a number of methodological considerations that are important for academic criminologists and policy-makers. The final chapter examines the theoretical and policy implications arising from the issues discussed in this and preceding chapters.

7
Conclusions and Reflections

It is perhaps a truism to say that social rented housing has failed to be embodied as a principal element of the welfare state; commodified housing forms are the norm under advanced capitalism. We can acknowledge that during 'abnormal' times decommodified, large-scale, mass models of social housing forms can emerge, because they hold significance for the dominant social and economic order (Harloe 1995), and do so without suggesting a crude determinism. Indeed, we should distinguish the role of reformers and the organized working class (and other interest groups). But we must, in so doing, appreciate the changing social, economic and political environments in nation-states that mould relationships between subordinate and dominant interests, which give rise to particular housing forms in general, and mass social housing in particular, in advanced capitalist societies. Moreover, we must understand that these struggles take place in a context where earlier developments have left ideological and concrete legacies (Harloe 1995). In this way, functionalist relationships between the needs of capital (accumulation and legitimacy) and social policy are not assumed, neither is social welfare seen simply as a product of working-class struggle, or benevolent states responding to reformist elites (Harloe 1995).

In recognizing these processes we can note the striking similarities found in analyses of the processes that have given rise to mass social housing, and its residualization, in many advanced capitalist countries, although transitions are temporally variable (Harloe 1995). Against this, we can note the significant differences between European nations, and the resistance to residualization of the social housing stock in Denmark and Holland, for example, can be encompassed. In the UK, the direct impact of war, and the indirect impact of wartime conditions, for example, are a notable divergence from the USA context, and are significant for understanding the rise of social housing on a mass scale in the UK and elsewhere. But even so, what is important about 'abnormal conditions' such as war (Harloe 1995) is that they disrupted the established social and political order in particular regions, and the broad tenets of this explanation for the rise of particular housing forms remains relevant. For our present purposes, it is important that studies of urban change and crime consider the processes that give rise to particular housing forms and the changing balance of tenure that results. For, in large part, these processes shape urban population settlements and 'community configuration' (Reiss 1986: 19), which, in turn, fashion community crime careers.

In the UK the pressure towards private consumption of housing, and public- and private-sector partnerships in housing (in housing association financial arrangements, for example) and urban regeneration need to be seen in this way: the role of private interests is standard. And the ways in which neighbourhoods are configured and reconfigured, socially, spatially and politically in this context need to be understood in our analyses of crime, though urban criminologists in the UK have tended to concern themselves with social housing provision.

National comparisons necessarily suppress regional and local differences (Hancock 1996a). Nevertheless, similar observations can be made: local housing forms are the product of conflicts between interests of both a party and non-party nature, and struggles between central and local government, which take place in particular social, economic and political environments. They leave their legacies in the physical landscape and the social histories of localities. In turn, subsequent positions of dominance and subordination (Massey 1995) shape further rounds of struggle and intervention.

This book was essentially concerned with local-level struggles between competing interests, mapped against wider regional- and national-level processes. The neighbourhoods in which the empirical work was conducted may at first appear anomalous, though close examination will show that they reflect many of the current pressures that are a feature of inner-city neighbourhoods in the UK: a housing stock where the private market has been elevated; public, private and voluntary sector partnership, in social housing and urban regeneration, for example, is promoted; and central government control over local housing provision and regeneration strategies has been a key feature. The aim of the research was to contribute to debates regarding the 'community crime career' idea in this setting. It sought to contribute to a research agenda that others have pointed toward (Bottoms and Wiles 1992; 1995) in which analyses of crime are linked to those urban change and urban policies. The processes involved in neighbourhood change (decline and regeneration) and the 'place' of crime and disorder in these processes were of particular interest.

During the empirical research it soon became clear that the idea of 'neighbourhood change' was complicated in the mixed-tenure settings chosen in this study. Simple notions of decline and regeneration, or 'gentrification', were challenged, for they failed to acknowledge the complexity of change uncovered in the study areas. Though regeneration initiatives had been present in, or near to, the neighbourhoods for a number of years, they were undermined by the contradictory aims of other urban or social policies or by wider economic conditions that remained unresolved. As a consequence, the main neighbourhoods studied in this research displayed evidence of both decline *and* regeneration, increases *and* decreases in the economic activity of their residents, improvement *and* deterioration in the physical appearance and desirability of property. The combination of housing and urban economic regeneration initiatives pursued in recent years, in the context of wider disadvantage in the city-region, resulted in further social exclusion and alienation for some and the betterment of others in the study areas, particularly in Earleschuch. There are a number of reasons why they took the form that they did in that neighbourhood. Unemployment and disaffection are deeper and more entrenched there, its surrounding area is poorer, despite its experience of regeneration. Without a substantial increase in pressure on the housing market, which would have required a tangible improvement in the local labour market, which has been elusive in the inner areas, gentrification was inevitably uneven and restricted to those who could take advantage of the limited opportunities on offer. The availability of unconverted houses in specific streets was important for understanding the uneven nature of gentrification in specific parts of the neighbourhood, for example, and is an illustration of the importance of the 'physical' or concrete legacies that shape contemporary developments. These properties presented more opportunities for private-sector interests (developers, owner-occupiers and housing associations drawing in part on private finance) to exploit the appeal of the neighbourhood for professional groups of incomers in a way that minimized some economic risk.

The large number of converted flats in the social and private rented sector, similarly, was significant for understanding the difficulties associated with regenerating other parts of Earleschurch. Housing associations were limited in their ability to respond to concerns about the older, deteriorating stock. Changes in housing association finance ushered in by the Conservative government, in the period from 1988, disfavoured the rehabilitated stock and thus constrained their efforts. At the lower end of the privately rented sector few landlords were willing to make significant investments in their properties. Yet, this sector was promoted by central government during the same period. Furthermore, those occupying these sectors increasingly lacked the wealth or political power to improve their properties.

Contemporary housing forms are a reflection of earlier processes of decline and differential investment in housing by the local authority, private-sector interests and housing associations. And, indeed, these forms were influenced by patterns of earlier modes of housing consumption: very large Victorian family houses, of high status, which were ideal for conversion for flats. What is significant is that earlier investment patterns influenced differential housing regeneration. Moreover, the mixed neighbourhoods that emerged, and are reconfiguring, pose special problems for crime prevention policy interventions. I examine these issues below. First it is necessary to summarize the key processes involved in the long-term decline of the main study areas.

Broadly speaking, in both localities, affluent middle-class occupiers began to leave, first in Earleschurch and later in Edgebank. Their properties were taken over, in large part, by private landlords, local authorities and housing associations in Earleschurch. Social housing (mainly housing association controlled in Earleschurch and local authority controlled in Edgebank) were built on slum-cleared spaces in the late 1960s and early 1970s. But perhaps most importantly, in both the social and private rented sector, existing houses were converted to either small flats to rent or for multiple occupation. Because its economy remained relatively bouyant for a while, Edgebank did not witness dramatic decline as early as Earleschurch, in part because it remained attractive for the incoming, upwardly mobile, respectable working-class or petty bourgeoisie, who, though being of lower status than the neighbourhood's original occupants, regarded it as being attractive and could afford to live there in a period of post-war expansion. Though many initially rented their dwellings they remained in single-family occupation. What is clear, however, is that the war exacerbated the process of decline. In Earleschurch, for example, rapid change took place as the population increased (because of pressure on the housing market that resulted from war damage and pent up demand as a consequence of curtailed building programmes) and movement outwards from it as people sought to flee the poor conditions. As the new public and private suburbs were developed in the post-war period the trajectory of decline continued in both areas.

Over more recent years there have been a myriad of central and partnership funded regeneration projects and a (reduced) amount of Housing Corporation funding spent in the study areas. Some property has improved and quantitatively at least there has been *some* improvement in employment prospects. However, there is a perception that the benefits are not being distributed equally, and Earleschurch especially is regarded locally as becoming more divided: socially, spatially and politically.

The building and refurbishment of property undertaken by some housing associations and other private interests around the town centre and its environs, including Earleschurch, has attracted young professionals and students into the central wards, which has influenced the social life of these neigbourhoods. Their local networks are differently organized. And, as some local respondents have noted, the incoming groups do not resolve problems of transience; they remain socially and geographically mobile. Their arrival, or consolidation in these areas, is also ushering in transformations in their localities of departure. The areas traditionally housing these groups to the the south and east of the neighbourhood, because they afforded cheap privately rented accommodation within easy reach of the town centre, have witnessed further decline in the late 1990s, both directly and indirectly. These localities, which are also characterized by a mix of tenures, are likely to present further problems for policy-makers. Streets are increasingly showing signs of further decay because of weak pressure on the market, indicated by boarded up houses and physical disorder. As a result, the desirability of these localities are likely to fall further and their property crime rates are likely to continue to represent the highest rates in the borough.

The 'place' of crime and disorder

Housing and planning policies (or their failure) and practices clearly played a role in the development of physical disorder in the study areas. The subdivision of property in Earleschurch took little account of the waste-disposal needs of the converted properties, resulting in waste being left on the streets, for example. Similarly the external appearance of properties deteriorated as a consequence of the change from single-family owner-occupation to furnished private rented dwellings, often in multiple occupation, in Edgebank. In this way, 'physical disorder' followed neighbourhood decline.

The longer-term residents in Edgebank, mainly older owner-occupiers, perceived a higher level of physical disorder (litter, poorly maintained houses, graffiti, and so on) and attributed this, and the growing problem of social disorder (young people hanging around – especially outside the pubs at the weekend – and people drinking on the streets) and crime to the change in the nature of the population. However, it is clear that the underlying causes of decline are linked to changes in the housing and labour market and the wider economic fortunes of the region.

This research has suggested that it is difficult to separate the impact of disorder from other conditions when we examine people's fear of crime. Similarly, 'disorder' did not appear to impact upon people's willingness to engage in collective anti-crime and disorder, or other activities in the study areas. Thus, this research gave some support to the view that 'middle ranging' levels of concern may not be destructive toward community group activities (Hope and Hough 1988 in Skogan 1990). Indeed, other local factors mediated their concern and promoted or undermined residents' action around crime and disorder in the study areas. Furthermore, they did so despite the areas being characterized by a fair degree of transience with consequent implications for social cohesion.

Changes in the use of housing had important implications for population turnover and residents' sense of social cohesion. The situation in Earleschurch was particularly acute. People wanted to remain in the area, but were often unable to do so because of unsuit-able family housing. The picture is not one of an inevitable downward spiral of decline, however. Many people cited a number of benefits associated with living in the two main study areas: the proximity to the town centres; cosmopolitanism (in Earleschurch especially); the amenities on offer to residents. In part because these neighbourhoods offered use-values to their residents, neighbourhood groups in Earleschurch and Edgebank lobbied to improve the quality of life in their neighbourhoods. They have been concerned to improve housing conditions, engender 'community spirit' and address both physical and social disorder. In most cases community groups exhibited a sophisticated understanding of the causes of local problems and those involved, and had preferred stragegies for managing them (see Chapter 6). Many community groups lacked the resources needed to bring their ideas to fruition, however.

Explaining disorder and victimization in the study areas: brief summary

This research supported the idea that certain kinds of areas, particularly city centres, need to be approached differently to those of, say, residential housing estates. Crime did not appear to be self-contained (people living in the areas and beyond them were responsible for the commission of crime in those localities), as in many studies of this sort (see Bottoms and Wiles 1986, for example). Since both key study areas were located near to town centres, we would expect each to have some of the 'offence-attracting' features of city centres (Bottoms and Wiles 1986). And, indeed, the proximity of the neighbourhoods to their town centres was argued to be important for understanding certain types of crime patterns in these areas (see Chapter 3).

The physical design of housing, and the prevalence of converted flats in particular, provided a number of opportunities for potential offenders. For many properties, the conversions took place many years ago, prior to the 1974 Housing Act, and their physical barriers to intruders (door frames, etc.) are rather poor. The conversion of property into a very large number of small flats in Earleschurch, and the prevalence of conversions, HMOs and private renting in certain sections of Edgebank, has promoted a high degree of internal and external migration. In this context, strangers and potential offenders are less likely to be identified, even in the communal areas of converted property, and bystanders are less likely to intervene in disorderly or criminal behaviour on the street.[1] Still, the organizational structure of these localities was not simply 'organized' or 'disorganized'; it was both. These localities, Earleschurch especially, exhibited a high level of population turnover *and* a stable community of residents some of whom were highly 'organized' – formally and informally. In this way, this research contributes to recent debates around the social disorganization, 'collective efficacy' model and supports analyses in which these complexities have been acknowledged (see Bottoms and Wiles 1997). Attempts to locate neighbourhoods in their wider urban political structure were supported in similar fashion (see Chapter 3). But the evidence in this volume suggests that we need to recognise the relationships that result as ones of negotiation, conflict and accommodation against their wider social, economic, political and ideological contexts, locally and nationally; for relations with external agencies may be important for the ability of neighbourhood groups to obtain funding for welfare-oriented projects and other provisions within communities. These may help to enhance neighbourhood use values (Taylor 1996), contribute to resident satisfaction and also provide a source, or sources, of 'social capital' (Portes 1998).[2] And relationships between communities and formal policing agencies beyond community boundaries, for example, may be important for crime control. However, it is necessary to examine the extent to which institutions that may direct resources into communities are considered legitimate or not (Bottoms and Wiles 1997). This research, therefore, exmined how external agencies, such as the police, local authorities and other agencies, are perceived by local people; and the extent to which external 'solutions' are regarded as appropriate at the local level.

Tackling neighbourhood decline, crime and disorder

This research was concerned in large part with how community groups perceive and/or respond to changes in their local enviornment, and some research attention was therefore focused upon the ways in which they responded to regeneration initiatives, including those associated with community safety. The empirical work revealed that the arrangements afforded some limited opportunities for community groups to address some of their concerns (the 'Safe and Warm' project and the community development worker, for example, in Edgebank). However, many commentators were concerned about the longevity of provisions. Furthermore, in general, residents' groups were, at best, supportive but sceptical and, at worst, cynical about the use of short-term funding to address deeply entrenched, long-term problems. Past experience had left groups with little faith in these bodies, not only to address crime and disorder but to make even marginal improvements in the economic well-being of local people. In some cases this reflected a dissatisfaction with the structures for their involvement and/or they regarded other, non-local people as being the main beneficiaries. Respondents indicated that there was little evidence that regeneration bodies were responsive to local community groups. Perhaps most worringly for community safety policies, all community groups were critical of the role of the local authority in their area. Indeed, most related crime and disorder to issues associated with housing, and none of the regeneration initiatives in the mixed-tenure study areas had a remit to address these concerns specifically.

Changes in the financial arrangements for housing associations over recent years meant that many rehabilitated properties had deteriorated. Furthermore, transience, increased management costs and the aging nature of property had further implications for maintenance costs. Should the housing stock in this sector become more undesirable there are clear implications for crime and disorder being concentrated in such areas.

In Earleschurch there have been some improvements over recent years. An improved security package was made available to tenants of one large housing association. The association managed to attract some funding to convert properties to family housing and to improve the general stock. Arrears declined and the 'turnaround' time between tenants vacating properties to the property being relet reduced. Tenants began to request Earleschurch as their first-choice area, for the first time, and anecdotal evidence suggested that the population was beginning to stabilize. This association was willing to use some of its reserves to fund improvements. There were other examples of good practice, though in areas located outside of the key study areas. However, some associations were not able, or keen, to commit the kind of funding needed to address the housing-based causes of instability, crime and disorder in the study areas, and elsewhere. Financial arrangements favoured new-build and new tenure types (shared owner-ship, for example). In this context, where residents were witnessing degeneration in *their* local housing stock and cuts were made to main-tainance budgets, for example, it was not surprising to find that some residents thought that some aspects of housing association activity was furthering a process of gentrification – in which they felt marginalized. At the lower end of the privately rented sector in both areas, few land-lords were willing (or able) to make significant investments in their properties, and many of the older owner-occupiers were clearly unable to do so. Thus, in the mixed housing areas, without substantial capital investment in the social and private stock the property is likely to dete-riorate further, with consequent implications for the social fabric of these areas.

Residents turned to other agencies to resolve some of their prob-lems. People remained reluctant to report incidents to the police, for a number of reasons, particularly in Earleschurch. In part these responses arose because some respondents felt there was little point reporting crimes or other problems to the police (see Chapter 5).

However, what was also clear was that residents were concerned about, and in some cases questioned the legitimacy of, particular policing styles: the Operational Support Division's interventions in economically marginal neighbourhoods was notable in this regard. However, it is not that the legitimacy of the police as a whole that was at issue. Rather, residents clearly distinguished between community policing styles and public-order tactics including the use of specialist squads (see also Gifford et al. 1987). Indeed, some distinguished between different community beat officers. Residents in the study areas felt that more foot-patrols would increase confidence in the police and the locality. But, perhaps more importantly, residents wanted Community Beat Officers (CBOs) that are sensitive and respond, fairly, to the needs of their communities.

Furthermore, there were clear divisions between people who reported getting a decent service from the police and those who did not in Earleschurch in particular. Those who reported receiving a poor service tend to be the more marginalized groups, black people and young poor people, for example. This was recognized even by those, in the same area, who said they recieved a satisfactory or good level of service. Residents in both areas were also generally positive about alternative ways of responding to incivility. Respondents said that they wanted help in dealing with neighbourhood problems.

Chapter 6 focused upon collective action around crime and disorder. It showed that community groups can, and do, take action around neighbourhood crime and disorder problems, even in impoverished communities and those that are rather transient. Key influences on mobilization and conditions which obstruct collective action were also discussed in Chapter 6. It argued that the historical experience of organizing was important to understanding community mobilization, and that one of the motivating factors behind residents' action was the failure of those agencies deemed officially responsible for resolving neighbourhood difficulties. It argued that an urban social movement analysis was perhaps the most important framework for understanding these phenomena. It testified to the importance of understanding the sensibilities that exist in communities and, perhaps more importantly, the conditions that underpin these.

Nevertheless, it was difficult to assess the impact of residents' actions (though some activists reported important benefits flowing from their action), or indeed the responses of other statutory and partnership activities. The police beats, which cross-cut Earleschurch, were reorganized in 1994, and the police stations responsible for policing Earleshurch changed. Different stations may have had divergent reporting cultures. This was an important limitation for the current study. To overcome some of these problems, data were supplemented with information gleaned from a variety of sources discussed in more detail in Chapter 2. By using these methods, though not ideal, strong impressions regarding the scale and nature of crime and disorder and about changes over time could be obtained. The strong argument that emerged from the analysis of the variety of data during the fieldwork was that crime and victimization's spatial pattern was being redrawn in Earleschurch in particular. Despite the 'hidden figure' (see Chapter 5), crime was found to be concentrated in those areas where residents had lost out in the housing market, the labour market and, now, in the quest for security. Less strong was some evidence of crime and disorder rates operating in a cyclical fashion, since this may be accounted for by these changes. Clearly there was a range of processes operating in each neighbourhood that *may* have impacted upon their crime and disorder rates – regeneration, housing improvement in small pockets, degeneration, the activities of the police and indeed the (cyclical) actions of residents themselves, but the data were insufficient to say which factors impacted upon crime and disorder rates for sure. Nevertheless, this did not stop a number of agencies and actors claiming that *their* actions were responsible for short-term falls in recorded crime!

Indeed, this research suggested that not only do community crime careers undergo movement from low-crime to high-crime status; in Schuerman and Kobrin's (1986) terms, three stages can be identified: emerging, transitional and enduring, but some encounter aspects of each of these stages. In any case we need to recognize the interactions between macro (including ideologies, power and resources), meso (for instance, the allocation and management of resources) and micro level social processes; patterns of local, social behaviour and responses, for example (Herbert 1982; Bottoms and Wiles 1997). Moreover, the ways in which actors and institutions operating at each level mediate the processes that occur between them, in different urban spaces and times, is clearly imporant for understanding 'community crime careers'.

In the mixed-tenure environments that formed the focus of this study there were a variety of macro level processes that impacted upon different tenures and resident groups; similarly at the meso level, there were a variety of allocation processes and different approaches to the management of urban resources. This is the nature of the mixed-tenure enviornments that are becoming a feature of life in inner areas in urban Britain. The policy interventions and community responses that resulted highlighted the importance of recognizing these processes as ones played out in a local 'policy arena' (see Chapter 4).

At the time of writing it is too early to say what the intermediate and long-term implications of the Crime and Disorder Act (1998) will be. But this research suggests that responses to crime and disorder in high-crime communities need to avoid the inexorable pressure for bureau-cratized, technical and managerial responses to local problems. Moreover, they should not be concentrated solely in local authority controlled 'estates'. The 'responsible authorities' have a duty to develop community safety strategies in their *area*, not limited to local authority stock. It is important that housing associations, and other less powerful agencies, are enabled to develop community stability and anti-exclusionary policies, including community safety and crime reduction activities. It is important also that the constraints presently placed on such activities are addressed.

There are a number of issues that need to be grappled with regard-ing the development of community safety plans in areas of mixed-tenure. Developing housing management models that are sensitive to community safety issues will be difficult to achieve when there are several non-local authority landlords operating in the neighbour-hood. In addition, it is difficult to envisage how the housing-based factors strongly associated with crime and disorder will be addressed without substantial capital investment in some areas. This research suggests, furthermore, that a simple focus on crime or disorder reduc-tion or indeed housing may be inadequate; rather it is important to address the unequal nature of victimization and the compounding effects of social exclusion in which crime contributes to and impacts upon other disadvantages. And, finally, this research supports calls for independent sources of support for community action, not simply over the short term. Residents groups, particularly in areas of high population turnover or that are otherwise distressed, need ongoing support.

There have been some interesting policy proposals over recent months, which (potentially at least) may help to ameliorate the prob-lems of poor or declining mixed-tenure neighbourhoods, including some the issues mentioned above. The Social Exclusion Unit has recently issued *The National Strategy for Neighbourhood Renewal* con-sultation document (2000), which proposes some interesting new developments. The Policy Action Teams' reports that have under-pinned the strategy (see *Joining It Up Locally* and *Unpopular Housing*, for example) have helped to put the issue of the mixed-tenure declining areas on the political agenda. Furthermore, the Local Government Bill (1999) placed a duty on councils to develop 'community strategies'. And the Housing Green Paper *Quality and Choice: a Decent Home for All* (DETR April 2000: 10) has prioritized the importance of 'authorities taking a strategic view of needs across all housing, public and private sector,' 'encouraging authorities to work in partnership with local communities, registered social landlords and other organizations' and 'ensuring that authorities link housing policies with planning policies and those of the wider social, economic and environmental well-being of the community'.

Of course developing inter-agency partnerships to address these problems is not new, as *Joining It Up Locally* acknowledges, along with the reasons for their failure. Notably that:

- communities were not adequately involved or empowered;
- initial joint strategies were not translated into sustained joined up-working;
- too much attention was driven by central funding rather than local needs; and
- central government policies and practices made local joint working difficult. (Report of the Policy Action Team, 17 April 2000: 10)

For the sake of these neigbourhoods, it is hoped that these problems are not repeated. And it will be the task of future research to evaluate the impact of these developments.

A number of other issues that require further research have been indicated in previous chapters. What is clear, however, is that there is a need to reinvigorate the study of communities in a variety of settings, which, while a popular focus of study during the 1950s and 1960s (see Bell and Newby 1971), has tended not to be seen as having the same degree of importance, for its own sake, in the modern period. Ethnographies that explore how people make sense of living in urban communities would add much to our understanding of urban change and crime. The Chicago School's studies were notable in this respect, together with the longitudinal studies that they played such an important part in developing. Unfortunately, in the UK, longitudinal studies of communities and crime have been rare, in part because of the funding arrangements relating to academic studies. Bottoms and his colleagues recognized the value of these approaches in Sheffield, but these tools of exploration have been underemployed elsewhere. Finally, as Bottoms and Wiles (1995: 1.38) suggested, we need to examine the 'consequences of late modernity for crime in our own city', exchange ideas, and formulate comparative research questions.

Notes

Chapter 1: Introduction: Urban Change and Crime

1. Department of the Environment, Transport and the Regions (14 July 1998), 'Prescot welcomes more money for priority areas' (Press Release); www.coi.gov.uk/coi/depts/GTE/coi3923e.ok p1–3
2. Department of the Environment, Transport and the Regions (May 1998), *Housing: Key Facts*; www.housing.detr.gov.uk/information/keyfacts/index.htm
3. Ibid.
4. Ibid.
5. Department of the Environment, Transport and the Regions 'Enfield tenants vote on housing transfer', 14 July 1998 (Press Release).
6. Department of the Environment, Transport and the Regions (May 1998), *Housing: Key Figures*; www.housing.detr.gov.uk/information/keyfigures/index.htm
7. Joseph Rowntree Foundation Housing Research Findings Paper 143, April 1995.
8. Home Office, '£250 million to develop an effective crime reduction strategy of the future' Press Release, 21 July 1998; www.coi.gov.uk/coi/depts/GHO/coi4182e.ok
9. *The Guardian* leader; 'Crime need not pay' 22 July 1998.
10. There is some evidence to suggest that many health trusts and education authorities were failing to take part in partnerships. See A. Travis, 'Crime up 20% under new system' *The Guardian*, 25 Aug. 1999 (page 2).
11. See also D. W. Osgood, 'Interdisciplinary integration: building criminology by stealing from our friends', *The Criminologist* 23:4 (1998): 1–4 & 41.
12. City of Liverpool, *Key Statistics, 1991 Census, Liverpool Wards 1971/81/91* (Liverpool: City of Liverpool, no date).
13. Merseyside Economic Assessment (1996); www.merseyworld.com.m.tec/mea/sect7.html
14. Liverpool City Council, Central Policy Unit, *Liverpool 1996: Social, Economic and Environmental Context* (Liverpool: Liverpool City Council, 1996); see also www.ds.dial.pipex.com/liv.cpu/cspr/needs.htm
15. Safer Merseyside Partnership, *New Solutions, Further Actions*, Challenge Fund Submission (Merseyside: Safer Merseyside Partnership, 1996).
16. Merseyside contains one of the largest proportions of cooperatively based housing in Britain.
17. Liverpool City Council, Central Planning Unit, *Liverpool 1996*.
18. Ibid., p. 5
19. Liverpool City Council Housing Department Figures (1991).
20. Housing Strategy for Wirral 1997–8, p. 13.
21. Ibid.

Chapter 2: Researching Neighbourhood Change, Crime and Disorder

1. A short discussion of the background to these research aims can be found in Hancock (2000).
2. In the context of urban policy-making and service delivery, excepting community safety and crime prevention, in which the local authority has diminished in its importance, other bodies, some of whom are funded by central government, together with voluntary and private sector interests, have seen their role augmented over recent years. Ostensibly, problem-solving is organized, and urban services are coordinated, through 'partnerships' and 'multi-agency' initiatives in this environment.
3. I follow Bell and Newby's view 'that "participant observation" is not a single technique but is rather variable depending on the social situation' (1971: 65), and concur with Burgess's argument that there is no simple dichotomy between observer and participant (Burgess 1984).
4. Following a burglary, for example, residents are likely to report to housing authorities in order to secure prompt repairs. In this research, residents were found to be more likely to report to landlords than to the police, though landlords in the social rented sector were encouraging tenants to report to the police and, in some cases, requiring residents to quote crime numbers before repairs were carried out.
5. P. Xanthos, *Crime, the Housing market and Reputation* (unpublished Ph.D. thesis, University of Sheffield 1981).
6. More so in Edgebank than in Earleschurch.
7. Validity is used in the technical sense as the relation between an indicator and a concept; it is associated with the 'accuracy of the report' (Zelditch 1970: 250) and is bound up with the idea of being sure that one is measuring what one thinks one is measuring.
8. There is also an emotional dimension in that I grew to know and like many of my respondents over the year-long fieldwork period.
9. A practice employed by many writers who have been concerned with similar research questions (Foster and Hope 1993; Bottoms et al. 1989; 1992; Xanthos 1981, for example).

Chapter 3: Crime and the Urban Area: Explaining Neighbourhood Change and Crime

1. Barke and Turnbull illustrate this by noting that even in 1985 85.7 per cent of tenants had no car and that by May 1990 no tenant had applied to buy their house/flat under the 1980 right-to-buy policy.
2. By the mid-1980s male unemployment was estimated to be 80 per cent in some parts of the estate (Archbishop of Canterbury's Commission 1985, cited in Barke and Turnbull 1992: 65).
3. S. Dow, 'Move on UP' *Roof* 17, no. 6 (1992): 18–19.

4. Ibid.
5. R. Sampson, paper presented to the Scottish Criminology Conference 'Community, Solidarity and Crime' held at the University of Edinburgh, 4–5 Sept. 1998.
6. Ibid.
7. A. Bottoms, paper presented to the Scottish Criminology Conference, University of Edinburgh, 4–5 Sept. 1998.
8. See Bassett and Short (1980) for a concise, if somewhat dated, discussion of how the processes of production, consumption and exchange in US housing markets differ to those in the UK.
9. At the small-area, enumeration-district level there are some extremely small gaps or disparities in the data. These are evident only when values are calculated for the neighbourhoods as a whole. Nevertheless, these data remain the most accurate available and for present purposes remain adequate.
10. The survey consisted of 100 postal questionnaires sent out to the oldest converted properties owned by one of the housing associations in the locality, i.e. those converted before the 1974 Housing Act. The survey was conducted for the tenants' association. In the sample 92.5 per cent were flats, the remainder being bedsits or maisonettes. The questionnaires were sent to all the oldest properties owned by the association but since this represents only 25 per cent of the stock owned by the housing association it cannot be seen as being representative. Similarly, since the response rate was 40 per cent there were a number of limitations on the generalizations to be made. Nevertheless the survey did reveal some interesting results which could be confirmed by other data.
11. These data are unable to illustrate the way that many residents distinguish between 'hard' and 'soft' drugs, yet this was evident in more recent work carried out by this author.
12. Personal communication, Rosie Campbell (Liverpool Hope University).
13. Juveniles aged 10–15 made up only 2.7 per cent of the population and youths aged 16–19 accounted for 3.1 per cent of the population, both considerably lower than the Merseyside average. Young adults aged between 20 and 30 years constituted 38 per cent of the population, which was above Meresyside's average (1991 Census).
14. This respondent's house is a three-storey terraced house containing approximately 9 rooms. In this street the houses are about 100–120 years old. The basement is used as the living area – this is where the interview took place. There is a gap between the window and the pavement, just above eye level. The respondent was pointing to this gap as she made this remark.
15. For example, no burglaries in Earleschurch appeared to be carried out by offenders living in the area for the period 1994–5. This may be because none occurred or simply because the data were inadequate, i.e. the offenders did not commit burglaries in the same time period, or maybe it was the case that there are problems linking offenders with offences (personal communication, URPERRL 8.7.96).
16. The long-established nature of the housing association movement is a distinctive feature of Merseyside's housing stock.

17. 27.5 per cent of respondents in the survey in 1992 referred to earlier, had been resident for less than a year; 35 per cent had been resident for 1–5 years; 15 per cent resident for 6–10 years; and 22.5 per cent had been resident for over 11 years.
18. The respondent is a private renter in a house in multiple occupation in Earleschurch.

Chapter 4: Regeneration, Community Safety and Local Governance

1. Launched by the Home Office in 1988, though later brought under the auspices of the Single Regeneration Budget (see Chapter 1 in this volume; Hughes 1998; Gilling 1997).
2. 'Quango': Quasi-autonomous national government agency. 'Quangocracy': a term used by Cohen et al. in 'What happened to democracy?', *The Independent On Sunday*, 28.3.93, p. 19, to refer to the proliferation of these bodies in contemporary governance. 'Qualgo': quasi-autonomous local government agency.
3. Department of the Environment, Transport and the Regions (1998), *Modern Local Government: In Touch With The People*; www.local-regions.detr.gov.uk/lgwp
4. Set up in the period from 1995, the 'Partnerships' referred to here involve the voluntary and public sectors; Training and Enterprise Councils, educational establishments, police authority and businesses. They draw upon European Objective One funding and, in some areas, Single Regeneration Budget moneys. In the Partnership areas unemployment is more than 31 per cent, 55 per cent of families have no earner, and 72 per cent of households have no car. More than 247,000 people in the local authority live in such areas. The aim of partnerships is to provide training and skills, environmental and housing improvements, and to attract new businesses.
5. F. Field (MP), 'How we can tame the new barbarians', *Daily Mail*, 3 Dec. 1996, p. 8.
6. A. Travis, 'Crime up 20% under new system', *The Guardian*, 25 Aug. 1999, (p. 2).
7. Ibid.

Chapter 5: Interventions in the Mixed Housing Areas

1. Merseyside Economic Assessment (1996); www.merseyworld.com.m.tec/mea/sect7.html
2. Government Office of the North West; www.gonw.freeserve.co.uk/synop.h.page 1
3. For the purposes of anonymity this name has been changed.
4. It is important to note that the depth of the economic problems in some communities in Merseyside has important methodological implications. Respondents, when asked 'what would you like to see to improve your

neighbourhood?' or 'Tell me about the problems in your area?', often do not include employment issues. This is not because employment (or lack of it) is not an important issue; this is seen in other aspects of their responses. Rather, people's expectations regarding improvement in employment prospects have systematically revised downward to the extent that for many the issue is beyond their frame of reference.

5. Draft Anti-Poverty Strategy and Action Plan 1996/7, Liverpool City Council (1996).
6. Domestic customers register their most frequently used numbers with British Telecommunications plc. and qualify for a discount on these calls.

Chapter 6: Community Responses to Crime, Decline and disorder

1. This residents group is also referred to in Chapter 2, as an illustration of how little some of the local agencies knew about the communities in their vicinity.
2. Many local authority residents associations have secured the right to be involved in lettings decisions. However, a significant number in this research said that 'problematic' tenants were made offers without the associations' knowledge – often when committee members were otherwise engaged or during periods when residents find it difficult to meet (Christmas and other holiday periods). There are a number of issues that could be discussed regarding this matter, but here we may note that one implication may be that the residents committee (and the council) increasingly lack credibility with the local tenancy, which may have ramifications for other (including community safety) activities.
3. Personal communication, Rosie Campbell, Liverpool Hope University.
4. No interviewees said that they reported prostitution-related offences to the police.
5. Area beat officer.
6. See also Chapter 2.
7. A number of writers have applied a social movement framework to the study of neighbourhood organizing and crime prevention efforts in the USA (see Donnelly and Majka 1998 and their references). Lowe's use of urban social movement analysis is preferred here because it is adapted for the UK setting.

Chapter 7: Conclusions and Reflections

1. See Skogan (1990).
2. 'The ability of actors to secure benefits by virtue of membership in social networks or other social structures' (Portes 1998: 6). Social capital can function as 'a) a source of social control; b) as a source of family support; c) as a source of benefits through extrafamilial networks' (1998: 9).

References

Anderson, H. et al., *Social Cohesion and Neighbourhood Change in Liverpool*. Liverpool: Department of Sociology, Social Policy and Social Work Studies (University of Liverpool and Joseph Rowntree Foundation, Draft Report, 1998).

Balchin, P., *Housing Policy: an Introduction*, 3rd edn (London: Routledge, 1995).

Baldwin, J. and Bottoms, A. E., *The Urban Criminal* (London: Tavistock, 1976).

Barke, M. and Turnbull, G. M., *Meadowell: the Biography of an Estate with Problems* (Aldershot: Avebury, 1992).

Bassett, K. and Short, J. R., *Housing and Residential Structure* (London: Routledge and Kegan Paul, 1980).

Becker, H. S., 'Problems of Inference and Proof in Participant Observation', in D. P. Forcese and S. Richer (eds), *Stages of Social Research: Contemporary Perspectives* (New Jersey: Prentice-Hall, 1970).

Bell, C. and Newby, H., *Community Studies: an Introduction to the Sociology of the Local Community* (London: George Allen and Unwin, 1971).

Bennett, S. F., 'Community Organizations and Crime' *The Annals of the American Academy of Political and Social Science*, 539 (May 1995): 72–84.

Blowers, A. and Raine, J., 'Local Democracy or Central Control', *Case Studies in British Social Policy*; unit 11, block 4 (Milton Keynes: Open University, 1984).

Bottoms, A. E., 'Environmental Criminology', in M. Maguire, R. Morgan and R. Reiner (eds), *The Oxford Handbook of Criminology* (Oxford: Clarendon Press, 1994).

Bottoms, A. E., Claytor, A. and Wiles, P., 'Housing Markets and Residential Crime Careers: a Case Study from Sheffield', in D. J. Evans, N. R. Fyfe, and D. T. Herbert (eds), *Crime, Policing and Place: Essays in Environmental Criminology* (London: Routledge, 1992).

Bottoms, A., Mawby, R. I. and Xanthos, P., 'A Tale of Two Estates', in D. Downes (ed.), *Crime and the City: Essays in Memory of John Barron Mays* (Basingstoke: Macmillan, 1989).

Bottoms, A. E. and Wiles, P., 'Housing Tenure and Residential Community Crime Careers in Britain', in A. J. Reiss and M. Tonry (eds), *Communities and Crime: Crime and Justice a Review of Research*, 8 (Chicago: University of Chicago Press, 1986).

Bottoms, A. E. and Wiles, P., 'Explanations of Crime and Place', in D. J. Evans, N. R. Fyfe and D. T. Herbert (eds), *Crime, Policing and Place: Essays in Environmental Criminology* (London: Routledge, 1992).

Bottoms, A. and Wiles, P., 'Crime and Insecurity in the City', in C. Fijnaut, J. Goethals and L. Walgrave (eds), *Changes in Society, Crime and Criminal Justice in Europe*, vol. 1 (The Hague: Kluwer, 1995).

Bottoms, A. and Wiles, P., 'Environmental Criminology', in M. Maguire et al. (eds), *The Oxford Handbook of Criminology* (Oxford: Clarendon Press, 1997, 2nd edn).

Bottoms, A. E. and Xanthos, P., 'Housing Policy and Crime in the British Public Sector', in P. J. Brantingham and P. L. Brantingham (eds), *Environmental Criminology* (Beverly Hills: Sage, 1981).

Bramley, G., 'The Enabling Role for Local Authorities: a Preliminary Evaluation', in P. Malpass and R. Means (eds), *Implementing Housing Policy* (Buckingham: Open University Press 1993).

Brantingham, P. J. and Brantingham, P. L., *Patterns in Crime* (New York: Macmillan, 1984).

Bridges, L., ' "The Ministry of Internal Security": British Urban Social Policy 1968–74', *Race and Class*, 16:4 (1975): 375–86.

British Sociological Association (BSA), 'BSA Statement on Ethical Practice', *Sociology*, 26:4 (1992): 703–7.

Burgess, R. G., 'The Unstructured Interview as a Conversation', in R. G. Burgess (ed.), *Field Research: a Sourcebook and Field Manual*, Contemporary Social Research Series (London: George Allen and Unwin, 1982a).

Burgess, R. G., 'Some Role Problems in Field Research', in Burgess (ed.), *Field Research: a Sourcebook and Field Manual*, Contemporary Social Research Series (London: George Allen and Unwin, 1982b).

Burgess, R. G., 'Elements of Sampling in Field Research', in Burgess (ed.), *Field Research: a Sourcebook and Field Manual*, Contemporary Social Research Series (London: George Allen and Unwin, 1982c).

Burgess, R. G., 'Keeping Field Notes', in Burgess (ed.), *Field Research: a Sourcebook and Field Manual*, Contemporary Social Research Series (London: George Allen and Unwin, 1982d).

Burgess, R. G., *In the Field: an Introduction to Field Research* (London: George Allen and Unwin, 1984).

Bursik, R. J., Jr., 'Social Disorganisation and Theories of Crime and Delinquency: Problems and Prospects', *Criminology*, 26:4 (1988): 519–51.

Bursik, R. J., Jr and Grasmick, H. G., *Neighborhoods and Crime: the Dimensions of Effective Community Control* (New York: Lexington Books, 1993).

Campbell R. and Hancock, L., 'Sex Work in the Climate of Zero Tolerance: Hearing Loud Voices and the Silencing of Dissent', paper presented to the *Sex Work Reassessed* Conference, University of East London, 9 Sept. 1998, unpublished.

City of Liverpool, *Key Statistics 1991 Census Liverpool Wards 1971/81/91* (City of Liverpool, n.d.).

Clarke, A., 'The Changing Balance of Central-Local Relations', *Case Studies in British Social Policy*, unit 11, Block 4 (Milton Keynes: Open University, Press 1986).

Coleman, A., *Utopia on Trial* (London: Hilary Shipman, 1985).

Cook, D., *Poverty, Crime and Punishment* (London: Child Poverty Action Group, 1997).

Crawford, A., *The Local Governance of Crime: Appeals to Community and Partnerships* (Oxford: Clarendon Press, 1997).

Crawford, A., 'Community Safety and the Quest for Security: Holding Back the Dynamics of Social Exclusion', *Policy Studies*, 19:3/4 (1998): 237–53.

Damer, S., 'Wine Alley: the Sociology of a Dreadful Enclosure', *Sociological Review*, 22 (1974): 221–48.

Darke, J., 'Local Political Attitudes and Council Housing', in S. Lowe and D. Hughes (eds), *A New Century of Social Housing* (Leicester: Leicester University Press, 1991).

Department of the Environment, Transport and the Regions Regeneration Research Summary: *City Challenge – Final National Evaluation*, no. 27 (1999); www.regeneration.detr.gov.uk/rs/02799/index.htm

Department of the Environment, Transport and the Regions, *Preparing Community Strategies: Draft Guidance to Local Authorities* (London: DETR, June 2000); www.regeneration.detr.gov.uk/consult/lgbill99/

Department of the Environment, Transport and the Regions Report of National Strategy for Neighbourhood Renewal Policy Action Team 17: *Joining It Up Locally*; www.regeneration.detr.gov.uk/ (April 2000).

Department of the Environment, Transport and the Regions, *Quality and Choice: a Decent Home for All: the Housing Green Paper* (London: DETR, April 2000); www.regeneration.detr.gov.uk/

Department of the Environment, Transport and the Regions Report of National Strategy for Neighbourhood Renewal Policy Action Team 7: *Unpopular Housing*; www.regeneration.detr.gov.uk/ (2000).

Donnelly, P. G. and Kimble, C. E., 'Community Organizing, Environmental Change, and Neighbourhood Crime', *Crime and Delinquency*, 43:4 (1997): 493–511.

Donnelly, P. G. and Majka, T. J., 'Residents' Efforts at Neighborhood Stabilisation: Facing the Challenge of Inner-City Neighborhoods', *Sociological Forum*, 13:2 (1998): 189–213.

Donnison, D., 'Crime and Urban Policy: a Strategic Approach to Crime and Insecurity', in C. Fijnaut, J. Goethals and L. Walgrave (eds), *Changes in Society, Crime and Criminal Justice in Europe* (The Hague: Kluwer, 1995).

Dow, S., 'Move On Up', *Roof* 17:6 (1992): 18–19.

Duncan, S. and Goodwin, M., 'Removing Local Government Autonomy: Political Centralisation and Financial Control', *Local Government Studies*, 14:6 (1988): 49–65.

Easterday, L., Papademas, D., Schorr, L. and Valentine, C., 'The Making of a Female Researcher: Role Problems in Fieldwork', in R. G. Burgess (ed.), *Field Research: a Sourcebook and Field Manual*, Contemporary Social Research Series (London: George Allen and Unwin, 1982).

Edwards, A. and Benyon, J., 'Networking and Crime Control at the Local Level', in M. Ryan, S. Savage and D. Wall (eds), *Criminal Justice Networks* (London: Sage, 1999).

Edwards, A. and Stenson, K., 'Crime Control and Liberal Government: the "Third Way" and the Shift to the Local', paper delivered at the *Crime, Neo-Liberalism and Risk Society* conference, John Jay College of Criminal Justice, City University of New York, 14–16 April (1999a).

Edwards, A. and Stenson, K., 'Crime Control and Advanced Liberal Government: the "Third Way" and the Return of the Local', paper presented to the British Society of Criminology Conference, Britannia Adelphi Hotel, Liverpool, 13–16 July (1999b).

Foster, J. and Hope, T., *Housing, Community and Crime: the Impact of the Priority Estates Project*, Home Office Research Study no. 131 (London: HMSO, 1993).

Fyfe, N., 'Crime', in M. Pacione (ed.), *Britain's Cities: Geographies of Division in Urban Britain* (London: Routledge, 1997).

Gans, H. J., 'The Participant Observer as a Human Being: Observations on the Personal Aspects of Fieldwork', in R. G. Burgess (ed.), *Field Research: a*

Sourcebook and Field Manual, Contemporary Social Research Series (London: George Allen and Unwin, 1982).

Gifford, Lord (QC), Brown, W. and Bundey, R., *Loosen the Shackles: First Report of the Liverpool 8 Inquiry into Race Relations in Liverpool* (London: Karia Press, 1989).

Gill, O., *Luke Street: Housing Policy, Conflict and the Creation of a Delinquent Area* (London: Macmillan, 1977).

Gilling, D., *Crime Prevention: Theory, Policy and Politics* (London: UCL Press, 1997).

Gilling, D. and Barton, A., 'Crime Prevention and Community Safety: a New Home for Social Policy?', *Critical Social Policy*, 17 (1997): 63–83.

Goldblatt, P. and Lewis, C. (eds), *Reducing Offending: an Assessment of Research Evidence on Ways of Dealing with Offending Behaviour*, Home Office Research Study 187 (London: Home Office, 1998).

Haddon, R., 'A Minority in a Welfare State Society: Location of West Indians in the London Housing Market', *New Atlantis* 2:1 (1970): 80–133.

Hancock, L., *Tenant Participation and the Housing Classes Debate*, Ph.D. thesis, University of Liverpool, 1995, unpublished.

Hancock, L., 'The People's Home? Social Rented Housing in Europe and America', Michael Harloe (1995), Book Review in *The Sociological Review*, 44:1 (1996a): 138–40.

Hancock, L., 'Housing, Crime and Social Exclusion', paper presented to the Housing Studies Association Conference *Housing and Social Exclusion*, 16–17 Sept., University of Birmingham (1996b).

Hancock, L., 'Community, Crime and Urban Policy in Merseyside, England', paper presented to the American Society of Criminology 48th Annual Meeting, *Controlling Crime and Achieving Justice*, 20–3 Nov. in Chicago, Illinois (1996c).

Hancock, L., 'Community and State Responses to Crime and Disorder: Conflict, Compromise and Contradiction', Paper Presented to the *British Society of Criminology Bi-Annual Conference* held at Queen's University Belfast, 15–18 July 1997.

Hancock, L., 'Going Around the Houses? Researching in High Crime Communities', in R. King and E. Wincup (eds), *Doing Research on Crime and Justice* (Oxford: Oxford University Press, 2000).

Harloe, M., *The People's Home? Social Rented Housing in Europe and America* (Oxford: Blackwell, 1995).

Herbert, D. T., *The Geography of Urban Crime* (London: Longman, 1982).

Her Majesty's Inspectorate of Constabulary (HMIC), *Calling Time on Crime* (London: HMIC, July 2000).

Hirschfield, A., *Crime and Disadvantage in North West England: An Analysis using Crime Statistics, Geodemograhics and Geographic Information Systems*, presentation to National Institute of Justice, Washington DC, 8 Nov. (1995).

Hirschfield, A., Bowers, K. and Brown, P. J. B., 'Exploring Relations between Crime and Disadvantage in Merseyside', *European Journal on Criminal Policy and Research*, 3:3 (1995): 93–112.

Hirschfield, A., Brown, P. J. B. and Todd, P., 'GIS and the Analysis of Spatially-Referenced Crime Data: Experiences on Merseyside', *International Journal of Geographical Information Systems*, 9:2 (1995): 191–210.

Hirschman, A. O., *Exit, Voice and Loyalty: Responses to Decline, in Firms, Organizations, and States* (Cambridge, Mass.: Harvard University Press, 1970).

Hope, T., 'Community Crime Prevention', in M. Tonry and D. P. Farrington (eds), *Building a Safer Society: Strategic Approaches to Crime Prevention, Crime and Justice*, vol. 19 (Chicago: University of Chicago Press, 1995).

Hope, T., 'Communities, Crime and Inequality in England and Wales', in T. Bennett (ed.), *Preventing Crime and Disorder: Targeting Strategies and Responsibilities* (Cambridge: Institute of Criminology, 1996).

Hope, T., 'Inequality and the Future of Community Crime Prevention', in S. P. Lab (ed.), *Crime Prevention at a Crossroads*, American Academy of Criminal Justice Sciences Monograph Series (Cincinnati, Ohio: Anderson Publishing, 1997).

Hope, T., 'Community Safety, Crime and Disorder', in A. Marlow and J. Pitts (eds), *Planning Safer Communities* (Lyme Regis: Russell House Publishing, 1998).

Hope, T. and Hough, M., 'Area, Crime and Incivilities: a Profile from the British Crime Survey', in T. Hope and M. Shaw (eds), *Communities and Crime Reduction* (London: HMSO, 1988).

Hope, T. and Shaw, M., 'Community Approaches to Reducing Crime', in T. Hope and M. Shaw (eds), *Communities and Crime Reduction* (London: HMSO, 1988).

Hughes, G., *Understanding Crime Prevention: Social Control, Risk and Late Modernity*, Crime and Justice Series (Buckingham: Open University Press, 1998).

Jarvie, I. C., 'The Problem of Ethical Integrity in Participant Observation', in R. G. Burgess (ed.), *Field Research: a Sourcebook and Field Manual*, Contemporary Social Research Series (London: George Allen and Unwin, 1982).

Joseph Rowntree Foundation *Housing Research Findings Paper 143, Housing Associations and Non-Housing Activities* (York: Joseph Rowntree Foundation, April 1995).

Joseph Rowntree Foundation, *Housing Research Findings Paper 219, Implementing 'Housing Plus' on Five Housing Association Estates* (York: Joseph Rowntree Foundation, July 1997).

Jupp, V., *Methods of Criminological Research*, Contemporary Social Research Series (London: Routledge, 1989).

Kelling, G. L and Coles, C. M., *Fixing Broken Windows: Restoring Order and Reducing Crime in Our Communities* (New York: The Free Press, 1996).

Kyprianou, P., *Community Participation and Partnership: a Review of Community Participation in the Liverpool Objective One Partnerships* (Liverpool: Liverpool Community Rights, 1997).

Lambert, J. and Filkin, C., *Ethnic Choice and Preference in Housing*, Final Report to the Social Science Research Council on the Pilot Research Project (London: Centre for Urban and Regional Studies, 1971, unpublished).

Lee, P. and Murie, A., *Poverty, Housing Tenure and Social Exclusion* (Bristol: Policy Press, 1997).

Lowe, S., *Urban Social Movements: the City After Castells* (London: Macmillan, 1986).

Lowe, S., 'Introduction: One Hundred Years of Social Housing', in S. Lowe and D. Hughes (eds), *A New Century of Social Housing* (Leicester: Leicester University Press, 1991).

Massey, D. *Spatial Divisions of Labour: Social Structures and the Geography of Production*, 2nd edn (Basingstoke: Macmillan, 1995).

Matthews, R., 'Replacing Broken Windows: Crime, Incivilities and Urban Change', in R. Matthews and J. Young (eds), *Issues in Realist Criminology* (London: Sage, 1992).

McConville, M. and Shepherd, D., *Watching Police, Watching Communities* (London: Routledge, 1992).

McGabey, R. M., 'Economic Conditions, Neighbourhood Organization and Urban Crime', in A. J. Reiss and M. Tonry (eds), *Communities and Crime: Crime and Justice, a Review of Research*, 8 (Chicago: University of Chicago Press, 1986).

Merton, R. K., 'The Bearing of Empirical Research upon the Development of Social Theory', in D. P. Forcese and S. Richer (eds), *Stages of Social Research: Contemporary Perspectives* (New Jersey: Prentice-Hall, 1970).

Middleton, M., *Cities in Transition* (London: Michael Joseph, 1991).

Mirrlees-Black, C., Budd, T., Partridge, S. and Mayhew, P., *The 1998 British Crime Survey: England and Wales* (London: Home Office, 1988).

Moore, R., 'Becoming a Sociologist in Sparkbrook', in C. Bell and H. Newby (eds), *Doing Sociological Research* (London: George Allen and Unwin, 1977).

Morgan, R. and Newburn, T., *The Future of Policing* (Oxford: Clarendon Press, 1997).

Osgood, D. W., 'Interdisciplinary Integration: Building Criminology by Stealing from Our Friends', *The Criminologist*, 23:4 (1998): 1–4 & 41.

Pacione, M. (ed.), *Britain's Cities: Geographies of Division in Urban Britain* (London: Routledge, 1997).

Pahl, R., *Patterns of Urban Life* (London: Longman, 1970).

Park, R., Burgess, E. and MacKenzie, R., *The City* (Chicago: University of Chicago Press, 1923).

Parker, H., *View From the Boys: a Sociology of Down-Town Adolescents* (London: David and Charles, 1974).

Parkinson, M., 'Power Plays', *New Society*, 84:1323 (1988): 12–13.

Pitts, J. and Hope, T., 'The Local Politics of Inclusion: the State and Community Safety', *Social Policy and Administration*, 31:5 (1997): 37–58.

Podolefsky, A. and Dubow, F., *Strategies for Community Crime Prevention: Collective Responses to Crime in Urban America* (Springfield, Ill.: Charles C. Thomas, 1981).

Portes, A., 'Social Capital: Its Origins and Applications in Modern Sociology', *Annual Review of Sociology*, 24 (1998): 1–24.

Power, A., 'Housing, Community and Crime', in D. Downes (ed.), *Crime and the City: Essays in Memory of John Barron Mays* (Basingstoke: Macmillan, 1989).

Power, A. and Tunstall, R., *Dangerous Disorder: Riots and Violent Disturbances in Thirteen aras of Britain, 1991–2* (York: Joseph Rowntree Foundation, 1997).

Reiner, R., *The Politics of the Police* (Hemel Hempstead: Harvester Wheatsheaf, 1992).

Reiss, A. J., 'Why are Communities Important in Understanding Crime?', in A. J. Reiss and M. Tonry (eds), *Communities and Crime: Crime and Justice, A Review of Research*, 8 (Chicago: University of Chicago Press, 1986).

Rex, J. and Moore, R., *Race, Community and Conflict: a Study of Sparkbrook* (London: IRR, 1967).

Rex, J. A., 'The Concept of Housing Class and the Sociology of Race Relations', *Race* 12:3 (1971): 293–303.

Rich, R. C., 'A Political Economy Approach to the Study of Neighbourhood Organizations', *American Journal of Political Science*, 24:4 (1980): 559–92.

Richardson, A., 'Thinking about Participation', *Policy and Politics*, 7:3 (1979): 227–44.

Richardson, A., *Participation Concepts in Social Policy*, 1 (London: Routledge and Kegan Paul, 1983).

Safer Merseyside Partnership (SMP), *New Solutions, Further Actions*, Challenge Fund Submission (Merseyside: SMP, 1996).

Sampson, R. J., Raudenbush, S. W. and Earles, F., 'Neighbourhoods and Violent Crime: a Multilevel Study of Collective Efficacy', *Science*, 277 (1997): 918–24.

Saunders, P., *Urban Politics: a Sociological Interpretation* (London: Hutchinson, 1983).

Saunders, P., *Social Theory and the Urban Question* (London: Hutchinson, 1986).

Schuerman, L. and Kobrin, S., 'Community Careers in Crime', in A. J. Reiss, Jr. and M. Tonry (eds), *Communities and Crime*, 8 (Chicago: University of Chicago Press, 1986).

Shapland, J., 'Policing with the Public?', in T. Hope and M. Shaw (eds), *Communities and Crime Reduction* (London: HMSO, 1988).

Shaw, C. R. and McKay, H. D., *Juvenile Delinquency and Urban Areas* (Chicago: University of Chicago Press, 1942).

Silverman, D., *Interpreting Qualitative Data: Methods for Analysing Talk, Text and Interaction* (London: Sage, 1993).

Sklair, L., 'The Struggle Against the Housing Finance Act', *The Socialist Register* (London: Merlin, 1975).

Skogan, W. G., 'Fear of Crime and Neighborhood Change', in A. J Reiss and M. Tonry (eds), *Communities and Crime: Crime and Justice, A Review of Research*, 8 (Chicago: University of Chicago Press, 1986).

Skogan, W. G., 'Disorder, Crime and Community Decline', in T. Hope and M. Shaw (eds), *Communities and Crime Reduction* (London: HMSO, 1988a).

Skogan, W. G., 'Community Organizations and Crime', in M. Tonry and N. Morris (eds), *Crime and Justice, A Review of Research*, 10 (Chicago: University of Chicago Press, 1988b).

Skogan, W. G., *Disorder and Decline: Crime and the Spiral of Decay in American Neighborhoods* (New York: The Free Press, 1990).

Skogan, W. G. and Maxfield, M. G., *Coping with Crime: Individual and Neighbourhood Reactions* (Beverly Hills: Sage, 1986).

Smith, J., 'Labour Tradition in Glasgow and Liverpool', *History Workshop Journal*, 17 (Spring, 1984): 32–56.

Smith, S. J., *Crime, Space and Society* (Cambridge: Cambridge University Press, 1986).

Smith, R. and Whysall, P., 'The Origins and Development of Local Authority Housing in Nottingham 1890–1960', in S. Lowe and D. Hughes (eds), *A New Century of Social Housing* (Leicester: Leicester University Press, 1991).

Social Exclusion Unit, *National Strategy for Neighbourhood Renewal* (Cabinet Office: London, April 2000); www.cabinet-office.gov.uk/seu/2000/ Nat_Strat_Cons/

Solomos, J., 'Policy Analysis and Research on "Race" ', *Foundation*, 5 (June 1989): 5–10.

Spencer, K. M., 'Local Government and the Housing Reforms', in in J. Stewart and G. Stoker (eds), *The Future of Local Government* (London: Macmillan, 1989).

Stoker, G., 'Inner-Cities, Economic Development and Social Services: the Government's Continuing Agenda', in J. Stewart and G. Stoker (eds), *The Future of Local Government* (London: Macmillan, 1989).

Stoker, G. and Wilson, D., 'The Lost World of British Local Pressure Groups', *Public Policy and Administration*, 6:2 (1991): 20–34.

Taub, R. P., Taylor, D. G. and Dunham, J. D., *Paths of Neighbourhood Change: Race and Crime in Urban America* (Chicago: University of Chicago Press, 1984).

Taylor, R. B., 'Neighbourhood Responses to Disorder and Local Attachments: the Systemic Model of Attachment, Social Disorganisation, and Neighborhood Use Value', *Sociological Forum*, 11:1 (1996): 41–74.

Taylor, R. B., 'Crime, Grime, and Responses to Crime: Relative Impacts of Neighborhood Structure, Crime, and Physical Deterioration on Residents and Business Personnel in the Twin Cities', in S. P. Lab (ed.), *Crime Prevention at a Crossroads* (Cincinnati, Ohio: Academy of Criminal Justice Sciences/Anderson Publishing, 1997).

Walklate, S., 'Crime and Community: Fear or Trust?', *British Journal of Sociology*, 49:4 (1998): 550–569.

Walklate, S. and Wardale, R., *'Zero Tolerance: Same Old Policework; Same Old Problems?'*, paper presented at the Institute of Criminology, University of Stockholm, Sweden, Nov. 1997, unpublished.

Wikström, P.-O., *Urban Crime, Criminals and Victims* (New York: Springer-Verlag, 1991).

Wilks, S., 'Networks of Power: Theorising the Politics of Urban Policy Change', in *Contemporary Political Studies*, Proceedings of the Political Studies Association Annual Conference, University of York, 18–20 April (1995).

Wilson, J. Q. and Kelling, G. L., 'Broken Windows: the Police and Neighborhood Safety', *Atlantic Monthly*, 249:3 (1982): 29–38.

Xanthos, P., *Crime, the Housing market and Reputation*, Ph.D. thesis, University of Sheffield, 1981, unpublished.

Zelditch, M., 'Some Methodological Problems of Field Studies', in D. P. Forcese and S. Richer (eds), *Stages of Social Research: Contemporary Perspectives* (New Jersey: Prentice-Hall, 1970).

Index